ROYAL LINE FROM
QUEEN VICTORIA AND PRINCE ALBERT

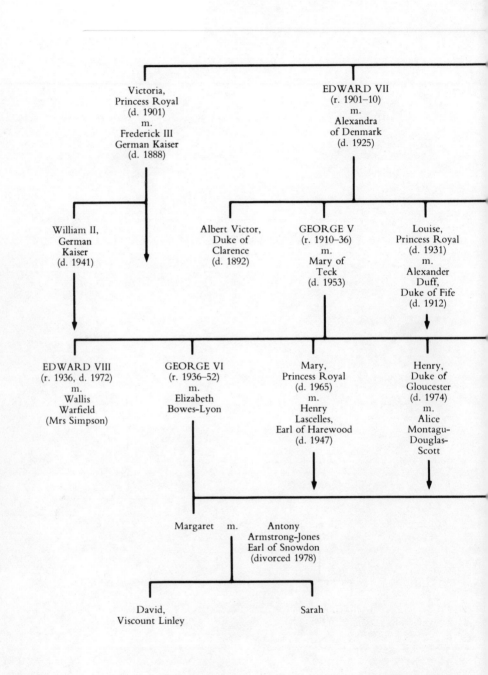

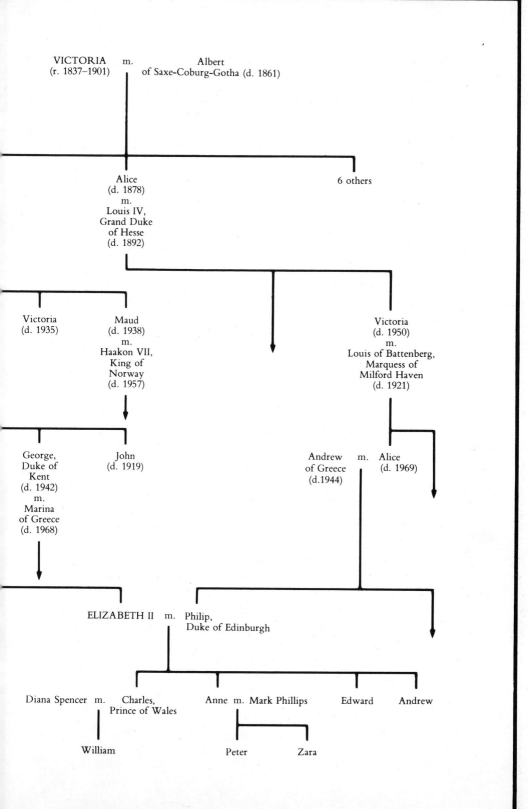

KING GEORGE VI

ALSO BY DENIS JUDD

Balfour and the British Empire
The Victorian Empire
Posters of World War Two
The British Raj
Livingstone in Africa
George V
The House of Windsor
Someone Has Blundered
Edward VII
Palmerston
The Crimean War
Eclipse of Kings
Radical Joe: A Life of Joseph Chamberlain
The Boer War
The Adventures of Long John Silver
Return to Treasure Island
Prince Philip
Lord Reading: A Biography of Rufus Isaacs
The Evolution of the Modern Commonwealth

KING GEORGE VI
1895–1952

DENIS JUDD

FRANKLIN WATTS
NEW YORK   1983

Copyright © 1982 by Denis Judd.

Printed in the United States.
First published in the United Kingdom in 1982 by
Michael Joseph Limited.
First United States publication 1983 by
Franklin Watts.

6   5   4   3   2   1

Library of Congress Catalog Card Number: 83-60015
ISBN: 0-531-09898-2

To
BRUCE HUNTER,
for twelve years of steady,
but not uncritical,
support and advice

CONTENTS

LIST OF ILLUSTRATIONS

Between pages 46 and 47

Between pages 206 and 207

[xv]

ACKNOWLEDGEMENTS

The author and publishers would like to thank the following for permission to reproduce extracts from the publications mentioned: Allen & Unwin, *Queen Mary, 1867–1953* by James Pope-Hennessy; Cassell, *The Little Princesses* by Marion Crawford; Constable, *King George V: His Life and Reign* by Sir Harold Nicolson; Hodder & Stoughton, *Prince Philip: A Family Portrait* by Alexandra, ex-Queen Consort of Yugoslavia; Hutchinson, *Thatched with Gold* by Lady Airlie and *Majesty: Elizabeth II and the House of Windsor* by Robert Lacey; Macmillan *King George VI: His Life and Reign* by Sir John Wheeler Bennett; Weidenfeld & Nicolson, *King George & Queen Elizabeth* by Frances Donaldson, *Edward VIII* by Frances Donaldson, *The Tongs and the Bones* by The Earl of Harewood and *The Queen Mother: A Biography* by Elizabeth, Countess of Longford.

PREFACE

THIS NEW BIOGRAPHY of King George VI has been written to commemorate the thirtieth anniversary of the death of a greatly loved and much admired monarch. Apart from Sir John Wheeler-Bennett's weighty official life, there have been no other full-length biographical studies of the King during the three decades since his death. In these circumstances, it seemed appropriate to take a comprehensive and fresh look at the life and reign of George VI and to examine, in particular, some of the less comfortable aspects of his personality and career. I have tried throughout to avoid the sycophancy that so often distorts royal biography, and to conduct an honest and unprejudiced appraisal of a man whose ultimate national and international reputation was achieved at the cost of consistent self-sacrifice in the name of duty, and after a lengthy struggle to overcome various personal disabilities. As well as extracting information from printed letters and speeches, works of autobiography, biography and historical analysis, I have examined a mass of contemporary newspapers and journals, both British and American, in order to see George VI from as many angles as possible.

In writing the book I have received a great deal of encouragement and support from Alan Brooke and Jennie Davies at Michael Joseph. I have also been fortunate in the promptness and skills of my typist Jill Fletcher, and in the supplementary secretarial assistance offered by my mother, aided by my father. Edda Tasiemka and her staff of the Hans Tasiemka Archives have efficiently provided me with access to much contemporary archival material. I am grateful, too, for the facilities offered by a number of national and public libraries and their staff. My friend Bruce Hunter, of David Higham's, has been, as usual, a source of invaluable advice and support, and I take great pleasure in dedicating this book to him.

DENIS JUDD
April 1982

I

A ROYAL,
AND DEPRIVED, CHILDHOOD
1895–1908

. . . my grandfather [George V] found it so easy to find fault with anyone that what was probably a basic kindness was quite lost in his gruff exterior . . . I don't think he really cared much for children and he had a positive mania for punctuality.

The Earl of Harewood

The child to whom I was most drawn was Prince Albert – Bertie – although he was not a boy who made friends easily. Intensely sensitive over his stammer he was apt to take refuge either in silence – which caused him to be thought moody – or in naughtiness. He was more often in conflict with authority than the rest of his brothers.

Mabell, Countess of Airlie

THE FUTURE KING GEORGE VI was born in 1895 at Sandringham on the blackest day in the calendar of the Royal Family – 14 December, the anniversary of the death of Prince Albert thirty-four years earlier, and of Queen Victoria's daughter Alice in 1878.

In a more superstitious age, soothsayers would have struggled to interpret the omen. As it was, there was much consternation within the Royal Family and early, anxious attempts to propitiate the imagined wrath of Queen Victoria, who was now in her seventy-sixth year, and, despite her physical infirmities, a matriarchal totem of great potency.

The baby's father, the Duke of York, later to become King George V, recorded in his diary the events of the momentous day in the spare prose of the naval log:

A little boy was born, weighing nearly eight lb. at 3.40 a.m. . . . Everything most satisfactory, both doing well. Sent a number of telegrams, had something to eat. Went to bed at 6.45, very tired.[1]

Among the telegrams was one addressed to Queen Victoria, mourning at Windsor. It read: "Darling May was safely confined of a son at 3.30 this morning both doing well. GEORGIE."

How would the old Queen respond? Early newspaper reaction to the birth met the problem head-on: the *Globe* believed that:

> Henceforth it is permissible to hope that the august lady, in whose joys and sorrows the nation claims a right to share, may find in the felicitous event of December 14, 1895, a solace for the mournful memories of December 14, 1861, and December 14, 1878.[2]

On 16 December the *Standard* weighed in with an editorial in which sound advice was presented in pompous and leaden prose:

> But, surely, the Fourteenth of December may, henceforth, bear its white mark. Not that the Past can ever be forgotten, not that even the sound of the joy-bells of the present hour can ever deaden our ears to the recollections of a sadder and graver note. It is the distinguishing characteristic of the higher natures, and equally of the more serious communities, never to part wholly with their reminiscences, even though these should give to existence a certain air of sombreness. But the "Too much sorrow", on which Shakespeare comments with disapproval, is incompatible with the healthy activities either of individual or of national life; and all of us, from our beloved Sovereign downward, will, we are quite sure, hail with eagerness the new cause given us by the Duchess of York for looking on the Fourteenth of December as not by any means one of the days devoted exclusively to mourning and regret.[3]

Within the family, Queen Victoria's eldest child, Victoria, the widowed mother of the German Kaiser Wilhelm II, was quick to put the best interpretation on the birth. Writing to her mother from Berlin on 17 December she said:

> I cannot say how much I rejoice! On the one hand I thought it rather to be regretted that the dear little Baby was born on a day of such inexpressibly sad memories to us – but on the other – it is a gift from Heaven and a very precious one – and there is something very touching in the thought – that on this *darkest* day of your Life a ray of sunshine is sent in after years! and I like to look at it in this light![4]

The new baby's grandfather, the Prince of Wales, had written in similar terms to the Duke of York from Windsor on 14 December.

While admitting that, "Grandmama was rather distressed that this happy event should have taken place on a darkly sad anniversary for us," the future King Edward VII added, "but I think – as well as most of us in the family here – that it will 'break the spell' of this unlucky date." The Prince of Wales followed up this letter with a second, written two days later, in which he reassured his son that, "Grandmama is not the least annoyed with you about anything, but she only regretted that the little boy was born on the fourteenth though we have all told her that it will dispel the gloom of that sad anniversary." In order to make the best of it, the Prince of Wales, after reminding the Duke of York that the Queen "is ageing rapidly – and has always been very kind and affecte. to you", suggested, "I really think it would gratify her if you yourself proposed the name of *Albert* to her."

Queen Victoria had probably already indicated the pleasure that naming the new baby Albert would give her. Indeed, it was difficult for her descendants to christen their male offspring without including Albert among the names. Thus the Prince of Wales' first name was Albert, as had been that of his eldest son, the Duke of Clarence, who had died of typhus in 1892; the Duke of York's fourth name was Albert, and his eldest son, later to be King Edward VIII, bore Albert as his second name. The name should, in Queen Victoria's view, be the distinguishing mark of the lineage that had sprung from her joyful union with the Prince Consort.

The Duke of York hastened to play the Albert card, and with some finesse. He wrote to the Queen, soon after the new prince's birth, repeating the family sentiment that "his having been born on that day may be the means of making it a little less sad to you", and then produced his trump: "Dear Grandmama, we propose with your permission to call him *Albert* after dear Grandpapa & we also hope that you will be his Godmother."

Queen Victoria accepted these offerings at the shrine of her dead husband with the warmth and spontaneity of the middle-European great-grandmother that she was. She replied immediately:

I cannot tell you how much pleased & gratified I have been by your dear letter [she wrote to her "Darling Georgie"]. But before I answer it let me express my joy at dear May's doing so well & recovering so quickly. Thank God! she is, *unberufen*, very strong. She gets through these affairs like nothing. It is a great satisfaction to us all that it should be a second boy & I need not say how delighted I am that my great wish – viz. that the little one born on that sad anniversary shd. have the dear name of Albert – is to be realized. Most gladly do I accept being Godmother & this dear little Boy born the day when his beloved great grandfather entered on a new greater life will be especially dear to me. – I thank you lovingly for your very kind letter &.will write again soon, but I must end to save the Post.

Ever Your devoted Grandmama

V.R.I.[5]

So excited was she by the birth that she confessed to the baby's mother, "I am all impatience to see the *new* one," and would dearly have liked the christening to have been held at Osborne so that she could have personally played the part of Godmother. The new prince was, however, christened at the Church of St Mary's, Sandringham, on 17 February 1895, taking the names Albert Frederick Arthur George. Within the family he was destined always to be known as Bertie.

The prospects for Prince Albert Frederick Arthur George were overwhelmingly favourable. Britain was still the greatest world power in 1895, her influence, like her Empire, far-flung and world-wide. The Royal Navy patrolled the seven seas and British exports still dominated the world's markets. Although Britain's commercial pre-eminence was shortly to be challenged by the rapidly growing industrial strength of Germany and the United States, and her military shortcomings cruelly exposed in the Boer War of 1899–1902, there seemed little cause for pessimism on these scores in 1895.

If Britain was the centre of a global imperial structure, the Royal Family were the unquestioned leaders of British society and the only viable focal point of imperial patriotism. The republican agitation of the 1870s had died away; indeed, a few months before Prince Albert Frederick's birth, Joseph Chamberlain, earlier a demagogic radical and republican, had taken the post of Colonial Secretary in a Unionist government dominated by the Tory party. Few in 1895 countenanced the overthrow of the British monarchy or imagined a bloody revolution that would plant the red flag amid the smoking ruins of Buckingham Palace.

In all these ways the new prince's future seemed secure, but Prince Albert Frederick's upbringing was little short of disastrous. A combination of circumstances robbed him of the consistently loving, intelligent support and guidance which should form the basis of childhood development. In a very real sense, his was a deprived childhood. To begin with, the Duke and Duchess of York had serious failings as parents. For those who remember them fondly as King George V and Queen Mary this may be difficult to accept. George V is recalled as a bluff, kindly, plain-spoken monarch, the embodiment of good sense, a father-figure to his people; Queen Mary, upright and alert, embodied family respectability and patriotic devotion, and was an emblem of stability amid much change.

All of this is true enough; it did not, however, make the Duke and Duchess of York good parents. Frances Donaldson, in her biography of Edward VIII, has even gone so far as to say that the couple "were for different reasons temperamentally unsuited to parenthood".[6]

The future George V, though amiable with the children of others, and a devoted father to his own children in that he watched carefully over their development and bathed and played with them when they were babies, was far too ready to criticise and control them. In part, the problem lay in his excessive respect for discipline and order. The naval career that had been cut short by the premature death of his elder brother the Duke of Clarence in 1892 had encouraged his passion for tidiness and hard work, and made him later inclined to see his children as the potentially mutinous crew of an unseaworthy vessel. George V's obsession with the formalities of dress, with doing things in the "correct" way, was an indication of a narrowness of outlook that sprang both from his strong belief in tradition and from feelings of intellectual inadequacy. He read very little and showed scant interest in artistic or cultural matters.

In addition to his need to control his children, he also gave way all too easily to fits of temper. He was, particularly as a young man, impetuous and unrestrained in giving vent to his feelings. So much so that his wife found it difficult "to stand between [the children] and the sudden gusts of their father's wrath".[7] Apart from these unpredictable outbursts, George V frequently hauled his children before him for formal rebukes, many of which added yet another "Don't" to an already lengthy list. The Duke of Windsor was one of the chief recipients of such rebukes, and recalled in his autobiography that nothing would ever be so "disconcerting to the spirit"[8] as the message delivered by a footman that his father wished to see him in the library.

George V may have had a deliberate policy of intimidating his children, particularly his sons. The evidence is confused, but Harold Nicolson probably came nearest the mark when he recorded in his diary:

At dinner I sit next to Cromer. He makes interesting points about George V.[1] He believed that Princes ought to be brought up in fear of their father: "I was always frightened of my father; they must be frightened of me."[9]

At the very least, it seems clear that George V could be a very forbidding father and one likely to undermine the self-confidence of his offspring. It has been said, on the other hand, that he got on well with other people's children. This is not the impression given by his grandson, the Earl of Harewood, in his recently published memoirs *The Tongs and the Bones*. Recalling his childhood contact with the King he wrote:

We saw our royal relations comparatively often and regarded them therefore with awe rather than dread, though my grandfather the King found it so easy to find fault with anyone that what was probably a basic kindness was quite lost in his gruff exterior, added to which the ritual good morning and goodnight peck had to be offered to a beard of astonishing abrasiveness. I don't think he really cared much for children and he had a positive mania for punctuality.

The only person who was allowed to be late for anything, even breakfast, was apparently my mother, who was of course his only daughter, and whose instincts must have been similar to those of her two grandmothers, Queen Alexandra and the Duchess of Teck, each of whom was capable of being up to a couple of hours late for meals, which must have been astonishing even in Victorian times.

We used at Windsor to come down at nine o'clock to breakfast, not to eat – we'd done that – but to play, visibly of course but if possible inaudibly. The King had an African Grey parrot called Charlotte of which he was very fond, it sat at a table by his side eating seeds or the apple core he gave it, sometimes perching on people's hands, including my mother's. Like all parrots, it clung on hard and we were scared of those pinching claws and that awesome beak so that my grandfather shouted: "The parrot will see that child's nervous – make him keep still. . . ."[10]

The possibility of getting something wrong was, where my grandfather was concerned, raised to heights of extreme probability, and our visits to Windsor for Easter usually provided their quota of uneasy moments. In 1931 he had been dangerously ill and was terrified of getting a cold. I had started to get hay fever and at the end of April, as we went to say goodbye to him in the sitting room after breakfast, I started to sneeze, either from the pollinating grass or sheer nerves, and no amount of assurance that I had hay fever could stop the shouts of "Get that damn child away from me", which made a rather strong impression on an awakening imagination.[11]

Marion Crawford, nanny to the princesses Elizabeth and Margaret Rose, has also left a graphic account of her awesome first meeting with George V soon after she had taken up her post:

King George grunted and prodded the ground with his stick. At first acquaintance he was rather disconcerting. He had a loud, booming voice, rather terrifying to children and young ladies who did not know him. After a moment he said: "For goodness sake, teach Margaret and Lilibet to write a decent hand, that's all I ask you. Not one of my children can write properly. They all do it the same way. I like a hand with some character in it" he added, and walked away.[12]

Interestingly, George V's own handwriting has been described as 'slow and laboured, like a schoolboy's'. Kenneth Clark has said he never saw an adult man write so slowly. It would seem, therefore, that the King's irascible condemnation of his children's handwriting may have sprung from his own inadequacies in the art. Perhaps many of his criticisms of others originated in an inner recognition of his own failings.

The novelist and statesman John Buchan, however, thought that George V "had one key of access to all hearts, his sincere love of his fellows". He acknowledged that the King "could be explosive and denunciatory", but added that it was "always with a twinkle in his eye".

Mabell, Countess of Airlie, a lady-in-waiting to Queen Mary, has also left an account of the royal parents which, though basically favourable, intentionally or otherwise contains some telling criticisms:

King George V and Queen Mary have often been depicted as stern unloving parents, but this they most certainly were not. Remembering them in my early days at Sandringham, before their family was even complete, [before the births of Prince George in 1902 and Prince John in 1905] I believe that they were more conscientious and more truly devoted to their children than the majority of parents in that era. The tragedy was that neither had any understanding of a child's mind. They themselves had been brought up in particularly loving homes – Queen Alexandra had an almost cloying affection for her son; the Duchess of Teck was an adoring mother to Princess May – but they did not succeed in making their own children happy.[13]

Lady Airlie also remarked that, "Prince George was fond of his sons but his manner to them alternated between an awkward jocularity of the kind which makes a sensitive child squirm from self-consciousness, and a severity bordering on harshness."[14]

If George V's failings as a father are plain enough, his wife's inadequacies as a mother were perhaps even more serious. Lady Airlie was sympathetic, though perceptive:

Princess May's [Mary's] attitude to parenthood I could well understand, for it was much the same as my own. Although she disliked the routine of child-bearing, and had no interest in her children as babies, she grew to love them dearly when they were older. But the difference between us was that while I, being a commoner, could keep in step with my children as they passed from babyhood into childhood and adolescence, she was prevented by her position and her public life from having this close contact with them. When they reached an interesting age, and began to develop personalities, her sons were taken from her and delivered over to tutors. Her only opportunity of getting to know them as individuals was during the hour they spent with her in the evening, and that is not enough to create a happy relationship between child and parent.[15]

The future Queen Mary was prey to acute shyness, and so reserved in her emotions that she found it almost impossible to express them freely to her small children. The Empress Frederick considered her to be 'very cold and stiff and very unmaternal". According to Frances Donaldson, "Someone who knew her in later life summed up what dozens of people bear witness to by saying: 'Queen Mary had nothing of the mother at all.' "[16] So crippling was her inability to communicate easily with others, at least during this early stage of her marriage, that it was left to her husband to rebuke servants or alter arrangements for the children. Between her young children and her there was a chilling distance, and it is significant that she once wrote to her husband of her eldest son: "I really believe he begins to like me at last, he is most civil to me." Later, "I have always to remember that their father is also their King."

Nothing illustrates the sorry lack of a close physical and emotional involvement between the royal couple and their young children more plainly than the fiasco over Prince Edward's first nursemaid. This woman who was, it transpired, emotionally unstable, was so possessive of the baby prince that whenever she brought him into his parents' presence for some rather ritualized formal contact, she pinched him so that his cries of pain and outrage ensured his speedy return to her care.

It is difficult to know what effect this sadistic treatment had upon the development of the future King Edward VIII, although the fact that it cut down to the absolute minimum his physical contact with his parents was damaging enough. More significant is the implication that neither of his parents wished to keep and comfort him when he was handed, bawling, to them. Instead, he was passed back quickly and whisked out of sight. How such a disturbed and manipulative nursemaid could have been appointed in the first place, let alone sustained in her appointment for three years, is an unpleasant mystery. Furthermore, only when the nursemaid eventually revealed the extent of her problems by suffering a nervous breakdown did it come to light that she had not had a single day's holiday during her three years of service.

Although the nursemaid was dismissed, and her place taken by the under-nurse Mrs Bill – the altogether more wholesome and stable "Lala" – she had not only helped to damage Prince Edward's emotional development, but had also so consistently neglected Prince Albert Frederick, feeding him carelessly and erratically, that he developed chronic gastric troubles.

The Duke and Duchess of York were away from their young children for lengthy periods, quite apart from only seeing them briefly during the day when they were at home. In 1897 the couple paid a state visit to Ireland, and between March and November 1901 they undertook an Empire-wide tour which culminated in the Duke opening the first parliament of the new commonwealth of Australia. On her return, it is hardly surprising that the Duchess of York should have felt that, "The younger children had grown and altered so much that, when I got back, they seemed like little strangers." In October 1905 the Yorks embarked on a six-month tour of the Indian Empire.

[11]

Although, as they grew up, their mother came to play a more conventionally maternal part in their lives, reading to them and helping them with their problems, the royal children's early years were passed in an inhibiting atmosphere. York Cottage, on the Sandringham estate, was the first home of the Duke and Duchess of York and did not exactly provide a liberating environment. Sir Harold Nicolson described it as:

> . . . a glum little villa encompassed by thickets of laurel and rhododendron, shadowed by huge Wellingtonias and separated by an abrupt rim of lawn from a pond, at the edge of which a leaden pelican gazes in dejection upon the water lilies and bamboos. The local brown stone in which the house was constructed is concealed by roughcast which in its turn is enlivened by very imitation Tudor beams. The rooms inside, with their fumed oak surrounds, their white overmantels framing oval mirrors, their Doulton tiles and stained glass fanlights, are indistinguishable from those of any Surbiton or Upper Norwood home. The Duke's own sitting-room, its north window blocked by heavy shrubberies, was rendered even darker by the red cloth covering which saddened the walls. Against this dismal monochrome (which was composed of the cloth used in those days for the trousers of the French Army) hung excellent reproductions of some of the more popular pictures acquired by the Chantrey Bequests. This most undesirable residence remained his favourite home for thirty-three years. It was here that five of his six children were born.[17]

Lady Airlie has left an account of York Cottage which first emphasizes the difference between the royal couple's quarters and those of their children and attendants, and then describes its orderly atmosphere:

> In spite of its disadvantages she had succeeded by the time I arrived there in 1902 in imprinting her own personality on the Cottage. Her boudoir, which had the exquisite daintiness and freshness which I grew to associate with her, was charming. But many of the other rooms were very badly planned. The lady in waiting slept in a bedroom little bigger than a cupboard, and the nursery and school-room quarters were dark and depressing.[18]

The children were expected to keep within their own domain, except when they had a legitimate excuse for leaving it – on their way to their mother's boudoir after tea, or for a less pleasurable interview with their father in his sitting-room. I never saw them run along the corridors; they walked sedately, generally shepherded by nurses or tutors.[19]

The future Queen Mary, according to Osbert Sitwell, was almost obsessionally tidy:

Certainly [she] disliked untidiness in every form, even in plants that grew in a dishevelled manner and harboured dirt or dust: for this reason, among others, she was an inveterate and implacable foe to ivy, advising always that it should be cut down, and pulling it off walls herself and making others do so.[20]

In these circumstances, it is hardly surprising that the York children were, in various degrees, inhibited. Lady Airlie considered "Prince Edward, always called David, and Princess Mary . . . the least inhibited of the children – the former because as the eldest son he had the highest status in the family; the latter because she was her father's favourite. Although his jokes at her expense often made her cheeks crimson she was rarely scolded by him."[21] If Prince Edward was the least inhibited of the boys, he certainly did not escape unscathed. Quite apart from the emotional needs that led him ultimately to sacrifice his throne for Mrs Simpson, he exhibited various nervous traits throughout his young manhood, like tugging at his tie and fiddling with his coat lapels; he also smoked very heavily.

Prince Albert was in a particularly difficult position in the family, sandwiched between Prince Edward and the only girl, Princess Mary. His elder brother was more self-confident and enjoyed a pre-eminence as the future monarch. His sister was doted upon by their father; indeed, the Duke of York had fervently hoped that his second child would be a girl. When the third baby proved to be the longed-for daughter, a tremendous amount of paternal emotion was invested in her. So deep was the attachment that when Princess Mary married Lord Lascelles in February 1922, George V recorded in his diary, "I went up to Mary's room & took leave of her & quite broke down . . . Felt very down and depressed now that darling Mary has gone."[22] This almost excessive emotional attachment was very similar to the bond that had existed between Prince George and his mother, Queen

Alexandra. Hating to be parted from his "Darling Motherdear", Prince George's emotional dependence upon his beautiful mother had only been broken by his marriage to Princess Mary of Teck in 1893.

The pinching nursemaid had "frankly ignored [Prince Albert] to a degree which amounted virtually to neglect".[23] Given this and the other vicissitudes of his early upbringing it is little wonder that his official biographer, John Wheeler-Bennett, has described him thus, "a shy, nervous and affectionate child, frightened and somewhat prone to tears, he compared unfavourably with the gaiety of his more forthcoming elder brother and the inevitable charms of his baby sister." Squeezed between these two attractive siblings, Prince Albert sometimes escaped notice altogether as when Queen Victoria recorded in her diary, "The dear little York children came, looking very well. David is a delightful child, so intelligent, nice and friendly. The baby is a sweet, pretty little thing."[24] The old Queen made no mention of Prince Albert, who perhaps compensated for his difficult position in the family by engaging in mischievous pranks, even though these were often inspired by his elder brother. His father's exhortations to be more obedient were even included in his fifth birthday greetings.

Lady Airlie has left a sensitive account of Prince Albert's "naughtiness", and of his attempt to make friendly contact with her:

> The child to whom I was most drawn was Prince Albert – Bertie – although he was not a boy who made friends easily. Intensely sensitive over his stammer he was apt to take refuge either in silence – which caused him to be thought moody – or in naughtiness. He was more often in conflict with authority than the rest of his brothers.
>
> He made his first shy overture to me at Easter 1902 – after I had been only a few weeks in the Household – when he presented me with an Easter card. It was his own work, and very well done for a child of six – a design of spring flowers and chicks, evidently cut out from a magazine, coloured in crayons, and pasted on cardboard. He was so anxious for me to receive it in time for Easter that he decided to deliver it in person. He waylaid me one morning when I came out of his mother's boudoir, but at the last moment his courage failed him, and thrusting the card into my hand without a word he darted away.
>
> When I succeeded later in gaining his confidence he talked to me quite normally, without stammering, and then I found that far from

being backward he was an intelligent child, with more force of character than anyone suspected in those days.[25]

Prince Albert's stammer was a symptom of those insecurities that his parents had done little to dispel and much, unwittingly, to increase. Classically, his stammer vanished when he felt at ease and valued. There is some dispute as to when the stammering first manifested itself. It has been claimed by Sir Louis Greig, his mentor, friend, and tennis partner, that Prince Albert's stammer only started when he "had to make public speeches . . . It was never a natural stammer",[26] but this seems to be quite wrong. Lady Airlie had noticed it when the child was six years old. Another theory is that it began to be a problem after the prince's tutors forced him during his seventh and eighth years to write with his right hand, rather than his left which came more naturally to him. This, according to his official biographer "would create a condition known in psychology as a 'misplaced sinister' and may well have affected his speech".[27] This speech affliction, according to one authority, was treated callously and unthinkingly at home:

> His brothers and sister were allowed to make fun of his stammering, ragging him without mercy after the style set by his father's quarter-deck chaff, and he withdrew still more tightly into himself.[28]

As if this was not enough, Prince Albert suffered from knock-knees, like his father and all of his brothers except the eldest. A set of splints was devised to correct a failing deemed inappropriate for princes of the blood royal, and at the age of eight, for many months, he had to spend some hours each day and every night in these contraptions. For much of the time it was a wearisome business and at worst like some mild form of torture. Once Prince Albert begged his manservant Finch to allow him to sleep without them. Finch relented in the face of his young charge's bitter weeping and one night was spent without the splints. The Prince's father heard of this act of compassion and, summoning Finch to the library, displayed his own, uncorrected, knock-knees and roared, "Look at me. If that boy grows up to look like this, it will be your fault."[29]

For the most part, Prince Albert bore the splints with fortitude, writing stoically to his mother in 1904, "This is an experiment! I am sitting in the armchair with my legs in the new splints and on a chair. I have got an invalid table, which is splendid for reading but rather awkward for writing at present. I expect I shall get used to it."[30] Prince Albert's courage was rewarded. His knock-knees were eventually straightened out. Unfortunately his stammer and his chronic gastric troubles were not as easily cured.

It is little wonder that his frustrations and disabilities sometimes erupted in fits of ungovernable rage. "I am very sorry to say that Prince Albert has caused two painful scenes in his bedroom this week," wrote his first tutor, Mr Hansell, on 16 January 1904. "On the second occasion I understand that he narrowly escaped giving his brother a very severe kick, it being absolutely unprovoked & Finch being engaged in helping Prince Edward at the time."[31]

Prince Albert and his siblings found some solace in the affection and relaxed attention of their grandparents, Edward VII and Queen Alexandra. In their presence it was possible to indulge in high-spirited romps and to escape from the watchful and disapproving eye of their father. These hours of condoned mayhem must have tasted like great gulps of freedom, and Prince Albert was quite a favourite of his grandfather. His great grandmama Queen Victoria, on the other hand, was held in great awe by the family, and seems not to have played any creative role in Prince Albert's development; on the contrary, he felt uncomfortable in her presence.

Apart from Prince Edward and Princess Mary, three other brothers were born: Prince Henry (later Duke of Gloucester) in March 1900, Prince George (later Duke of Kent) in 1902 and Prince John in 1905. Although Prince Albert was to find much joy in his relationships with Prince Henry and Prince George, his youngest brother's life was a tragic one and ended in his sudden and premature death in 1919. Nothing much is known of Prince John. He is almost a skeleton in the Royal Family's cupboard. Sir John Wheeler-Bennett mentions him twice in his official biography of George VI, saying, of his death in January 1919:

> This handsome and lovable, but unfortunately quite abnormal, boy had lived in complete seclusion at Sandringham in the charge of Mrs Bill and a male attendant, and his sudden and peaceful death could only be regarded as a release from further suffering and misery.[32]

No one has ever disclosed the precise nature of Prince John's abnormality. He appears as a bouncing baby in a few family photographs.

Sir Harold Nicolson's official life of George V refers to him once in the text at the time of his death saying, simply but obscurely, that he "had for long been an invalid".[33] In James Pope-Hennessy's *Queen Mary* there is a brief footnote which informs us that, "Prince John . . . had early developed epilepsy and was segregated from his brothers and sister."[34] Later, there is a fuller description of his death.

Epilepsy seems to be the most commonly recorded description of Prince John's disability. Whether the epilepsy was the result of a difficult birth, an accident in infancy, or some undiagnosed mischance it is difficult to establish. What is certain is that Prince Albert's youngest brother lived the latter part of his brief life segregated from his family on medical advice. He has been described as living:

> . . . as a satellite with his own little household on an outlying farm on the Sandringham estate under the care of a nurse Lala [Mrs Bill]. When the family went to Scotland little Prince John would follow them, though at a distance. Guests at Balmoral remember him during the Great War, a distant figure, tall, muscular but always remote, who would be glimpsed from afar in the woods escorted by his own retainers.[35]

Apparently, Prince John "was a friendly, outgoing little boy, much loved by his brothers and sister, a sort of mascot for the family, who treasured his naïve little sayings in later years". His eventual exclusion from their company must have been a cause of sadness, perhaps even of feelings of guilt, but since he was only born in 1905 and had in any case lived for several years in the family home, his elder siblings in particular would have been able to understand and adjust to his predicament.

Still, at one level, his segregation and "abnormality" must have been disturbing to his brothers and sister. At the news of his death, Queen Mary was both grief-stricken and somewhat relieved, writing in her diary, "The news gave me a great shock, tho' for the poor little boy's restless soul, death came as a great relief. I broke the news to George & we motored down to Wood Farm. Found poor Lala very resigned but heartbroken. Little Johnnie looked very peaceful lying there."[36] Queen Mary also put her feelings into a letter written to her old friend Emily Alcock:

> For him it is a great relief, as his malady was becoming worse as he grew older, & he has thus been spared much suffering. I cannot say

how grateful we feel to God for having taken him in such a peaceful way, he just slept quietly into his heavenly home, no pain no struggle, just peace for the poor little troubled spirit which had been a great anxiety to us for many years, ever since he was four years old – The first break in the family circle is hard to bear but people have been so kind & sympathetic & this has helped us much.[37]

Although the immediate family circle (if Prince John can fairly be described as belonging to that circle) was thus broken in 1919, the wider family circle had suffered the far more momentous losses of Queen Victoria in 1901 and Edward VII in 1910. The five-year-old Prince Albert had stood among a host of domestic and foreign dignitaries on a bitingly cold afternoon in early February 1901 and watched the burial of his great-grandmother, the revered and awe-inspiring "Gangan". At least he would no longer have to suffer the ordeal of being presented to the old Queen, a contact which had almost invariably reduced Prince Albert (and Prince Edward) to frightened weeping, causing Victoria to ask "with the petulance of old age, what she had done wrong now".

Prince Albert first knew of the death of his greatly loved "Grand-papa" when, looking out of a window of Marlborough House on 7 May 1910, he saw the royal standard flying at half-mast over Buckingham Palace. There is no doubt which of the two monarchs the children mourned most sincerely.

Prince Albert's early education was as erratic and flawed as his upbringing. The year 1902 marked the ending of "Lala" Bill's benevolent reign, and two new influences entered his life. One was his manservant, Frederick Finch; the other was his tutor, Henry Peter Hansell.

Finch, who took charge of both Prince Edward and Prince Albert in 1902, was a great success. Described as "handsome, stalwart and muscular", he was also "naturally respectful but without a trace of servility".[38] He was thirty years old when he became, in effect, the two princes' "nursemaid", and for the next eight years he was responsible for their care, supervising their clothes, ensuring that they had washed properly, hearing their prayers, and coping with their tantrums and anxieties. There is no doubt that Finch was a good influence: fair, concerned, consistent and unruffled.

The same cannot be said for Mr Hansell. Appointed by the boys' father chiefly on account of his enthusiasm for yachting, Hansell, though tall and good looking, a competent academic and a keen sportsman, was often detached, much given to staring into space with his pipe in his mouth. Mr Hansell had neither a sense of humour nor any great insight. He expected obedience and hard work, but seems to have manifestly failed to captivate or stimulate his young charges' imaginations. It is perhaps symptomatic of Hansell's virtuous and humourless disposition that he was later to make Prince Edward head-boy in a "school" consisting of two pupils. When, in the spring of 1907, Prince Edward left for the Royal Naval College at Osborne, Prince Albert was appointed head-boy over his brother Prince Henry, who constituted the rest of the school. Such dizzy promotion did not increase Prince Albert's sense of responsibility, and in December 1907 Hansell told the Prince of Wales, "I should say that Prince Albert has failed to appreciate his position as 'captain'."

In fairness to Hansell, he did tell the Princes' father that his pupils might benefit more from contact with boys of their own age in a preparatory school. The Prince of Wales, however, recalling his own close attachment to his tutor the Reverend John Dalton, refused to consider such a move. So Hansell plodded on, aided with varying degrees of success by Walter Jones, the schoolmaster at Sandringham, Monsieur Hua who taught the royal children French, Professor Oswald the German tutor, and their maths teacher Martin David.

Prince Albert was not the ideal pupil. His stammer made foreign language practice an agony, his maths were at first very weak, and, in general, he found concentration difficult:

Driven in upon himself, he alternated between periods of dreamy abstraction, during which it seemed impossible to command his concentration, and outbursts of emotional excitement, sometimes of high spirits and exuberance, sometimes of passionate weeping and depression.[39]

Added to this, his father's testy and regular exhortations to do better and to "no longer behave like a little child of 6" could not have encouraged him to gain in confidence.

In 1908, he took the entrance examination for the Royal Naval College at Osborne. Thanks to some heavy cramming in mathematics, he passed the written examinations in December with some ease – having done "extremely well" in English, History and French. His interview, a month earlier, also went well after a bad start when he stammered and exhibited tremendous shyness.

It was clear, therefore, that despite his disabilities, Prince Albert could rise to a challenge and acquit himself with credit. It was a pattern that was to be characteristic of his later career.

2

THE NAVAL CADET

1909—1913

Now remember everything rests with you, and you are quite intelligent and can do well if you like.

George V to Prince Albert while
a naval cadet at Osborne, 1910

I am afraid there is no disguising to you that P[rince] A[lbert] has gone a mucker. He has been quite off his head, with the excitement of getting home, for the last few days, and unfortunately as those were the days of the examinations, he has come quite to grief. . . .

James Watt, Second Master at Osborne, to Mr Hansell, 1910

DURING HIS FIVE YEARS OF NAVAL TRAINING, Prince Albert progressed from the Royal Naval College at Osborne, to Dartmouth, and finally to the training ship HMS *Cumberland*. Prince Albert's father had received what was probably the most formative part of his education as a cadet in the Royal Navy, it seemed natural to him that his two eldest sons should follow his example. There was no featherbedding for princes in the Royal Navy. King George V later recalled:

It never did me any good to be a Prince, I can tell you, and many was the time I wished I hadn't been. It was a pretty tough place and, so far from making any allowances for our disadvantages, the other boys made a point of taking it out on us on the grounds that they'd never be able to do it later on . . . they used to make me go up and challenge the bigger boys – I was awfully small then – and I'd get a hiding time and again.[1]

Prince Albert was hardly better equipped to cope with the rigours and demands of life at the Royal Naval College at Osborne. To begin with, he was shy, nervous and particularly homesick. He had never before sat in a class of more than three, and never played a serious game of cricket or football in his life. In addition, the fact that he was a prince of the blood, and one who suffered from a stammer, encouraged his fellow cadets to taunt and tease him.

Despite the fact that in his first letter home to his mother, Prince Albert wrote "I have quite settled down here now", it is quite evident that it took him from January 1909 well into the summer term of the same year to adjust to the demands of his new environment. By that summer term, however, his friendly and open personality, and his growing skill at rugby and cricket, had made him more popular with his fellow cadets. Captain Christian, the Captain of Osborne College, said of him, "He shows the grit and never-say-I'm-beaten spirit which is strong in him – it is a grand trait in anybody's character." Later, at Dartmouth, another naval officer recalled, "One knew, instinctively, that he would never let you down . . . he never once asked for a favour all the time he was at Dartmouth, nor did he once use his position to gain a favour from anybody else."[2]

Prince Albert, despite his natural shyness and the disability of his stammer, proceeded to make a number of friends at Osborne. These included Jimmie James, Colin Buist, George Cavendish, Bill Slayter and Miles Reid. He continued to keep in touch with all of these throughout his naval career, and did not forget them in later life. For their part, they enjoyed his sense of fun and what has been called his complete lack of "side". He was also known for his integrity and courage, and for his general capacity for good fellowship. When he was with these friends, Prince Albert's stammer more or less disappeared.

Unfortunately, this was not so in class. He frequently found it impossible to participate in group discussions, and several of his masters were annoyed and impatient at his hesitation, failing to understand the cause of it. His father showed a deeper understanding of what was going on. Writing to Mr Hansell, "Watt thinks Bertie shy in class, I expect it is his dislike of showing his hesitating speech that prevents him from answering, but he will, I hope, grow out of it."

Towards the end of the summer term of 1909, and just before the State Visit of the Tsar of Russia, Prince Albert developed whooping cough. He was quickly put into quarantine, and the illness, though denying him the opportunity of meeting his royal Russian relatives, brought him into contact with a young Scotsman, Surgeon-Lieutenant Louis Greig. Greig was the Assistant Medical Officer at Osborne, and he was a hero to the cadets, more for his skill at coaching rugby football, than for his medical expertise. Prince Albert took an instant liking to this self-confident and tough young man, and a friendship developed between them which was to play a significant part in the later life of the Prince.

In May 1910, Prince Albert's grandfather, King Edward VII, died, and on 9 May the accession of King George V was proclaimed on the balcony of Friary Court, St James's Palace. Prince Edward and Prince Albert, dressed in naval uniforms, witnessed the ceremony from the garden wall of Marlborough House. Prince Edward now became Prince of Wales, and Prince Albert second in line to the succession to the throne.

There were, however, more pressing concerns for Prince Albert. In particular, it was not certain that he would make the grade for the transfer to Dartmouth at the end of 1910, as his academic perform-ance at Osborne had not been impressive and he had frequently been bottom of the class, or near the bottom, in many subjects. Captain Christian had written, "He is always very penitent with me, assures me that he is doing his best, and so on. I am sure the boy has determination and grit in him, but he finds it difficult to apply it to work, tho' with games it comes out strongly." One of his tutors commented, "With Prince Albert's mercurial temperament, all things are possible . . . I don't think he regards a rebuke any more seriously than his work." His father, though earlier prepared to be understanding, had consequently issued him with a stern reprimand on the subject:

"My dearest Bertie,
I am sorry to have to say that the last reports from Mr Watt [the Second Master] with regard to your work, are not at all satisfactory, he says you don't seem to take your work at all seriously, nor do you appear to be very keen about it. My dear boy, this will not do, if you go on like this you will be at the bottom of your Term . . . and you won't pass your examination, and very probably will be *warned* this term if you don't take care. You know it is Mamma's and my great wish that you should go into the Navy, and I believe that you are anxious to do so, but unless you now put your shoulder to the wheel and really try and do your best to work hard, you will have no chance of passing any of your examinations. It will be a great bore, but if I find that you have not worked well at the end of this term, I shall have to get a Master for you to work with all the holidays, and you will have no fun at all. Now remember, everything rests with you, and you are quite intelligent, and can do very well if you like. I trust that you will take to heart what I have written, and that the next report will be a good one, and the others to come, until the end of the term."[3]

Although Prince Albert avoided the necessity of having a home tutor, his academic performance during his last few months at Osborne was far from satisfactory. In the end of term examinations in December 1910, he did very badly indeed. The excitement engendered by the prospect of returning to Sandringham for the Christmas holidays had apparently destroyed his powers of concentration. Mr Watt wrote despairingly to Mr Hansell:

> ... I am afraid their Majesties will be very disappointed, and I can well understand it. But after all, the boy must be at the least stable part of his mental development, and I expect another year will produce a great change in him."

There could be no disguising the fact that Prince Albert's final position at Osborne was sixty-eighth out of sixty-eight.

Despite these lamentable results, Prince Albert *was* allowed to proceed to the Royal Naval College at Dartmouth. He arrived there on a grey January afternoon in 1911. Here he joined his brother, the Prince of Wales, who was in his last year. Prince Albert did not make a brilliant start at Dartmouth. He was at once assigned for extra tuition in mathematics and engineering to a Lieutenant Start. Start, who was another of the Prince's tutors with a distinguished sporting reputation, at least succeeded in encouraging Prince Albert to make some academic headway. Indeed, as a reward for his pupil's hard work, shortly before the beginning of the holidays Start gave him a set of teaspoons made of an amalgam of metals which looked very like silver, but which would melt at 160°F. These trick spoons would dissolve in a cup of tea, as the tea was stirred. The Prince reported to Start on his return to Dartmouth after the holidays that he had tried the trick at Sandringham, with excellent results, although his father had not been amused.

Prince Albert's first six months at Dartmouth were marked by two occurrences, one potentially lethal, the other more satisfying. In the first instance, an epidemic of measles and mumps swept through the naval college, and both princes were among the victims of both diseases. They were sufficiently ill for bulletins to be issued to the press, but by the beginning of March they were discharged from medical attention and went to recuperate at Newquay, at the Headlands Hotel, under the supervision of their old tutor, Mr Hansell.

In June 1911, Prince Albert participated in the great ceremonials attending the Coronation of his father as King George V. Dressed in naval cadet's uniform, he drove to the Abbey in the Prince of Wales' procession, where, with his three brothers and sister, he watched the age-old and majestic ceremony of the Coronation, and saw his elder brother pay homage to their father. They then took part in the lengthy ceremonial drive back to Buckingham Palace through the cheering crowds, and appeared with the King and Queen on the balcony.

When he returned to Dartmouth, he went straight back to his studies, but his tutors still found him wanting in concentration. One of them wrote, "He can concentrate, but at present he will not force himself to do so for more than a minute or two; it is a spasmodic effort to satisfy us, not the deliberate choice of his own mind." Therefore, during the summer vacation at Balmoral, Mr Watt was engaged to tutor Prince Albert in physics and mathematics. In view of the fact that Prince Albert had finished sixty-seventh out of sixty-eight at the end of the summer term at Dartmouth, this extra tuition was very necessary.

Although some progress was made in the offending subjects during the summer vacation, King George took his second son to task before his return to Dartmouth, urging upon him the virtues of hard work and self discipline. He followed this up with a letter:

I trust you will take to heart all I told you before you left, & remember yr. position, & that is for you to set an example to the others, & you must really work hard & try your best and soon I hope go up several places, as it does look so bad that you are practically last in your term, & everyone says that you can do much better if you like.[4]

By the end of the Christmas term, Prince Albert had satisfied his father's demand to some extent. He was now marked sixty-third, a rise of four places, and his tutor's reports were encouraging.

Life at Dartmouth did not consist only of hard academic work. It seems that Prince Albert had the opportunity to get up to mischief as well. On Guy Fawkes night, 1912, he and some sixteen other cadets let off fireworks in the college's lavatories. Together with the others, the Prince was given six strokes of the cane, although he was later to complain that since the cane had broken at the fourth stroke, he should not have received the remaining two.

In April 1912, at the Parish Church at Sandringham, where he had been baptized, Prince Albert was confirmed by Bishop Boyd-

Carpenter, the Clerk of the Closet. The Prince was apparently greatly moved by the ceremony of confirmation, and two years later wrote to Bishop Boyd-Carpenter, "It will be just two years ago tomorrow that you confirmed me at the small church at Sandringham. I have always remembered that day as one on which I took a great step in life. I took the Holy Sacrament on Easter Day alone with my father and mother, my eldest brother and my sister. It was so very nice having a small service, quite alone like that, only the family."

During his last six months at Dartmouth, Prince Albert continued to make steady, though unspectacular, academic progress. His final position was sixty-first, which was a moderate improvement. None of his tutors yet considered him to be outstanding, either in academic work or even in games. On the other hand, he had acquired an admirable reputation for generosity, loyalty and the capacity for sharing in fun. One of his tutors summed him up by saying, "Quite unspoiled, and a nice honest, clean-minded and excellent-mannered boy." It was a judgement which must have pleased his father.

The final part of Prince Albert's naval training took place aboard the 9,800-ton cruiser *Cumberland*, which he joined at Devonport on 17 January 1913.

Aboard HMS *Cumberland*, Prince Albert had to put into practice the theoretical training he had acquired at Osborne and Dartmouth. Quite apart from this, he was obliged to experience, at first hand, the various tasks of those whom he would one day have to command. Thus he coaled the furnaces, like everybody else on board, and went on watch under the supervision of his officers. More important, perhaps, the cruise on HMS *Cumberland* brought him into contact with the world outside. A further advantage, since Prince Edward was not aboard *Cumberland*, was that he no longer was likely to be compared unfavourably with his elder brother. One contemporary, remembering them both at an earlier stage of their naval training, recalled, "It was like comparing an ugly duckling with a cock pheasant." The ugly duckling was now about to strike off into the world in his own right.

The *Cumberland*'s cruise lasted from 18 January to 8 July 1913, and took her from Tenerife to the West Indies, Halifax, Nova Scotia, Quebec, St John's, Newfoundland and finally back to Plymouth. Prince Albert was thus able to witness the enthusiasm of many of his father's subjects at first hand. In Jamaica, he faced the ordeal of officially opening the new wing of the Kingston Yacht Club, of which the main building had been opened by his father in 1901. The speech was not a great success. Quite apart from Prince Albert's anxiety lest he should stammer, several young Jamaican women stood round him on the platform as he spoke, and prodded his ankles and thighs. One whispered to her friend, "Say, have you touched the Prince?" Her friend replied rapturously, "Yes, three times." At the very least, this was a new experience.

Later, in Canada, Prince Albert was pursued by the press. He wrote in his diary, "I was hunted all the time by photographers, and also by the Americans, who had not manners at all, and tried to take photographs all the time." He went salmon fishing on the Gaspe peninsular, and in Newfoundland, his hosts noticed that he seemed completely at ease while engaged in this sport, and that his stammer was not in evidence.

When Prince Albert returned to England in July 1913, his father noticed on greeting him that he had changed a great deal. He seemed more grown up, with more self-confidence, and was able to express himself more fluently. A little later, King George met Prince Albert's Term Officer aboard HMS *Cumberland*, and said to him, "Thank you. I am pleased with my boy." It was sufficient.

3

THE ROYAL NAVY

1913–1917

At the commencement I was sitting at the top of A turret, and had a very good view of the proceedings. I was up there during a lull, when a German ship started firing at us, and one salvo "straddled" us. We at once returned the fire. I was distinctly startled, and jumped down the hole in the top of the turret like a shot rabbit!
Prince Albert on his part in the Battle of Jutland, 1916

PRINCE ALBERT WAS APPOINTED MIDSHIPMAN on 15 September 1913, barely eleven months before the outbreak of the First World War. Halfway through that conflict, the Prince took part in the Battle of Jutland, thus becoming the only British monarch in recent history to have been on active service. It cannot, however, be claimed that Prince Albert's naval career was an unqualified success. Although between 1913 and 1916 he rose from the rank of midshipman to lieutenant, his progress was dogged by chronic seasickness, and other disabilities.

His first appointment was in the 19,250-ton battleship *Collingwood*, commanded by Captain James Ley. Midshipman Prince Albert was accorded no special privileges, as this rank were at the beck and call of their superior officers aboard ship. Even when off duty, he and a dozen others shared a flat outside the gun-room, where all his clothes and personal belongings were stored in a tea-chest, above which he slung his hammock at night. In addition, he carried out the daily routine of the midshipman, such as standing watch, taking his picket boat to shore, and working hard at coaling the battleship. He was known aboard ship simply as Mr Johnson, a further indication of his lack of privilege. Being, at seventeen, one of the lowest forms of life in the Royal Navy could not fail to be an excellent training for a prince. As a result, and despite his innate conservatism, Prince Albert was always able to demonstrate that he had the common touch. At the same time, his naval duties imposed a considerable degree of responsibility, and there was soon ample evidence that the experience was maturing and developing his personality.

At the end of October, 1913, *Collingwood* sailed as part of the first battle squadron, from Devonport, to take part in manoeuvres in the Mediterranean, and then to cruise in Egyptian and Aegean waters.

During this voyage, Prince Albert saw Alexandria where the fleet docked after its manoeuvres. He stayed with Lord Kitchener of Khartoum, the British Agent and the effective ruler of Egypt. Kitchener presented Prince Albert to the Khedive, Abbas II, who must have wondered at the sight of the second son of the King-Emperor serving in so humble a position aboard a British warship. While he was in Egypt, Prince Albert was taken by a guide to the top of the great Pyramid, where the initials 'AE' were pointed out to him, scratched into the stone. They were the mark of his grandfather, King Edward VII, made there fifty years before.

After Alexandria, the fleet sailed to Greece, where it anchored in the Bay of Salamis. Despite suffering from a cold, Prince Albert was able to make some contact with his Greek relatives, particularly King Constantine and Queen Sophie. He recorded in his diary, "I saw Uncle Tino, Aunt Sophie and the cousins, and then I went with George and Alexander to see the Acropolis and museums. After lunch I looked at some photographs of the War. After tea I motored down to Piraeus with Aunt Sophie, and returned to the ship in the barge. I changed and then helped with the main derrick. After supper, we left Salamis Bay for Malta. I turned in at 9.30."[1]

By December 1913, *Collingwood* was back at Gibraltar. There, Prince Albert celebrated his eighteenth birthday, the first birthday and the first Christmas he had spent away from home. The entry in his diary read, "My eighteenth birthday, and I am allowed to smoke." In celebration of his birthday his mother had sent him a cigarette case, which he acknowledged in a grateful letter, written from Toulon. Thus began Prince Albert's long addiction to nicotine, a taste which was eventually to lead to lung cancer and his premature death in 1952. At the end of December the first Battle Squadron returned to its home base, and Prince Albert was able to join his family at Sandringham for the new year celebrations. His father was pleased with further signs of his son's growing maturity.

For the next six months, Prince Albert served aboard his ship, with routine periods of leave with his family. That he lived a very ordinary life aboard HMS *Collingwood* is indicated by the account he sent to his father of a minor injury he suffered as a result of being tipped out of his hammock by another midshipman. ". . . hit my left eye on my chest. It swelled up very much, and yesterday it was bandaged up. I did not touch it, or actually hurt the eyeball, but it was very sore all round. It is much better today, but I expect I shall have a black eye for a few days."[2] King George V replied sympathetically, "Sorry that with the help of someone else you fell out of yr. hammock, and hit your eye on yr. chest, it must have hurt a good deal, but glad it didn't damage yr. eye permanently. I should do the same to the other fellow, if I got the chance."

Meanwhile, the old order in Europe was passing. The assassination in June 1914 of the Archduke Franz Ferdinand, at Sarajevo, began the lengthy and in some ways unnecessary descent into full-scale hostilities. On 15 July 1914 the Naval Reserve began a test mobilization on the orders of Winston Churchill, the First Lord of the Admiralty. On 28 July, Austria declared war on Serbia in retaliation for the assassination of the Archduke. On the very same day, the British fleet was despatched to its war station, and the battle squadrons began to leave Portland to concentrate at Scapa Flow. *Collingwood* took part in this great naval migration, and Prince Albert reported in his diary, "After dinner, I kept the first watch, and we went to night defence stations. The four-inch guns were all ready for a destroyer attack. We passed the Straits of Dover at 12.00. I then turned in."

On 4 August, Britain declared war on Germany. Aboard HMS *Collingwood*, Prince Albert recorded, "I got up at 11.45, and kept the middle watch till 4.00. War was declared between us and Germany at 2.00 am. I turned in again at 4.00 until 7.15. Sir John Jellicoe took over the command from Sir George Callaghan. After divisions, we went to control. I kept the afternoon watch till 4.00 pm. Two German trawlers were captured by destroyers. Papa sent a most interesting telegram to the Fleet. I put it down in words."

Back in London, George V wrote in his diary, "Please God it may soon be over, & that he will protect dear Bertie's life." As it happened, there was no immediate cause for alarm. *Collingwood* played her part in the routine patrolling of the coast and Prince Albert performed his routine duties as midshipman in the 'A' turret of the battleship. For the most part, these duties consisted of enduring lengthy periods at sea, interspersed with brief bouts of shore leave at Rosyth.

With his second son at sea in the Royal Navy, the King found it easier to express the growing warmth of his regard, writing, "It has all come so suddenly . . . always do your duty. May God bless and protect you, my dear boy, is the earnest prayer of your ever devoted Papa." A few days later the King was reminding his son that "you can be sure that you are constantly in my thoughts". In fact, the main hazard which Prince Albert faced in these early months of the war came not from the German High Seas Fleet, but from a series of gastric illnesses. Doubtless the tensions of war service revived the gastric ailments that had characterized his childhood.

On 23 August, however, something more serious occurred. Prince Albert noted in his diary, "I then went to the sick bay with a violent pain in the stomach. I could hardly breathe. They put hot fomentations on it, which eased it. . . . Morphia was injected into my arm. I was put to bed in the Commander's cabin at 8.00 and I slept the whole night." Within two days, appendicitis had been diagnosed. Prince Albert was moved from *Collingwood* to the hospital ship *Rohilla*, at Wick. Eventually, despite the menace of a German submarine in the vicinity, *Rohilla* was sent to Aberdeen on 28 August. The next day Prince Albert was occupying a bed in the Northern Nursing Home. On 9 September he was operated on by Professor John Marnoch of Aberdeen University. The operation was perfectly straightforward and successful, and within a few days Prince Albert was writing to his parents:

> I am afraid you must be rather frightened when you heard I was ill. I am much better now, and feel quite happy . . . the pain has practically gone away, although it hurt a good deal last Sunday . . . you must be very sorry at not being able to go up to Scotland this year as usual. You must be very tired after all this very trying time with so much work to do, and so many people to see, and never getting a rest. . . .
>
> Best love to you dearest Papa, Mama and Mary, and my thoughts are always with you. Your most devoted son, Bertie.

Because of his appendicitis, Prince Albert had missed the first engagement of the war, when the fleet had encountered the enemy at the Battle of Heligoland Bight. Moreover, for a time it seemed that he might never go to sea again. Sir Frederick Treves, the King's surgeon, was adamant that the convalescence should be a protracted one, even arguing that the Prince should not be allowed to go back to the Navy. Eventually it was arranged that he should go to work on the War Staff at the Admiralty, and on 2 December 1914 he reported there and was received by Winston Churchill, the First Lord of the Admiralty, and taken to see the War Room, where the great charts showed the position and movement of every British warship. Shore work, however, did not appeal to him, and he was soon showing his eagerness to get back on active duty. At length, in February 1915, after an interview with the Second Sea Lord, he was given permission to return to sea. He wrote to his father, "I was really very sorry to leave last Friday, and I felt quite homesick the first night, not being used to a hammock. But of course I knew that it was quite right for me to go back, now that I have quite recovered from my appendicitis." His father replied, somewhat oddly, a few days later, "I miss you still very much, especially at breakfast."

Back aboard the *Collingwood*, Prince Albert now took up the post of senior midshipman. His new duties included being in control of searchlights and in charge of submarine lookouts during the daytime. The pattern of the naval war had changed since his sick leave. Now, units of the Fleet only went out into the North Sea for three-day tours of duty, remaining in harbour at Scapa Flow for ten days. This meant that a good deal of Prince Albert's new responsibilities were undertaken on shore. While ashore, he worked as an assistant to the gunnery and torpedo lieutenants, and commanded a variety of small boats, servicing the Fleet. For the most part, the Prince's routine was a dreary one, but he was able to correspond regularly with his father and mother, and it is from these letters that we learn of the exciting or dramatic incidents of these months. The nearest that Prince Albert came to experiencing a taste of real action was when *Collingwood* and other warships bumped into several German submarines, one of them being sunk from a blow from the *Dreadnought*'s bow. The appalling losses being suffered by the British Army on the western front were brought home at a personal level to Prince Albert with the death in action of John Bigge, son of King George V's Private Secretary, Lord Stamfordham. Later, the sinking of the *Lusitania* on 7 May 1915, with the loss of 1198 lives, caused Prince Albert to write to his father, ". . . a terrible catastrophe, with so much loss of life. It makes one angry to think that after a thing like *Lusitania* going down, we cannot do anything in revenge. Here we are, absolutely ready the whole time, and still we have to wait."[3]

Prince Albert was further frustrated by the return of his gastric troubles three months after his return to the *Collingwood*. By the middle of May 1915, he was complaining of the attacks. They were particularly trying in that he never knew when to expect them, and they might seize him while on duty. By the beginning of July he had lost so much weight, and was exhibiting so much anxiety, that he was transferred to a hospital ship for a period of observation and recuperation.

Prince Albert's second bout of sick leave was no more comprehensible than the first. What was really wrong with him? The diagnosis was of a weakening of the muscular wall of the stomach, resulting in a catarrhal condition. The treatment of this condition was hardly agreeable: a quiet, regular life, careful dieting, and the pumping out of the contents of his stomach every night – a process which he described in great detail to his mother in a letter of 21 July 1915. Recovery was not easy and there were frequent relapses. His failure to recover as quickly as expected put his medical advisers into a quandary. However, Prince Albert had received assurances from his father, his captain, and from the consultant to the Fleet, Sir William Watson Cheyne, that if the Fleet put to sea for action, he would immediately be recalled for duty.

On 10 August 1915, Captain Ley, commander of the *Collingwood* told King George V of his anxiety about Prince Albert's health. Expressing his misgivings over his undertaking to summon Prince Albert back to the *Collingwood* in the event of naval action, Captain Ley wrote:

> Ten days ago Dr Sutton told me that it would be most unadvisable, even dangerous to his health, to do so. Since then he has been improving steadily, but today he has again informed me that, taking everything into consideration, he does not consider that the Prince's condition would allow of his being embarked at the present time. . . .
>
> At the same time I feel strongly that should I . . . go to sea without him, I should be breaking my word to Your Majesty and Prince Albert. Nevertheless, I consider that this would be my right course.[4]

King George would have none of this. Convinced that his son would not want to miss any great sea action, and doubtless, with his own naval career behind him, wishing to experience any moment of glory vicariously through Prince Albert, the King told Captain Ley that:

> He attached the utmost importance to keeping faith with Prince Albert, with regard to the promise given HRH that in the event of the Fleet putting to sea, he should return to *Collingwood*.

. . . there is in the King's opinion only one alternative, and that is to declare that the Prince is medically unfit for service; to send him on sick leave and place him in a nursing home under special treatment.

This course His Majesty would however strongly deprecate.

. . . HM also remembers that you think that the Prince's illness gets somewhat on his nerves, which seems to be another reason for refraining from any action likely to upset HRH.[5]

Here, encapsulated in his father's letter, was Prince Albert's problem. That he wanted to return to sea was not in doubt. That his nervous and anxious disposition had exacerbated his physical ailments seems very likely. At the same time, the Prince knew how dearly the King wished him to participate in some great high seas naval action. He was aware that his father was investing more and more in him, in his reliability, obedience, and the capacity to mirror the paternal image. All of this must have put an enormous pressure upon the young naval officer. His father swung between consideration, understanding and impatience, on the one hand writing to his son, "you can't expect to get well in a minute, anything to do with the stomach must take a little time to get right," and on the other, expressing his exasperation to his old friend Admiral Sir Stanley Colville at his son's continuing indisposition.

At length a compromise was found. In mid-September 1915 Prince Albert was sent to convalesce at Abergeldie in the Highlands, where he was joined by Mr Hansell for a month. In October, however, he was still declared unfit for duty. His anxious state was not improved by the news of his father's accident in France at the end of October: the King had been pitched from his horse while inspecting men from the first Wing of the Royal Flying Corps, and had received serious injuries. By the end of 1915 Prince Albert, still unwell, was granted three months' sick leave by the Naval Medical Board.

Although he was officially attached to the Admiralty for light duties, these amounted to very little, and Prince Albert's spirits remained depressed. One breath of fresh air, bringing him near to real action in the war, occurred at the end of January 1916 when he went to spend four days with the Prince of Wales, who was attached to the Head-quarters Staff of the Army in France. He returned to London with more self-confidence, and with fresh determination to fight off his illness.

While on sick leave, Prince Albert began his official career as a working member of the Royal Family, although his duties were not particularly onerous. On 17 March 1916 he performed his first public function when he opened a new rifle range installed for the use of Members of Parliament in the Palace of Westminster. He concluded his short speech by saying, "I shall declare the range open by firing the first shot, and I will try my very best to obtain a bull's eye." (The shot was, in fact, an inner, just above the bull's eye.) A little later, he welcomed the Crown Prince of Serbia on his arrival at Charing Cross for a visit to Britain. Despite having to converse in French, he did well enough, though writing to his friend Louis Greig, "I am still leading the quiet life, with a Serbian Prince thrown in last week. Pretty stiff time with him, as he can't talk English."

At the beginning of May 1916 he was at last allowed to rejoin *Collingwood*. A few weeks earlier he had passed his examinations to be an acting sub-lieutenant, and was later made up to substantive rank. He rejoined the Fleet only just in time. It was clear, by the spring of 1916, that the German High Seas Fleet could no longer skulk within the safety of harbour, and the failure of the German army to make a dramatic breakthrough on the Western Front accentuated the demand for victorious action at sea. On 30 May the British Battle Fleet from Scapa and Cromarty under Sir John Jellicoe, and the Battle Squadrons from Rosyth under Sir David Beatty, put to sea, knowing that the German High Seas Fleet was steaming into the North Sea off the Norwegian coast.

The scene was now set for the most significant naval confrontation of the war. It was the day for which the Royal Navy, and, perhaps with less enthusiasm, the German navy, had thirsted since the beginning of hostilities. The Battle of Jutland, brief, oblique, and ultimately indecisive, was about to take place. Ironically, when *Collingwood*, with the first Battle Squadron, put to sea, on the night of Tuesday 30 May, Prince Albert was in the sick bay. Whether his indisposition was the result of his old gastric and nervous problems, or the effect of eating too much soused mackerel with a fellow lieutenant on the previous Saturday night, is not clear. What is clear is that he was revived by the call to action early in the afternoon of 31 May. A fellow lieutenant, Tait, serving on *Collingwood*, sent an amusing account of Prince Albert's recuperation to his brother, the Prince of Wales:

Suddenly, at about 2.00 pm a signal was received that the German High Seas Fleet was out, and engaging our battle cruisers only forty miles away, and that the battle was coming in our direction. Huge excitement. Out at last. Full speed ahead. Sound off "action" – you can imagine the scene! Out of his bunk leaps "Johnson". Ill? Never felt better! Strong enough to go to his turret and fight a prolonged action? Of course he was, why ever not?[6]

Sub-Lieutenant "Johnson" remained in his turret until the action finally ceased the next day. *Collingwood*, in fact, had little contact with the main German Battle Fleet apart from seeing the distant flashes of their guns. She was, however, attacked by torpedo craft, and saw the destruction of HMS *Defence*, and then *Black Prince*, uncomfortably near at hand.

HMS *Collingwood*'s great moment came when the German warship *Derfflinger* suddenly emerged from the mist leading a division of the enemy's ships. *Collingwood*'s great guns fired three salvoes, at eight thousand yards' range at *Derfflinger*. Huge gaps were torn in the enemy's side, and flames flickered through a hole in her quarter deck. But *Collingwood* was unable to finish her off. It was nine o'clock, and the darkness was closing in. Everywhere the action died away, and men in both battle fleets manned their guns, waiting for attacks which never came.

Prince Albert left a graphic account of his experiences in a letter written to his parents:

I was in A turret, and watched most of the action through one of the trainer's telescopes, as we were firing by Director, when the turret is trained in the working chamber, and not in the gun house. At the commencement I was sitting at the top of A turret, and had a very good view of the proceedings. I was up there during a lull, when a German ship started firing at us, and one salvo "straddled" us. We at once returned the fire. I was distinctly startled, and jumped down the hole in the top of the turret like a shot rabbit!! I didn't try the experience again. The ship was in a fine state on the main deck. Inches of water sluicing about to prevent fires getting a hold on the deck. Most of the cabins were also flooded.

The hands behaved splendidly, and all of them in the best of spirits, as their hearts' desire had at last been granted, which was to be in action with the Germans. Some of the turret's crew actually took on bets with one another that we should not fire a shot. A good deal of money must have changed hands, I should think, by now.

My impressions were very different to what I expected. I saw visions of the masts going over the side and funnels hurtling through the air etc. In reality, none of these things happened and we are still quite sound as before. No one would know to look at the ship that we had been in action. It was certainly a great experience to have been through and it shows we are at war and that the Germans can fight if they like.[7]

It seemed clear that this active involvement in the Battle of Jutland had helped Prince Albert to cast aside illness and depression. In the process, he had gained immeasurably in self-knowledge. Writing to the Prince of Wales, he said, "when I was on top of the turret I never felt any fear of shells or anything else. It seemed curious but all sense of danger and everything else goes except the one longing of dealing death in every possible way to the enemy." There is no doubt that Prince Albert had enjoyed his taste of action, and that it enabled him to identify more strongly than ever with the wartime experiences of his father's subjects. For his part, King George V said simply, "I am pleased with my son."

The Battle of Jutland provided the high point of Prince Albert's war. Indeed, the German High Seas Fleet never put to sea again, not wanting to risk an engagement with the Royal Navy. In that sense, Jutland was a British victory, although the Navy's losses had in fact been more serious than those suffered by the enemy.

Despite the exhilaration he experienced as a participant in the Battle of Jutland, Prince Albert's low resistance to illness had not vanished. Perhaps the monotony of Naval service after Jutland had something to do with it. At any rate, on the evening of 26 August 1916, he went sick, complaining of severe pains in his stomach, and was transferred to the Naval hospital at South Queensferry, and later to Windsor, where his mother described him as looking 'rather thin' and in need of rest. His illness was shortly diagnosed as a duodenal ulcer. This, at the very least, necessitated a lengthy period of rest. Although he did not know it, he was never to rejoin *Collingwood.*

Apart from being once more shorebound, Prince Albert seems to have been relieved at the diagnosis. The abdominal pains from which he had been suffering were not due to some malignant growth, as he had feared, and there was every chance that routine and rest would cure the ulcer. At the beginning of November 1916, moreover, he was appointed to the staff of the Commander-in-Chief at Portsmouth, Sir

Stanley Colville, his father's old friend. So for nearly six months he was deskbound, but as his health continued to improve he waged a persistent campaign to be recalled to his maritime duties.

In December 1916 Prince Albert celebrated his twenty-first birthday at Buckingham Palace, and was invested by his father with the Order of the Garter. Prince Albert was deeply touched by the award, taking it as an indication of his father's confidence and esteem. He wrote to his mother, "you don't know how proud I felt when Papa gave me the Garter." He told King George, "I cannot thank you enough for making me a Knight of the Garter. I feel very proud to have it, and will always try to live up to it."

In May 1917, Prince Albert's wish to return to active service was granted. He reported for duty aboard the 27,500-ton battleship *Malaya*, commanded by Captain Boyle. He now had the rank of acting lieutenant, and was delighted that later Dr Louis Greig was appointed the ship's second surgeon. The Prince wrote to his mother, "It is so nice, having a real friend as a mess mate, and he is very cheery." The Prince and Greig were to remain close companions for the next six years. Alas, by the end of July 1917 the Prince was once more suffering from his gastric troubles, and early in August he was transferred to South Queensferry Hospital from the *Malaya*. Louis Greig went with him. Those who visited him found him deeply depressed, very thin and ill.

Prince Albert had reached a point of crisis in his life. It had become clear that the strains of naval duty were too much for his constitution and for his temperament. He now felt able to write to his father, "personally, I feel that I am not fit for service at sea, even when I recover from this little attack". During the autumn of 1917 Prince Albert agitated for an operation, which he believed would remove the cause of his medical troubles. King George V's medical advisers were divided as to whether this was necessary, and while the wisdom of an operation was being debated, Prince Albert was transferred to the Royal Naval Air Service Station at Cranwell, where he was gazetted on 13 November 1917. The idea had originated with Prince Albert himself and, in his own words, "Papa jumped at the idea." The faithful Louis Greig was due to accompany him.

Unfortunately, before the transfer to Cranwell could be made, the Prince suffered a further serious attack of duodenal pain. On 29 November 1917 he was operated upon, and according to Queen Mary's diary, "the operation was very successful, and they found the cause of all the trouble he's been having since 1915." Here was an irony indeed. If these gastric troubles had been correctly diagnosed earlier, Prince Albert would have been spared many months of humiliation and depression. On the other hand, he had suffered both physical pain and much emotional distress, and had in the end won through. It had been an experience that he was never to forget.

4

FURTHER EDUCATION

1918–1920

*The work is entirely new to me and I find it rather difficult to begin with,
but I shall get used to it.*

Prince Albert as Officer Commanding no. 4 Squadron,
Boy Wing, Cranwell, 1918

We're not a family, we're a firm.

Prince Albert at Cambridge, 1920

PRINCE ALBERT WAS APPOINTED to HMS *Daedalus* on 1 January 1918; a month later he reported there to begin his duties. Despite its nautical name, HMS *Daedalus* was simply a rambling training station for pilots and aerial gun-layers in aeroplanes and airships, set on a windswept plateau in Lincolnshire, twelve miles to the north-east of Grantham. Although naval discipline and terminology were much in evidence, *Daedalus* consisted chiefly of hangars for the aircraft, and corrugated iron huts which housed some thousands of officers, men and boys, drawn from both the Royal Naval Air Service and the Royal Flying Corps.

From this jumble of temporary accommodation, and from two distinct air services, great things were to develop. On 1 April 1918 a unified air service was created, and named, by Royal Proclamation, as the Royal Air Force. Also, on 5 February 1920, the Royal Air Force Cadet College was inaugurated at Cranwell, although it was not until October 1934 that the new and imposing buildings of the college were officially opened by the Prince of Wales.

King George V had considered it entirely appropriate that one of his sons should be closely identified with the new service, and Prince Albert's transfer to HMS *Daedalus* was rendered even more apt by the entry of the King's fourth son, Prince George, later Duke of Kent, into the Royal Navy as a cadet. (Prince George, incidentally, left Dartmouth in May 1920, causing his brother Prince Albert to write to a friend, "he has kept up the best traditions of my family by passing out of Dartmouth 1 from bottom, the same place as I did!!!!")

Soon Prince Albert was hard at work as Officer Commanding no. 4 Squadron, Boy Wing. It was a challenge to his powers of leadership and organization, and provided him with his first real experience of responsibility for a large number of subordinates. Soon he was writing proudly to his father:

> I am going to run them as an entirely separate unit to the remainder of the men, and I am known as the Officer Commanding Boys. I shall have to punish them myself, and grant their requests for leave, etc. At present I have not got a proper office but I hope to get one shortly. The work is entirely new to me and I find it rather difficult to begin with, but I shall get used to it. They live in small huts, 20 boys in each, and these give me the most trouble as they won't keep them clean without my constantly telling them off to clean them out of working hours.[1]

The anxiety and sense of inadequacy which he still undoubtedly felt at one level explains his tendency to be a strict disciplinarian at Cranwell. Certainly the obsession with correct uniform and displays of decoration, a trait which he shared with his father, and which was to be a characteristic for the rest of his life, does not indicate a relaxed and fully coping personality. However, Prince Albert seems to have been happy at Cranwell. He threw himself enthusiastically into his new duties, rode a horse, played a lot of tennis in his spare time, and also learned to drive a car – sometimes with reckless abandon. It is, however, significant, and an indication both of his frail health and his lack of complete self-confidence, that the Admiralty had arranged that his close friend, Staff Surgeon Louis Greig should have been seconded to the same branch of the service with him.

The first months of the RAF's existence were bedevilled by a series of crises and much confusion. During April 1918, the Chief of the Air Staff, the Vice President of the Air Council, and finally the Secretary of State for Air, Lord Rothermere, resigned in succession. Prince Albert much regretted this disruption, writing to his father, "Everything here, as you may imagine is in a very unsettled state, owing to the changes in the Air Board, and nothing is settled yet as to what routine we are working under. We are now having a mixture of naval and military routine, which is not a great success." Later, in May 1918, he wrote again clearly resentful at the bewildering series of changes in policy and training methods which threatened to disrupt his work at Cranwell, "I am rather depressed about the whole affair, as you may imagine, as I was very keen on this job, and was doing my best to make it a success. Now I am afraid I have rather lost interest till I know exactly what is going to happen. I am telling you all this as I am certain you would want to know what sort of things do go on, and this is quite a serious question, and I am involved in it personally."³ A month later he wrote gloomily to a friend, "the whole of my show is upside down, and no one knows what is likely to happen. I am pretty fed up, and don't feel like staying here for good."

Fortunately, by the middle of July 1918, it was decided to move him to the cadet unit at St Leonard's-on-Sea, and on 1 August Prince Albert and Louis Greig were both transferred there. At St Leonard's, Prince Albert came under the command of Brigadier General Critchley, a dynamic man of great enthusiasm. After passing through the cadet school, the Prince was given command of a squadron. If his spirits had flagged at Cranwell, they were dramatically revived at St Leonard's. On 30 August 1918, King George inspected his son's training centre, afterwards writing:

> I was quite delighted with my visit to you last Friday, and I must say Genl. Critchley is a wonderful man, the very man for the job. Tell him from me that I never saw such keen boys as his cadets, & I thought his system of training quite first rate, & that I consider his by far the best training establishment that I have seen & I have seen a great many in the last 4 years. . . . I thought your squadron did wonderfully well considering they had only been at drill for a week.

The spirit of the RAF Headquarters at St Leonard's, dedicated to physical fitness and to technical and professional efficiency, was an inspiration. These fulfilling experiences were to provide the stimulus for the Prince's later involvement in his work with the Industrial Welfare Society, the National Playing Fields' Fund, and in his own Duke of York's Camp.

The First World War was now drawing to its close. The great German Spring Offensive of 1918 had been contained by the Allies, and with the advent of hundreds of thousands of American troops on the Western Front, the balance of power was irrevocably tilted against the Central Powers. By the early autumn of 1918 the German armies were being driven back along the whole of the Western Front, and Prince Albert was allowed to see something of the work of the Royal Air

Force in France before the final collapse of Germany. In October 1918, he and Louis Greig were flown across the Channel to the headquarters of the RAF at Autigny and the Prince was able to see both daytime and night-time operations. He was greatly impressed by the dedication and courage of the Flying Officers, writing to his mother, "the officers all seem in very good spirits, and never look upon a raid as more than an ordinary flight, which of course is only right."

Barely a fortnight after he had reported to RAF Headquarters, the war ended, at the eleventh hour of the eleventh day of the eleventh month. "The great day has come, and we have won the war," wrote King George to his son. "It has been a long time coming, but I was sure if we stuck to it, we should win, and it is a great victory over one of the most perfect military machines ever created."

Eleven days after the Armistice, Prince Albert was entrusted with the mission of representing his father when King Albert of the Belgians made his official re-entry into Brussels on 22 November 1918. The Prince was impressed by the warmth of the welcome which awaited the Belgian Royal Family in Brussels. He was also proud to represent his father, writing to him that, "the King told me how delighted he was that you had sent me to represent you. I rode at his right side. It was a very impressive sight, and he received a wonderful welcome from his people." From 27 November to 11 December 1918 King George V himself came to France where he was greeted by great crowds in Paris, and later toured the battlefields and war cemeteries, accompanied by the Prince of Wales and Prince Albert.

The King was determined that neither the Prince of Wales nor Prince Albert should make an embarrassingly hasty return to civilian life. There had already been a certain amount of malicious gossip, particularly during the winter of 1917, about Prince Albert's prolonged absence from active service. In order to give no ammunition to the uncharitable, the King therefore decided that both of his eldest sons should remain in France at least until the spring of 1919. That Prince Albert's reputation had suffered in some eyes as a result of his enforced inactivity during the early part of the war can be seen in a letter written by the Prince of Wales to his mother on 6 December 1918: "Bertie can be of far more use in this way than sitting in England, where he has spent most of the war, not that this was his fault!! But by remaining with the armies till peace is signed he will entirely erase any of the very unfair questions some nasty people asked last year as to what he was doing, you will remember."

[43]

During the Christmas festivities of 1918, therefore, Prince Albert was transferred to the staff of Major General Salmond, the Commander of the Royal Air Force on the Western Front, at Spa. From Spa, before the end of the year, he went to visit General Currie, Commander of the Canadian Corps, whose headquarters were at the Schaunburg Palace at Bonn, the residence of Princess Viktoria of Prussia. This meeting with his father's cousin, for Princess Viktoria was the sister of the ex-Kaiser Wilhelm II, was to prove most instructive for the young prince. Prince Albert was soon writing in amazement to his parents:

> She seemed to have very little idea of what our feelings are towards Germany. All the atrocities and the treatment of prisoners seemed to be a revelation to her, as everything like that has all been kept a secret from them. . . . She asked after you and the family, and hoped that we should be friends again shortly. I told her politely I did not think it was possible for a great many years!!!! She told everybody here that her brother did not want the war or any Zeppelin raids or U-Boats, but that of course was only a ruse to become friendly with us. . . .

Back at the RAF Headquarters at Spa, in the second half of January 1919, Prince Albert learned of the death of his youngest brother, Prince John. While sharing the family's grief at this loss, Prince Albert did not return to Britain for the funeral, instead, writing a letter full of sympathy to his parents. By the end of January however, Prince Albert had made it plain that he wished to return home as soon as possible. He did not believe that his presence in France was fulfilling any useful function, and, moreover, he had now decided that he should learn to fly as soon as possible, and that this could best be done back in the United Kingdom. It is also clear that he continued to find the problem of his stammer embarrassing, and wished to take advantage of a new specialist in speech defects whose name had been sent to him.

By the end of February 1919, Prince Albert was back in London, where he was given a position in the Air Ministry, presumably to acquaint himself more thoroughly with the Civil Service. According to Sir John Wheeler-Bennett, "His contact with the Civil Service brought him a wider vision and a greater wisdom." Prince Albert later gave his own version of his experiences at the Air Ministry, saying "I found myself being moved from one branch to another, rather like a human 'buff slip', marked 'Passed to you for action, please'." He also seems to have entertained a rather romantic view of Civil Service functionaries, a view not necessarily shared by his fellow countrymen, and later said of them "they never spare themselves, but continue to serve their country until at last the sad day comes when they, like their files, must be stamped with the fatal letters P.A. [Put away] and disappear."

During the spring and summer of 1919, Prince Albert gave practical effect to his earlier expressed desire to learn to fly by taking instruction at the Waddon Lane Aerodrome at Croydon. It is interesting that the devoted Louis Greig, although then nearly forty years of age, took the course with him, and also qualified as a pilot. By the end of July 1919 Prince Albert received his wings as a certified pilot – the only member of his family to be so qualified, for although his brothers the Prince of Wales, Prince Henry (later Duke of Gloucester) and Prince George (later Duke of Kent) were taught to fly, none of them received an official Pilot's Certificate. However, Prince Albert's medical examiners, "basing their judgement on his general physical and psychological condition, advised that he should not fly solo".

Despite his conscientious and determined approach to flying, Prince Albert was never an enthusiastic aviator. After his first flight, he had written to his mother, "it was a curious sensation, and one which takes a lot of getting used to. I did enjoy it on the whole, but I don't think I should like flying as a pastime. I would much sooner be on the ground!! It feels safer!!"[2] The eventual attainment of his wings was essentially a reflection of his determination to complete a task already begun.

In the same month that he gained his wings, Prince Albert, on the advice of his father, decided to give up his service career. The King had come to believe that it would be useful if Prince Albert and his brother Prince Henry were to complete their education by spending a few terms at Cambridge as members of Trinity College. Prince Albert seemed relieved at leaving the Air Ministry, particularly since he equated his return to civilian life with the task of standing in for his brother, the Prince of Wales, at public functions in the United Kingdom, when the latter was called upon to undertake tours of the Empire overseas. To his old Term Officer at Dartmouth, he wrote in July 1919, "I am giving up a Service career now, and go to Cambridge in October for a year, to learn everything that will be useful for the time to come. My brother is so overwhelmed with work that I am going to help him with it now. It is really the best thing to do, now that there is so much going on in every way."[4]

[45]

Prince Albert was not the first member of the Royal Family to have attended one of the older universities. Albert, the Prince Consort, had deemed it necessary that his eldest son, the future Edward VII, should attend no fewer than three universities, Edinburgh, Oxford and Cambridge. Prince Albert's elder brother, the Prince of Wales, had spent a short period at Magdalen College, Oxford. There is no evidence that their brief experience of university life did either of these Princes of Wales much good: Gladstone had said of King Edward VII that he knew everything except what was in books, and the President of Magdalen College, Oxford, Sir Herbert Warren, had said of the future King Edward VIII, "bookish he will never be."

How was Prince Albert to succeed, where his brother and his grandfather had failed? As his scholastic performances at Osborne and Dartmouth had revealed, he was no academic high-flyer. He would certainly not be able to hold his own with the best academic minds among his undergraduate contemporaries. His brother, Prince Henry, was even less likely to make a mark. It was perhaps as well that the most that was being proposed was that both young men should spend a year at Cambridge.

The two princes were to be attached to Trinity College, but there was some disagreement about where they were to live. The Vice-Master, J. R. M. Butler, son of the great Master of Trinity, believed, together with Dennis Robertson, a Fellow of Trinity College, that, "the Princes would gain educationally if it were possible for them to live in college. They would certainly see more of men of their own age, and so would get more of that mixing with other minds and similar interests that is a very important part of the university system of education." However, King George V was not of the same opinion and his secretary, Lord Stamfordham, wrote to Mr Butler, informing him of the King's decision: "Though the King realizes the obvious advantages to be gained by residence in College, he feels that both Princes, having already passed through the disciplinary period *in statu pupillari*, it would be hardly fair to ask them again to give up just that little extra freedom which is enjoyed by living outside walls and gates!"

What was behind the King's insistence that his sons should not reside in college? Although he leased "Southacre" for them, a small, ugly, but comfortable house in pleasant surroundings, about a mile from Trinity College, it is unlikely that this gave them more freedom. For one thing, Louis Greig (now a wing-commander) and his wife went up to Cambridge in mid-October 1919 also to live at "South-

1 Prince Albert, aged one year

2 Prince Albert (left), with the future King Edward VIII, and an admiring Princess Mary

3 Prince Albert, aged four, in early training for his naval career

3

5

4 The York children (Princess Mary, Prince Albert, Prince Henry and Prince Edward) with their grandparents, Queen Alexandra (centre) and Edward VII. Far left is Princess Maud, one of Edward and Alexandra's three daughters.

5 Left, the naval sub-lieutenant in 1916, and (6) serving tea to wounded soldiers at Buckingham Palace

7 In the background, Prince Albert as he leaves the Stock Exchange at the heels of a vivacious Prince of Wales

8 The top-hatted Duke of York leads in one of the winners at the St Dunstan's sports, 1920

8

RTING DUKE

9 The Duke of York kicks off at an ill-attended football match between St Barnabas and Silver-town Athletic in 1922

10 About to play a doubles match at Wimbledon, partnered by his friend Louis Greig

10

11 Industrial relations on the golf course, May 1924: from left, winning partners Sir Evan Williams (for the mine owners) and Frank Hodge, MP, (for the miners), the Duke of York. Sixth from left, Colonel David Davies, Liberal MP for Montgomeryshire

12 Some harmless fun at the Duke of York's Camp, 1936. The campers were an equal mixture of young workers and public schoolboys.

13 A beguiling Lady Elizabeth Bowes-Lyon, aged seven

14 Wedding day for the Duke and Duchess of York, April 1923

15 Wedding party on the balcony of Buckingham Palace. From left, Queen Alexandra, Queen Mary, the Duchess of York, the Duke of York and a benign King George V

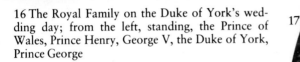

16 The Royal Family on the Duke of York's wedding day; from the left, standing, the Prince of Wales, Prince Henry, George V, the Duke of York, Prince George

17

17 Honeymoon couple walking in the grounds of Polesden Lacey, April 1923

18 Confetti flies as the Duke and his bride set off for their honeymoon

18

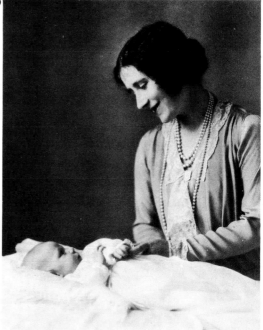

20

19 Princess Elizabeth, born April 1926, with her parents, and (20) exchanging looks with her proud mother

21 The christening of Princess Elizabeth. Among the group are the Duke of Connaught (far left, standing), the Earl and Countess of Strathmore (to the right of the Duke and Duchess of York) and Princess Mary (seated, far right).

21

22 A fifteen-month-old Princess Elizabeth surrounded by adoring parents and
grandparents in July 1927

23 Princess Elizabeth driving with the
King and Queen back to Balmoral after
attending a service at Crathie church,
September 1932

23

24 Evident public adoration for the little
princesses as they visit the Royal Tournament at Olympia with their parents in
1935

24

acre". Although Greig's friendship with Prince Albert was a stabilizing and creative factor in his life, it is obvious that neither of the Princes could step very far out of line with the Greigs as watchdogs. Residing in Trinity College, on the other hand, would have enabled them to have far more frequent contact with their fellow-undergraduates, with all the temptations and possible pitfalls that this would have involved.

Perhaps George V's insistence that his sons should live under careful supervision at Cambridge owed something to a murky piece of family history. In November 1861, while the future Edward VII was an undergraduate at Cambridge, the Prince Consort had been obliged to visit the university to confront his son over the rumours of his liaison with the actress Nellie Clifden. While staying at Cambridge for this heavy paternal duty, Prince Albert, who was overtired and somewhat depressed, caught a chill, and two weeks later developed typhoid fever. On 14 December 1861 he died at Windsor, in the arms of his distraught wife. It is therefore likely that at some level, George V made a connection between Cambridge, licence, disgrace and death.

Prince Albert's studies at Cambridge were very basic, which was perhaps inevitable as he had only a year at his disposal. Nonetheless, it was very much as if he was serving an academic royal apprenticeship; his studies were centred on history, economics and civics, with particular concentration on the development of the constitution. Like his father before him, he studied Bagehot's seminal work, *The English Constitution* and doubtless absorbed aphorisms like, "royalty is a government in which the attention of the nation is concentrated on one person doing interesting actions." Or, "royalty will be strong because it appeals to diffused feelings." Or again, on the subject of monarchy, "its mystery is its life. We must not bring in the daylight upon magic." In more homely vein, Bagehot insisted, "a *family* on the throne is an interesting idea also. It brings down the pride of sovereignty to the level of petty life . . . a princely marriage is the brilliant edition of a universal fact, and as such it rivets mankind . . . a Royal Family sweetens politics by the seasonable addition of nice and pretty events. It introduces irrelevant facts into the business of government, but they are facts which speak to 'men's bosoms', and employ their thoughts."[5] Bagehot's writings also stressed the need for morality in the monarchy, "we have come to regard the Crown as the head of our *morality*. We have come to believe that it is natural to have a virtuous sovereign, and that domestic virtues are as likely to be found on thrones as they are eminent when there."

Walter Bagehot's exhortations and advice had brought forth a strong response from George V. His son, who was striving to please his father in all things, was no less affected. Indeed, both as prince and monarch, it is as if Bagehot's conception of kingly deportment provided the brief by which Prince Albert carried out his official duties and his private obligations.

Prince Albert and his brother seem to have taken some advantage of the pleasures offered by Cambridge life. They rode recklessly round the countryside on motor-cycles, they punted on the Backs, they entertained their contemporaries hospitably at "Southacre". Prince Albert indeed, with his already well-developed taste for tobacco, was fined the sum of 6s.8d for smoking while in academic dress. He later recalled, "I was made to regard the cigarette which I was then smoking as one of the most expensive I have ever sampled." According to one version of the incident, "an officious mentor" described his offence as being worse than usual, because he was a member of the Royal Family, thus allegedly prompting the young prince to say bitterly, "we are not a family, we are a firm."[6] Despite this minor incident, when Prince Albert went down from Cambridge at the end of the Easter Term, 1920, he expressed his regret in a letter to Mr Butler, saying, "I am very sorry at leaving after the splendid time I have had." Throughout the rest of his life, he proudly considered himself a Cambridge man, and took particular pleasure when, as Duke of York and later as King, he was called upon to visit the university city.

While in residence at Cambridge, Prince Albert continued to undertake duties for the family firm. Even during his first term, and within a few days of going up, he returned to London on 24 October 1919 to become a member of the Worshipful Company of Drapers, and four days later to receive the Freedom of the City of London. At the end of October he had a more daunting task, which was to act as the King's representative, and to greet the Shah of Persia, Sultan Ahmed, at Dover at the beginning of his official visit to Britain. The Prince was obliged to act as companion and guide to the Shah during various visits to the City of London, to Windsor Castle, and even to the ballet at Covent Garden, managing to keep up a fairly fluent conversation in French with the young monarch. No sooner had he returned to Cambridge, than he was summoned to carry out another official duty: this time greeting the President of the French Republic and Madame Poincaré when they arrived on 11 November at Dover. His first term at Cambridge, therefore, was hardly one of uninterrupted academic study.

As his public duties increased in number, Prince Albert was obliged to make more speeches – ordeals which he approached with dread. Although he continued to consult various specialists in speech therapy, there was no marked improvement, but he was relieved to discover that if he spoke in public more or less impromptu, he stammered and hesitated less. Ironically, though, the public demands that were now being made upon him made impromptu speechmaking impossible, and he was obliged to struggle through a prepared text.

While he continued to grapple with his speech impediment with considerable courage and determination, he was apt to be easily depressed in the face of less serious difficulties and setbacks. Even in sports like tennis and golf, where his performance was well above average, he was inclined to take defeat and his own poor performances far too much to heart. His anxieties and lack of self-confidence, which he for the most part kept bottled up, sometimes exploded in outbursts of temper, and irrational self-criticism. As in earlier years, Louis Greig helped Prince Albert enormously in coming to terms with his own inconsistencies and fits of depressed irritability. Greig was later to say, "my principal contribution was to put steel into him." At Cambridge, Greig certainly worked hard at this task. In the process, Prince Albert, who, despite his military career, was still immature for his years, became somewhat more self-possessed and self-sufficient.

George V, at any rate, was pleased with the progress made by his second son. To mark his appreciation, the Birthday Honours List for 3 June 1920 carried the following announcement:

The King has been pleased to direct Letters Patent to be passed under the Great Seal of the United Kingdom of Great Britain and Ireland, to bear this day's date, granting unto His Majesty's Son, his Royal Highness Prince Albert Frederick Arthur George, K.G., and the heirs male of his body lawfully begotten, the dignities of Baron Killarney, Earl of Inverness and Duke of York.

These were the very same titles that King George himself had held, and his son was quick to take this as a sign of parental approval, writing, "I . . . thank you again ever so much for having made me Duke of York. I am very proud to bear the name that you did for many years, and I hope I shall live up to it in every way." His father's reply indicated the affection and regard which the King bore for his second son:

[49]

Dearest Bertie,

I was delighted to get your letter this morning, & to know that you appreciate that I have given you that fine old title of Duke of York, which I bore for more than 9 years, & is the oldest Dukedom in this country. I know that you have behaved very well, in a difficult situation for a young man & that you have done what I asked you to do. I feel that this splendid old title will be safe in your hands, & that you will never do anything which could in any way tarnish it. I hope that you will always look upon me as yr. best friend & will always tell me everything & you will find me ever ready to help & give you good advice. . . .

Ever my dear boy

Yr. very devoted Papa
G.R.I.[7]

In 1920 the new Duke of York reached the age of twenty-four years. He had now received all the military and academic training that he was likely to get, had earned his mother's and his father's approval, and had fought in the war. He had learned how to command men, and how to accept orders from superior officers. He was essentially modest, likeable and sincere. By the end of the year he was about to enter one of the most creative, formative and satisfying periods of his life.

5

THE DUKE OF YORK
AND ELIZABETH BOWES-LYON

1920—1923

"Lady Elizabeth was very unlike the cocktail-drinking, chain-smoking girls who came to be regarded as typical of the nineteen-twenties. The radiant vitality, and a blending of gaiety, kindness and sincerity, made her irresistible to men."

Lady Airlie

"I trust they will be very happy. We are delighted, and he looks beaming."

Queen Mary, 1923

DESPITE THE ENORMOUS PLEASURE he took in being created Duke of York, Prince Albert probably did not feel entirely fulfilled and secure in 1920. His naval career had been interrupted by illness, rendered piecemeal in nature, and had hardly been brought to an end in fully satisfying fashion. Although he had served in the infant RAF, and had learned to fly, he had not been allowed to take an aircraft up by himself. His year at Cambridge University, though enjoyable, had essentially been an artificial and incomplete episode; the tuition he had received had been of a very specific, utilitarian nature, which in any case had frequently been interrupted by the demands of his official position. Apart from the faithful Louis Greig, he had no really close friends, and must have continued to feel that he was living in his elder brother's shadow. Although he was undoubtedly sincere and kindly, he was also inexperienced, somewhat naïve about human relationships, and apt to be very conventional in his judgements. Beneath a normally rigidly controlled exterior, there lurked a host of anxieties and insecurities. He was prone to bouts of self-pity, fits of explosive rage, and he still found frustration difficult to bear.

The problems posed by his nervous disposition were illustrated when he took his seat in the House of Lords on 23 June 1920. As Prince Albert advanced towards the Woolsack to be received by the Lord Chancellor, Lord Birkenhead, he was so nervous that "he was almost tottering". Lord Birkenhead, who as F. E. Smith had been one of the great advocates of his day, quickly summed up the situation, and as he bent forward to take the new peer's hand in his own, whispered to him, "Been playing much tennis lately, Sir?" This act of solicitous kindness revived Prince Albert's spirits.

Sport was one of the areas in which he excelled. He was a very good cricketer, the best in his family, and this prowess had given him one unchallengeable claim to fame: as a youth, he had once bowled out King Edward VII and the future monarchs George V and Edward VIII, one after the other. This kingly hat-trick stands unrivalled in the records of English cricket. He was also an extremely competent golfer, his expertise on the golf course apparently causing a certain amount of rivalry between himself and his elder brother. The Prince of Wales, it seems, prided himself on his golf, and boasted a handicap of eleven. The national press took a benevolent and enthusiastic view of his golfing career, treating any victory "as an event of national importance".[1] According to one authority, however, "There was one thing which dimmed the mirror of his glory. His brother Albert, who never bothered much about golf, had a handicap of nine, and with very little trouble could have come down to scratch. The newspapers knew nothing of this family rivalry. Albert never played in tournaments. He just shot a consistent 81 to 83, and was content."[2]

The Prince of Wales went at his sports with great dash, alternating between enthusiasm and despair, but nonetheless persevered with his golf, and was a keen huntsman. Tennis, however, he discarded, which was just as well because his younger brother became a first-class tennis player. On 8 July 1920, a fortnight after he had taken his seat in the House of Lords as Duke of York, Prince Albert, partnered by Louis Greig, had won the doubles finals of the RAF Tennis Tournament. Prince Albert also entered the singles competition, but was defeated in the semi-final by his doubles partner. Pleased by news of his son's success, King George V sent a telegram of congratulations, to which, on 9 July, the Duke of York replied:

My dearest Papa,
    Very many thanks for your telegram, which I received last night. We are both very pleased at having won the Air Force Cup for the Doubles. Our hardest match was the semi-final as we lost the 1st set and after winning the 2nd easily we only just won the 3rd, after our opponents were 4–1 in games.

I was very surprised to get through the 3 rounds of the Singles into the Semi-Finals. The 1st round was a walkover as my opponent scratched.

The 2nd & 3rd rounds were all very long matches, & I lost the 1st in each, but won the last 2 sets.

Greig defeated me easily in the semi-final, which I knew he was sure to do. Greig scratched in the finals of the singles as he had played 4 matches in a day, and was very tired. As it was, in the Doubles, we both nearly collapsed from fatigue. I don't think I have ever played so well in my life, and I did not lose my head at the critical moment, which was very lucky . . .

I remain, Ever

Your very devoted son
Bertie[3]

The Duke of York hunted with the Pytchley whenever he could, proving himself, no doubt to the Prince of Wales' chagrin, to be the best horseman in his family. He was also an excellent shot with gun and rifle, a skill which must have gratified his father, who was a crack shot himself. It was the Duke of York's success at sport that showed he had put behind him the illnesses and physical frailties of his earlier years.

Less gruelling than his sporting exploits, but nonetheless demanding, were the ever increasing number of official engagements that he carried out. In July 1920, for the first time he held an Investiture at Buckingham Palace in place of his father, who had been obliged to attend the funeral of the Empress Eugénie, the widow of the Emperor Napoleon III. In February 1921, his father sent him to Belgium to present the Distinguished Flying Cross to King Albert, and to confer other decorations on Belgian citizens, in recognition of their services to Britain during the war. In his first experience as acting Head of State, the Duke of York made such a favourable impression that the British Ambassador wrote to Lord Stamfordham saying, "I cannot conclude this long letter without telling you how well the Duke of York played his part here. He talked in the most pleasant way to the Belgians, whom I had the honour of introducing to him, and many of them told me afterwards how pleased they had been to have had the opportunity of meeting His Royal Highness."

Less than a year later, in June 1922, the Duke of York was sent as the King's representative to Romania, to be the chief sponsor or "Koom" at the wedding of Queen Marie of Romania's daughter, Princess

Marie, to King Alexander of Yugoslavia. Pitched into the somewhat unpredictable circumstances of a Balkan royal wedding, the Duke of York impressed the crowds in Belgrade with his determined and skilful handling of an exceedingly restive mount. Queen Marie was to write appreciatively to George V, "he did his part beautifully, & his presence was most popular in Serbia. Everyone much appreciated that you sent one of your sons, and was awfully pleased . . . Somehow, your boy in some way reminded me so much of you, though he has exactly May's smile, but his movements were yours, and his hands . . ."[4]

Building on this success, the Duke of York was to become something of an ambassador to the Balkans. In October 1922 he attended the special coronation of King Ferdinand and Queen Marie of Romania, which marked the creation of an enlarged Romanian state after the First World War. Both here and in Bucharest, he made a very favourable impression as the King's representative, causing the British minister in Romania to write to Lord Stamfordham, "the Duke's soldier-like appearance, his bearing, his good looks, and horsemanship during the procession through the entire town as well as in the parade at Alba Julia, were all the subject of many flattering observations . . . I hope you will be good enough to tell His Majesty that in my long experience of such ceremonies I have never experienced greater pride in recognizing the suitability and complete popularity of my country's Special Representative." It is incidentally interesting that George V found it difficult to accept this apparently unqualified praise at its face value. Perhaps he considered the tribute too fulsome, or failed to recognize his son as being the recipient of such lavish praise.

Exactly a year later, in October 1923, the Duke of York was back in the Balkans. On this occasion, he once more represented his father at the christening of the infant son of King Alexander of Yugoslavia and Princess Marie of Romania. The ceremonies began on 21 October, and the Duke of York, still possessed of a somewhat shy and retiring disposition, was obliged to receive a set of hand-embroidered underwear from the child's parents. He also had entire charge of the baby during the ritual. This was just as well, for the aged Patriarch dropped the Crown Prince in the font, whence he was scooped up by his alert "Koom". The Duke of York later wrote his father an account of this testing experience, saying, "you can imagine what I felt like, carrying the baby on a cushion. It screamed most of the time, which drowned the singing, & the service altogether."

Within the more secure and predictable environment of Britain, the Duke of York was laying the foundations of those interests which were to characterize him before his accession to the throne. In particular, he was involving himself in the field of industrial relations, taking a particular interest in trades union activities, and undertaking various tours of industrial areas. He was also developing the ideas which were later to come to fruition in the Duke of York's Camp.

1920 was to be a year of the utmost significance in the young Duke of York's development, for in May of that year he fell in love with Lady Elizabeth Bowes-Lyon. The relationship that was to develop between the two was destined to be the most stabilizing and creative factor in his life.

According to one version, he fell in love with Lady Elizabeth at a dance given by Lord and Lady Farquhar on 20 May 1920. Seeing her dance with his equerry, he is supposed to have said, "That's a lovely girl you have been dancing with. Who is she?" As Elizabeth Longford has pointed out in her biography of the Queen Mother, this legend can scarcely be accurate – for one thing, Prince Albert had met Lady Elizabeth Bowes-Lyon before. The first occasion was at a children's party, when she was five and he was ten, and at which she showed her generosity by giving the shy boy the cherries off the top of her cake. In 1913 it is likely that she partnered him at a junior dance while he was still a naval cadet at Osborne. Lady Elizabeth had also become a close friend of Prince Albert's sister, Princess Mary, so she was certainly no stranger to him in May 1920.

Nonetheless, on 20 May 1920, he saw her with new eyes. He was not alone. Lady Elizabeth was a girl of striking beauty: she had a slim, attractive figure, a sensitive and sometimes pale face, dark hair and very beautiful violet-blue eyes. According to Elizabeth Longford, "all the men were at her feet. One devoted admirer still remembers the magical atmosphere she created, 'I was madly in love with her. Everything at Glamis was beautiful, perfect. Being there was like living in a Van Dyck picture. Time, and the gossiping, junketing world stood still. Nothing happened . . . after that, but the magic gripped us all. I fell *madly* in love. They all did.' "[5]

Who was this vital, attractive girl, who as a debutante had taken London by storm, and had now caught the eye of King George's second son? Lady Elizabeth Bowes-Lyon was the youngest but one of the ten children of the fourteenth Earl of Strathmore. Born in August

1900, Lady Elizabeth was fortunate to have been a member of a very united, loving, self-confident and largely unpretentious family. Her mother has been described as "a large, stocky presence, with a square jaw and bright eyes, a great flywheel maintaining the momentum and balance of the household. Nothing could fluster her. Guests at Glamis remembered a tipsy footman, who seemed always to be falling about and pouring wine down people's backs, but with whom Lady Strathmore coped quite unruffled."[6] The Earl of Strathmore took pride in the sensible handling of his estates; he also spent a lot of time chopping wood. According to one authority:

> The Strathmores were a pious family. Prayers were said every day in the little chapel at Glamis. The women would wear white caps made of thick crochet lace, fastened on to the head with hatpins. The cap was provided in the bedroom of each woman guest for her to wear every day, and on Sunday Lady Strathmore, with one such cap on her head, used to sit at the harmonium and accompany the little congregation of friends as they sang hymns. Upright, open and straightforward, the Bowes-Lyons lived by a simple, upper-class code, which made them at once fun-loving, considerate, unaffected – and totally self-confident.[7]

It was no coincidence that while staying at Balmoral in the autumn of 1920, the Duke of York paid a visit to Glamis Castle. There seems little doubt that he enjoyed the experience, writing to his mother, "It is delightful here, & Elizabeth is very kind to me. The more I see of her, the more I like her." Queen Mary's impressions of Lady Elizabeth Bowes-Lyon were favourable enough, for at this time she confided to Lady Airlie, her lady-in-waiting, "I have discovered that he is very attracted to Lady Elizabeth Bowes-Lyon. He is always talking about her. She seems a charming girl, but I don't know her very well."[8] Lady Airlie replied that she had known Elizabeth Bowes-Lyon all her life, and could say nothing but good of her. In Lady Airlie's view, "One knew instinctively that she was a girl who would find real happiness only in marriage and motherhood. A born homemaker."[9] By the spring of 1921, the Duke of York was sufficiently sure of his feelings to tell his parents that he was going to propose marriage to Lady Elizabeth. King George V's response was direct and encouraging, although not demonstrating full confidence in his son's capacity to win Lady Elizabeth's hand, "You will be a lucky fellow if she accepts you."

George V's doubts that the enterprise would run smoothly were more than justified, for when Prince Albert proposed to Lady Elizabeth in the spring of 1921, she refused him. Lady Strathmore was moved to write of the disconsolate young man, "I do hope he will find a nice wife who will make him happy. I like him so much, and he is a man who will be made or marred by his wife." Of Lady Elizabeth's refusal of the Duke of York's proposal, Lady Airlie wrote in her memoirs, "she was frankly doubtful, uncertain of her feelings, and afraid of the public life which would lie ahead of her as the King's daughter-in-law." These were indeed powerful reasons to give a vital and vivacious twenty-year-old girl pause. It is also probable that the Duke of York did not immediately fulfil Lady Elizabeth's ideal as to what a suitor should be. Compared with some of the other well-born young men who were paying court to her, he must have seemed rather uncertain of himself, and fundamentally unaccomplished. Lady Airlie described him as being "deeply in love, but so humble". These were not necessarily the qualities to sweep a young and eligible young girl off her feet.

Some hard work had to be done before the match could be made. Lady Airlie was one who used her good offices to great effect, recalling that "the Duke and Lady Elizabeth started dropping into my flat on various pretexts, always separately, but each talked of the other." Queen Mary was also determined to help her second son achieve a happy marriage if possible, and in the summer of 1921, the Queen together with the Duke of York, visited Glamis Castle. There they found that Lady Strathmore was ill in bed, but that Lady Elizabeth was acting as hostess on her behalf. Lady Airlie noted her impressions of this visit:

> Queen Mary was by then her son's ally. I always felt that the visit to Glamis was inspired by her desire to help him, although she was much too tactful to let it be apparent.
>
> In the setting of the grim old castle, where the traces of past bloodshed and terror can never be completely banished by any cosiness of the present, Lady Elizabeth filled her mother's place as hostess so charmingly that the Queen was more than ever convinced that this was "the one girl who could make Bertie happy", as she told me afterwards. "But I shall say nothing to either of them," she added. "Mothers should never meddle in their children's love affairs."[10]

In February 1922, another member of Prince Albert's family took a hand in advancing his cause. His sister, Princess Mary, who was to be married on 28 February to Viscount Lascelles, invited twenty-one-year-old Elizabeth Bowes-Lyon to be her bridesmaid. The participation in Princess Mary's wedding provided Lady Elizabeth with a first-hand experience of what a royal public event could be like. Dressed in a beautiful silver gown, she was much admired, and finding the event so enjoyable perhaps encouraged her to reconsider her earlier refusal of the Duke's proposal of marriage.

For the rest of 1922, the Duke of York persevered in his suit. Slowly he became more at ease at Glamis and at St Paul's, Walden Bury, the Bowes-Lyons' other family home; but his own upbringing, with its lack of freely and openly expressed emotion, had ill-prepared him for the courtship of a lively and spirited girl. Gradually, however, the Duke of York became more at ease, and, according to his official biographer, "the relations of Lord and Lady Strathmore with their children, and the happy badinage and affection of a large and closely knit family were a revelation to him, providing a climate of ideas to which he instantly responded, and in which his own personality throve and blossomed."[11] During this period, an odd reversal of roles took place between the Duke of York and Lady Elizabeth Bowes-Lyon. Prince Albert became the more assured of the two, whereas Lady Strathmore noticed for the first time that her daughter Elizabeth was "really worried". According to her mother, Lady Elizabeth "was torn between her longing to make Bertie happy and her reluctance to take on the responsibilities which this marriage must bring."[12]

Quite apart from mutual physical attraction, for just as Lady Elizabeth was acknowledged to be beautiful, the Duke of York was slim, handsome and youthful, there was a further bond between them, as both believed in fidelity in relationships. In the words of one of Lady Elizabeth's companions of the early 1920s:

Her circle wasn't more moral in a "Pious" way. It just never occurred to us that unmarried people should go to bed together. It was unthinkable, especially within our own group of very good friends. With the Prince of Wales we knew it was always married ladies. But Prince Bertie's circle were all "gals", nice "gals", that was the difference between the two men. The basis of their lives was completely different, and Prince Bertie would never have suggested that he might go to bed with anyone. Holding hands in a boat, *that* was courting.[13]

The protracted and not always easy courtship came to a climax in January 1923. Lady Airlie recalls in her memoirs that Lady Elizabeth continued to visit her for counsel:

> When she came to tea at my flat one afternoon at the beginning of January, 1923, I meant to make one final effort. But instead I found myself talking of my own marriage – of how much I had hated the Army life at first, and had tolerated it for David's sake, but how I had grown to love it. After she had gone, I feared I might have bored her by bringing up a chapter of my past which had closed before she had been born, and wished that I had talked more of the Duke.[14]

Whether Lady Airlie's recollections did the trick or not is unclear, but when, a few days later, the Duke of York once more proposed to Lady Elizabeth as they walked through the winter woods at St Paul's, Walden Bury, she accepted him. That afternoon, 13 January 1923, a telegram was sent to King George and Queen Mary at Sandringham. It contained three words: "All right. Bertie."

Prince Albert was relieved and beside himself with happiness. On 16 January, he wrote to Queen Mary, "I know I am very lucky to have won her at last." In response to a letter of congratulation from Lady Airlie, he replied, "How can I thank you enough for your charming letter to me about the wonderful happening in my life which has come to pass, and my dream which has at last been realized. It seems so marvellous to me to know that my darling Elizabeth will one day be my wife. We are both very, very happy, and I am sure always will be. I owe so much to you, and can only bless you for all that you did."

On 15 January, Prince Albert and Louis Greig arrived at Sandringham. King George wrote in his diary, "Bertie with Greig arrived after tea, and informed us that he was engaged to Elizabeth Bowes-Lyon, to which we gladly gave our consent. I trust they will be very happy." Queen Mary recorded, "We are delighted, and he looks beaming." Back in London the next day, Prince Albert wrote to his mother, "You & Papa were both so charming to me yesterday about my engagement, & I can never really thank you properly for giving your consent to it. I am very, very happy, & I can only hope that Elizabeth feels the same as I do. I know I am very lucky to have won her over at last."

Although the Duke of York had once been the rejected suitor, struggling to win the hand of the girl whom he wanted for his bride, once the engagement was announced the rightful relationship between the two families was reasserted. On 20 January, Lord and Lady Strathmore and Elizabeth were invited to spend the weekend at Sandringham, to meet King George V and Queen Mary, and also Queen Alexandra. According to all accounts it was a very successful meeting. In particular, Elizabeth Bowes-Lyon won universal praise. Queen Mary wrote in her diary, "Elizabeth is charming, so pretty & engaging & natural. Bertie is supremely happy." George V commented with a naval economy of sentiment, "She is a pretty & charming girl, & Bertie is a very lucky fellow."

Once the engagement had been announced, the royal ceremonial machine swung into action and preparations were made to solemnize the marriage with due splendour. The wedding was to take place on 26 April 1923 at Westminster Abbey.

6

ROYAL WEDDING
1923

A princely marriage is the brilliant edition of a universal fact, and as such it rivets mankind.

Walter Bagehot, *The English Constitution*

THE BRITISH PUBLIC REACTED with predictable enthusiasm to the prospect of the royal wedding between the Duke of York and Lady Elizabeth Bowes-Lyon. Although Prince Albert's sister, Princess Mary, had been married to Lord Lascelles at Westminster Abbey on 28 February 1922, the wedding of George V's second son caught the imagination rather more. It was left to *The Times* to point out, with editorial weightiness, that there remained "one wedding to which the people looked forward with still deeper interest – the wedding which would give a wife to the Heir to the Throne and, in the course of nature, a future Queen to England and the British People".

Since the Prince of Wales seemed as far as ever away from finding a bride, however, the people of Britain and the Empire made the most of the prospective marriage of the Duke of York. One writer remarked that, "whilst the Princes of Wales have almost invariably been compelled to accept the brides that State policy selected, the Dukes of York have nearly always obeyed the dictates of their hearts."[1] Others pointed out that the last time a King's son had been married in Westminster Abbey had been in the year 1382, when the youthful King Richard II had married Anne of Bohemia. This precedent was not an encouraging one: King Richard II's reign had been turbulent, ending in his own violent death, and his marriage had been marred by his continuing attachment to male favourites. Fortunately, King Richard II's unhappy history worried nobody in 1923, and genealogists were soon delving into Lady Elizabeth's background, soon managing to prove that both she and the Duke of York were descended from King Robert I of Scotland. The fruits of these genealogical labours were not wasted upon Buckingham Palace, and on the Duke of York's wedding day, George V conferred upon him the Order of the Thistle.

The general enthusiasm with which the news of the royal engagement was greeted undoubtedly owed a great deal to the qualities of the betrothed couple – young, attractive, and apparently very much in love. No scandal was attached to either of their names, and they seemed to symbolize an uncontaminated and hopeful future. Many knew that the Duke of York had been obliged to wage a lengthy war against ill-health and the disability of his speech impediment. On the day of the wedding, *The Times* pointed out in a supplement, "young as he is, and great as is his station, [the Duke has] known enough of frustration to make all admirers of pluck and perseverance the more anxious to wish him happiness and success in the venture."[2] Certainly, the great crowds that assembled to cheer the Duke of York and his bride on their wedding progress indicated considerable popularity. There were few who could find reason to dislike either bride or bridegroom, apart from those who felt both monarchy and aristocracy to be irrelevant anachronisms.

Despite the inevitable expense and the lavish display which were bound to attend the wedding, Lady Elizabeth clearly tried to limit any ostentation or signs of extravagance. Post-war Britain had not been made a "fit land for heroes", and the poverty and economic distress which characterized the lives of many of the people would provide an uncomfortable enough contrast with the pomp and opulence of a public royal occasion. Thus, when the people of Forfarshire asked Lady Elizabeth what she would like as a wedding present, she replied that she would prefer an illuminated scroll to a costly gift. Although King George V gave her an ermine coat as a wedding present, she declined other proffered gifts of mink and sable in favour of squirrel and rabbit fur. These gestures did not make Lady Elizabeth a child of the proletariat, but they did indicate a sensitivity allied to prudent good sense.

The bride's wedding dress had to be a deep ivory in colour, to tone with the old lace she had been lent by Queen Mary for the occasion. There were no floral decorations in Westminster Abbey and, "the bride had managed to get rid of her bouquet before even stepping into the aisle. With the delightful impulsiveness that was never to be totally repressed, she placed her white York roses and Scottish heather on the Tomb of the Unknown Warrior, instead of waiting to lay it on the Cenotaph in Whitehall."[3]

The wedding day was a great success. Although the April weather remained true to form, alternating showers of rain with sudden bursts of sunshine, at about 9.30 am the rain ceased, and as the bride entered the Abbey, the sun came out. At 11.12 am precisely, Lady Elizabeth left 17 Bruton Street, the family's new London home, accompanied by her father, Lord Strathmore. Such punctuality was not typical of Lady Elizabeth, but she did manage to leave her small handbag behind in the carriage which took her to Westminster Abbey, just as her daughter was to do nearly a quarter of a century later.

At the Abbey, Lady Elizabeth was attended by six bridesmaids, and the bridegroom by two of his brothers, the Prince of Wales and Prince Henry. The wedding service was read by the Archbishop of Canterbury, and the address given by the Archbishop of York. In the course of the Archbishop of York's address, the young couple were told, "You have received from Him at this Altar a new life, wherein your separate lives are now, till death, made one. With all our hearts we wish that it may be a happy one. But you cannot resolve that it shall be happy. You can and will resolve that it shall be noble. The warm and generous heart of this people takes you today unto itself. Will you not, in response, take that heart, with all its joys and sorrows, into your own?"[4] The Archbishop also made a point of referring to the Duke of York's activities in industrial welfare, "You, sir, have already given many proofs of your care for the welfare of our working people. You have made yourself at home in the mines and shipyards and factories. You have brought the boys of the workshop and the public school together in free and frank companionship. You have done much to increase the public sense of the honour and dignity of labour."[5]

Happy and cheering crowds greeted the married couple as they drove through silver-garlanded streets to Buckingham Palace. As she sat beside her husband, the Duchess of York smiled and waved with unaffected happiness, amply justifying the press's description of her the next day as "the smiling Duchess".

The wedding breakfast was a somewhat formal affair, consisting of an eight-course meal, which lasted an hour and a half. At the end of it, the bride "cut" a pre-sliced nine-foot cake. There was no speech-making, the guests being content with a toast by George V, offered in his homely voice, and with evident sincerity, "I ask you to drink to the health, long life and happiness of the bride and bridegroom." In the late afternoon, escorted by the Prince of Wales, the Duke and Duchess of York left Buckingham Palace for Waterloo Station, and started their honeymoon. The bride's going away outfit, designed in crêpe material in subdued shades of grey and beige, was very much what any comfortably off young woman in 1923 might have worn. Significantly, she chose for her hat a small, off-the-face model, rather than a larger hat which would have partially concealed her face – the new Duchess of York was clearly determined to show herself to the people. Elizabeth Longford believes:

> Perhaps to dwell on this little hat is to trivialize the Duchess's wedding-day. But it was symbolic of her life-long resolve to maintain her "place in the people's life". She would let them see her clearly, and would herself look them in the face. Lady Strathmore had long ago impressed on her "never look at your feet". Queen Mary was so shy that she rarely looked anywhere else. It was for the Duchess of York to bring a new look into the Royal Family.[6]

The first part of the honeymoon was spent at Polesden Lacey, near Dorking, which was the home of Mrs Ronald Greville, one of those friends who had worked hard at promoting the engagement of Lady Elizabeth to the Duke of York. Later parts of the honeymoon were spent at Glamis, and at Frogmore where the Duke had spent parts of his childhood. The Duchess developed whooping cough at Glamis. "So unromantic to catch whooping-cough on your honeymoon," the Duke of York was to write to his mother. The Duchess's illness probably reflects the enormous pressures and tensions which had been building up in the pre-wedding period. Both bride and bridegroom must have approached the honeymoon with some anxiety, as well as anticipation. After all, neither of them were experienced in matters of love – part of their appeal as a bridal couple had rested upon this very freshness and apparent innocence.

That their marriage was an immediate success need not be doubted, as their evident happiness and involvement in each other could not be simulated. The only anxiety expressed by the Duke in the aftermath of his marriage, came in a letter written to his mother the day after his wedding, when he said, "I do hope you will not miss me very much, though I believe you will, as I have stayed with you so much longer really than the brothers."[7] Perhaps these filial sentiments begged a warm and reassuring response from his parents. Certainly George V replied promptly, and at length:

Dearest Bertie,
. . . you are indeed a lucky man to have such a charming & delightful wife as Elizabeth & I am sure you will both be very happy together & I trust you both will have many, many years of happiness before

you, & that you will be as happy as Mama & I are, after you have been married for 30 years, I can't wish you more . . . It must have been with a pang that you left your home after 27 years. I miss you very much & regret your having left us, but now you will have your own home, which I hope will be as happy as the one you have left. You have always been so sensible, & easy to work with & you have always been ready to listen to any advice & to agree with my opinions about people & things, that I feel that we have always got on very well together (very different to dear David). I trust that this state of affairs will always remain the same between us, & that you will come to me for advice whenever you want it . . . By your quiet useful work you have endeared yrself to the people, as shown on Thursday by the splendid reception they gave you. I am quite certain that Elizabeth will be a splendid partner in your work, & share with you & help you in all you have to do.

Wishing you & Elizabeth every good luck & a very happy honeymoon.

Ever my dear boy

Yr. most devoted Papa
G.R.I.[8]

At the beginning of June 1923, the Duke and Duchess of York returned from their honeymoon and took up residence at White Lodge in Richmond Park. Built between 1727 and 1729, during the reign of King George II, White Lodge was set amidst the beautiful deer park which had once been Henry VIII's hunting ground. Although lent to the Duke and Duchess of York as a grace-and-favour house by George V, it was not altogether convenient as a first home; it was too big for their purposes, expensive to keep up, and lacked a proper heating system. It had, however, a special significance for the Duke of York's parents, having been Queen Mary's childhood home; she had returned there for the birth of her first son, the Prince of Wales. Her parents, the Duke and Duchess of Teck, had died at White Lodge. Indeed, it seems that Queen Mary was anxious that the Duke and Duchess of York should make their first home there, and she had certainly done her best while they were on honeymoon to supervise the organization and decoration of the property.

Shortly after the Duke and Duchess of York had returned from their honeymoon, they invited King George and Queen Mary to lunch at

White Lodge on the Thursday of Ascot Week, 28 June 1923. They were as anxious as any newly-married young couple to impress their in-laws, and the Duke wrote to his mother in advance warning her, "that our cook is not very good, but she can do the plain dishes well, & I know you like that sort." As it happened, the visit was a great success. The King and Queen evidently enjoyed the plain lunch, and also toured the whole house, reacting very favourably to what they saw. In his diary that evening, George V wrote, "May & I paid a visit to Bertie and Elizabeth at White Lodge, & had luncheon with them. They have made the house so nice with all their presents."

There is no doubt that both King George and Queen Mary thought very highly of their new daughter-in-law, and the Queen was lavish in her praise, declaring her to be pretty, charming and very well brought up. Between the King and the Duchess of York a very special relationship sprang up almost immediately. Whereas George V had earlier been an irascible and over-critical father, especially to his sons, with his daughter-in-law he was quite transformed. Rather like a legendary dragon confronted by a beautiful maiden, the King's harsher qualities became magically transmuted. Nothing illustrates better the hold which the Duchess of York had over her father-in-law than the occasion when she and the Duke arrived two minutes late for dinner, and, when she apologized for their lateness, the King mildly replied, "You are not late, my dear, I think we must have sat down two minutes too early." The King was quick to tell his son of his good opinion, writing from Balmoral shortly after the marriage, "the better I know & the more I see of your dear little wife, the more charming I think she is, & everyone fell in love with her here."

Quite apart from the fact that the Duchess of York was extremely attractive and attentive, she was also unafraid of her new father-in-law. This meant that her contact with him was natural and unaffected. She did not need to mask her feelings in his presence, and doubtless her lack of anxiety and her openness appealed to the King's better nature. She was also an extremely good listener. One of her rejected suitors remembers, "She had frightfully good manners, and gave the impression of being riveted by what you said."[9] Since George V was fond of holding forth at length, often denouncing the iniquities of the modern world, his daughter-in-law's receptive qualities must have been doubly appealing. That the Duchess of York held her father-in-law in equal affection is proved by a letter she wrote to his doctor, Lord Dawson, after his death, in which she said, "I miss him dreadfully . . .

He was so *dependable* and when he was in the mood, he could be deliciously funny too! Don't you think so?"

If the Duchess of York's joining the Royal Family brought deep pleasure to the King, it enhanced immeasurably the happiness of his son. The Duke of York now had a relationship which gave him the love, closeness, sympathy and support that he had for so long desperately needed. As their relationship developed, he was largely able to rid himself of the tendency to morbid self-pity and of the anxious introspection that had hitherto marked his personality. Secure in a loving marital relationship, he was able to survey the world anew, and found it a less threatening and a more joyous place. Having previously lacked a secure foundation for his life's work, the Duke of York was now sustained and stimulated by a family life that was to become the very core of his happiness. George VI's official biographer has summed up the state of affairs thus:

> The Duchess was not only to be the partner of his happiness and his inspiration of encouragement in the face of adversity, his enduring source of strength in joy and sadness. Hers was the ability to sustain or reward him by a single smile or gesture in the public battles which he waged with his stammer; hers the capacity to calm with a word the passionate temper which ever and anon would burst its bounds. Their marriage was not only an auspicious union of complementary personalities and attributes, but also a fusion of soul and spirit in dedication to the joys of family life in the service of the State.[10]

It would be tempting to dismiss such an assessment as an example of over-romanticized eulogy, but for the fact that every piece of available evidence confirms it. The House of Windsor, after all, has had its share of marital disharmony, including Princess Margaret's divorce from Lord Snowdon in 1978. Gossip in the domestic and foreign press has affected other members of the Royal Family. The private lives of British royalty have been, and continue to be, the subject of intense press speculation and interest. Given their superstar status, it is understandable and perhaps inevitable that this should be so. It is the price to be paid for a privileged lifestyle and much public adulation.

However, in the case of the Duke and Duchess of York, their marriage seems to have been above suspicion or reproach. There was no muck-raking done at their expense. Their relationship remains enshrined in the nation's memory as, at the best, ideal, and, at the very least, as solid, satisfying and mutually supportive. It was a marriage that quite clearly transformed for the better the life of a prince whose earlier life had been characterized by ill health and trauma.

7

DUKE AT WORK:
INDUSTRIAL RELATIONS

It may not have been the case that industry was actually despised, but that members of the Royal House had not found a way to intimacy of touch with it . . . the wisest influences in the ranks of industry are nowadays turned to the cultivation of pride in work well done rather than to shame of an overall and grimy hands. And the Duke is taking his part in this task.

The Yorkshire Post, 1928

THE TRIUMPHANT SURVIVAL of the House of Windsor into the last two decades of the twentieth century has been based not merely upon the conservatism of the British people, but also on a form of monarchical Darwinism. The British monarchy has shown the capacity to adapt successfully to changing circumstances, and to follow an evolutionary path which has kept it, for the most part, in favour with the majority of British citizens.

When George V acceded to the throne in 1910, although the fiction of monarchical constitutional power remained, with speeches from the throne, Prime Ministers hastening to Buckingham Palace to kiss hands on forming administrations, the monarch dissolving Parliament and so forth, the reality was quite different. Essentially, any British monarch was obliged to stick closely to the three inalienable rights described by Walter Bagehot in *The English Constitution* – the right to be consulted, the right to encourage, and the right to warn.

If the British royal house had thus demonstrated its capacity for self-effacing constitutional adaptability, its social position by the end of the First World War remained unchanged. Quite simply, the British monarch stood at the pinnacle of society's pyramid. While the monarchy remained, the peerage must also remain, and if the peerage were to endure, there was no prospect of any revolutionary process of social levelling. There could be some mobility within the classes below the peerage, and it was possible – and in the Edwardian age had been commonplace – for successful plutocrats in business and finance to be elevated to the peerage. But what could be done to improve the conditions of Britain's poor, short of taking from the rich to give to those most in need? The ferocious controversy that had surrounded David Lloyd George's People's Budget of 1909, and which had overflowed into the subsequent drive to limit the delaying powers of the House of Lords, had posed some awkward questions for the monarchy. If the issue could be presented, as Lloyd George chose to present it, as "the Peers versus the People", where did the monarchy stand in this confrontation? George V had succeeded his father at the height of the controversy over the Parliament Act of 1911 which proposed to restrict the veto of the Upper House. He eventually and reluctantly agreed to create enough Liberal peers to overwhelm the opposition of the Tory peers in the House of Lords. This compromise had worked, and the opposition of the Tory peers had melted away, allowing the Parliament Act to be put on to the Statute Book.

Apart from showing an appropriate concern and sympathy, members of the Royal Family had as yet done little to alleviate poverty. As Prince of Wales, Edward VII's response to being shown the London poor in their slums had been an impulse to throw a handful of gold sovereigns among them. Before the First World War, King George V and Queen Mary, although deploring unemployment and giving money privately to allay its effects, seemed to have viewed strike action chiefly as an unfortunate disruption of national activity. For example, when in 1912 the strike of transport workers followed hard on the heels of a national railway stoppage, Queen Mary wrote, "now we have a transport strike, which may become very serious – really we have no luck, one tiresome thing after another." Although before 1914 George V did pay some visits to industrialized areas, these ritual demonstrations of royal humanity did nothing to provide any improvement in the material wellbeing of his poorer subjects. The dissatisfaction of organized labour came to a head in 1913 and 1914 when the "Triple Alliance" of the three great unions of the miners, railwaymen and dockers began to discuss a common and militant approach to the solution of their members' problems. The outbreak of the First World War served to divert the unions' energies from such schemes, but this was to prove only a respite.

The war, though providing a reassuring rallying of the British working man to King and Country, also demonstrated what perils were abroad. The Russian revolution of 1917 overthrew the Romanovs, and a year later the Imperial Russian family was murdered at Ekaterinburg. As the First World War came to a close, two of the other great ruling houses of Europe had come crashing down: the Hohenzollerns in Germany, and the Habsburgs in Austria. Where was it all to end?

In the immediate aftermath of the First World War there were dangerous signs in Britain for the monarchy. In the second half of November 1918, as the Labour Party prepared to fight the imminent General Election, Mr Bob Williams, Secretary of the Transport Workers' Union, announced at a rally at the Albert Hall, "I hope to see the Red Flag flying over Buckingham Palace." Willie Gallacher, from the Red Clyde, glad to describe himself as "a Bolshevik from Glasgow", admitted openly that he was out for revolution. There had been much singing of "The Red Flag" at the Albert Hall rally, and the audience had given "hearty cheers for 'the Bolsheviks', 'Lenin and Trotsky', and, amid much laughter, 'The Bloody Revolution.'"[1]

On 23 November 1918, King George and the Prince of Wales, accompanied by other members of the Royal Family, reviewed some 35,000 Silver Badge ex-servicemen in Hyde Park. Although the King received an enthusiastic reception, with men breaking through the lines, surrounding him and nearly pulling him off his horse, it did not escape notice that various banners bearing slogans complaining at their poor pensions, lack of housing and work had been unfurled by the ex-servicemen. After the police had extricated the King from the mélée, he rode with the Prince of Wales to Buckingham Palace, and there dismounting had said, shaking his head, "those men were in a funny temper."

The "funny temper" of the electorate was not reflected in any dramatic sense in the election results of 1918. The Lloyd George coalition was returned to power, but with the Liberals split and much reduced in numbers in the House of Commons, which was now dominated by Conservative members. The Bloody Revolution had clearly been postponed.

King George V, through his two eldest sons, nevertheless responded quickly to the new spirit of the age. Prompted by the Prime Minister, Lloyd George, by leading members of the establishment, and by prominent industrialists and labour leaders, the following strategy was evolved. The Prince of Wales was to embark upon a series of Empire-wide tours, ostensibly to thank the people of the Empire for their contribution to the war, but also to show the future King's face to his father's subjects. At home, an active royal patron of schemes of industrial welfare was needed. In 1919 it was proposed that one of the King's sons should become President of the Boys' Welfare Association,

[71]

which was to be "an organization through which industry itself might be responsible for the development of the growing movement for the betterment of working conditions, the setting up of works' committees, the provision of health centres and canteens in factories, and of proper facilities for the maximum of enjoyment in the workers' free time."[2] Prince Albert was the obvious candidate for the position. His father believed that it would be good experience for him, and also beneficial to the monarchy. The Prince accepted the invitation with the one proviso, arising from his shyness and consciousness of his stammer, that the work should not be of too ceremonial a nature. As he put it, "I'll do it, provided that there's no damned red carpet about it."

Thus began Prince Albert's involvement with industrial welfare. The Boys' Welfare Association, soon after the Prince agreed to become its President, was renamed the Industrial Welfare Society, and Prince Albert's association with this organization provided him with an excellent opportunity to see at first hand the great industrial centres of Britain. He approached his task in a spirit of earnestness and goodwill. Insisting that he must always see factories and work-places under normal conditions, free of any special preparations on his behalf, he proceeded to go down coal-mines, drive railway locomotives, to climb up scaffolding, to sit at the controls of tramcars and buses. He took no short-cuts. Once, when visiting a soapworks, he was told that the factory had a glue department, which had an almost unbearable smell. His reply was "that if the place was good enough for the people who worked there, it was good enough for him to see – and in he went".

There was a lighter, although sometimes disconcerting, side to his visits to industry, as it soon became apparent that he had only to inspect a piece of machinery for it to go wrong. He once described what happened:

It seems that I place an evil spell on machines in which I show a special interest, and they sometimes break down and stop. Once, to my surprise and dismay, I was dropped in a lift. Another time, a fool-proof stamping machine threw out forty unstamped letters for my benefit. The threads of looms seem to break whenever I approach those machines. And yet, I find that industrialists are ready to welcome me in their midst.[3]

Despite this, the British press soon nicknamed him "the Industrial Prince". His father was delighted with his work, ". . . and on one occasion when the Prime Minister of the day brought up in audience some question of industrial relations, His Majesty replied, 'Oh, that's my second son's department,' and chuckled; and the Duke's brothers referred to him as 'the Foreman'." During his work for the Industrial Welfare Society, Prince Albert showed a capacity to ask intelligent and relevant questions, often of a technical nature, and gained the ability to talk unpretentiously and directly to ordinary men and women often without a hint of a stammer, demonstrating an idealism which had not previously been associated with the Royal Family. He communicated to his father the very real problems which faced so many British subjects, and described the unrest and unhappiness which he perceived in many parts of the country. In public, his views were encapsulated in a speech he made at the general meeting of the Industrial Welfare Society in 1920:

> To me the importance of the welfare questions lies in the fact that it helps the worker to free himself from the grip of the machine and enables him to make fuller use of his leisure.
>
> There is a new industrial philosophy abroad with which we must identify ourselves and of which we must be pioneers.
>
> The saving and brightening of the worker's life should be, and must eventually be, an industrial issue, and when the community realizes that the country is richest which nourishes the greatest number of happy people, a big step will have been taken towards the contentment and prosperity of the nation.[4]

Prince Albert's involvement with industrial welfare continued, and even grew, after his marriage, but it is difficult to agree with his official biographer's view that, "the Duke's influence made itself felt through the industrial life of Britain." Certainly, factory conditions were not improved overnight, nor were the wages of British workers miraculously increased. Indeed, the nineteen-twenties were marked by a series of bitter industrial disputes, culminating in the great General Strike of 1926. Measured in these terms, therefore, Prince Albert's public work could not be said to have brought about an amelioration in industrial conditions. Some trades union leaders even saw the Industrial Welfare Society as a bosses' device, a public relations exercise designed to divert attention from the real problems of poverty and unemployment. The fact that the Duke of York developed a close relationship with Frank Hodges, the General Secretary of the Miners'

Federation of Great Britain, did not prevent the mine owners threatening, in 1925, to cut miners' wages, a threat which was carried out after the General Strike of 1926 had ended in failure and the miners had been driven back to work after a further unsuccessful six months' strike.

Instead, it is tempting to see the Duke of York's well-publicized contact with Frank Hodges as being merely cosmetic in quality. It was, of course, all good copy for the press. Nothing illustrates this better than the golf match arranged in May 1924 at the Ton Pentre Welfare Scheme golf course in the Rhondda Valley. The golf club had been founded in 1922 with the active co-operation of two local mining companies, and had been laid out by the miners themselves, working voluntarily and after hours. The chief participants in the game arranged for May 1924 were the Duke of York, his comptroller Captain Basil Brooke, Frank Hodges representing the unions, and Mr Evan Williams, the President of the Mining Association of Great Britain, for the coal owners. The game itself, and the history of the course on which it was to be played, was thus meant to symbolize the harmony and co-operation possible between management and workers in the coal industry. The most that could be said for it, and for similar ventures, was that it offered a non-violent approach to what were potentially very violent disputes. Still, it was better that the Duke of York should be associated with such displays, even if they were essentially rather self-conscious exercises in industrial window-dressing, than not.

Much attention was focused on the match. "Even before the train had reached its destination, the loyal Welsh people all along the line had put out their flags and cheered the Duke as he passed. A good deal of washing was hanging out also, and occasionally this included a red petticoat, on the appearance of which the Duke would say: "Hodges, another member of your party!'." At the lunch arranged before the game, the Duke was welcomed by Colonel David Davies, a Welsh landowner and industrialist, and Liberal MP for Montgomeryshire. Speaking of the work of the Industrial Welfare Society in providing common ground where both sides of industry could meet, Colonel Davies said, "today is symbolic of that work. Not always, Sir, have your opponents, Mr Evan Williams and Mr Frank Hodges played together. I have known them, doughty warriors both of them, in other fields, fighting hard, stern battles – you have created this partnership".

The Duke of York was President of the Industrial Welfare Society from 1919 to 1935. Indeed, but for his accession to the throne, it is likely that he would have remained closely associated with the organization. In November 1935, speaking at the general meeting of the Industrial Welfare Society, he reviewed the sixteen years of his Presidency, saying:

I feel there is a change of spirit abroad, recalling many of the best features of working life in the Middle Ages, a spirit which, to a large extent, was lost in the development of the factory system. We must prove that throughout history there has always been an impulse to make a society in which men are able to work together in harmony.

In days gone by, the master craftsman lodged his apprentices. Today the employer has to provide houses for his work-people. The master was responsible for feeding his hands. Today he installs a canteen. . . . The master watched over the health of his work-people. Today the employer develops medical services and sickness funds. In those far-off days the master was responsible for the discipline of his young people during their leisure. Today, that responsibility exists no longer, but the wise employer provides, where there is need, facilities for recreation. I may even suggest that the modern works council is in direct following of the close domestic tie which existed between the master and the apprentice which, if the story-books are to be believed, often led to a happy marriage with the employer's daughter.

Through the advent of large industrial groups, many of these old human associations disappeared, and with them nearly all sense of partnership. Since our work began, however, we have shown that partnership promotes the well-being of the workers and adds to the efficiency of the enterprise. Much that was best in the relations that existed in the age of the Craft and the Guild is being reestablished today.[5]

Much of the Duke's speech could be dismissed as tendentious, pious and superficial. Certainly, a survey of Britain's industrial relations today, nearly half a century after the speech was made, does not justify the optimistic and rather romantic views expressed. Nonetheless, the Duke's involvement with British industry between the two world wars was sincere and thorough – during these years he visited up to one hundred and fifty work-sites and factories, showing a genuine interest and a praiseworthy competence. The human touch which he developed through these activities undoubtedly made him an acceptable successor to his more obviously popular and dashing elder brother when the latter abdicated at the end of 1936.

According to one writer, the Duke's response to the General Strike of 1926 was by no means typical of the reaction of other members of the ruling order:

> The Duke was furious with the cry of "Reds". Better than any member of the Royal Family, he knew the character of the British working men, with their tolerance, their common sense, their innate courtesy and their humour. Those nearest to the Duke were startled at the transformation in him. His novitiate was over. He was meeting the onslaught of events and making up his own mind as a man.[6]

Perhaps, above all, it was the Duke of York's consistency of interest in industrial matters that was so impressive. His brother, the Prince of Wales, also visited industrial areas, particularly in the early nineteen-thirties, during the worst years of the Depression. Indeed, the future King Edward VIII gained a considerable contemporary reputation as a Prince deeply sympathetic with the plight of unemployed workers. During his brief reign, in November 1936, he visited the depressed region of South Wales, saying to the chairman of the Unemployed Mens' Committee at Blaenavon, "something will be done about unemployment." A little over a month later, he abdicated.

The Duke of York, on the other hand, shrugged off none of his royal obligations, and assumed no shallow enthusiasm for the difficulties of working people. He was not identified in the public imagination as an open sympathizer with left-wing political movements, as his elder brother, quite unjustifiably, was. Nonetheless, he had established a relationship with British working men which was to endure. This link was neatly symbolized in November 1940 when, as King George VI, he was presented with a gold medal by George Gibson, the chairman of the General Council of the Trades Union Congress. On being handed the medal, the King said with a smile, "That means I can attend any T.U.C., does it?" To which Gibson replied benignly, "Yes, Sir, that's right."[7] It was an exchange which indicated a mutual warmth of regard.

8

THE DUKE OF YORK'S CAMP

The Camp, I have always felt, is my own private enterprise . . .
                                    The Duke of York, 1930

So he comes down without any fuss or bother for one day . . . before he
arrives we have a great clean-up of Camp . . . four hundred boys are lined
up and walk slowly over the site, picking up litter as they go.
                                    Robert Hyde, *The Camp Book*

THE DUKE OF YORK'S INVOLVEMENT in the Industrial Welfare Society
did not, of course, please everybody. Although the majority of British
newspapers were content to call him the "Industrial Prince", the *Daily
Worker* derided him as an old fashioned paternalist. In 1921 however,
he had begun a more personal contribution to the promotion of better
employer-worker relations in British society. Evidently conscious of
the grave threat posed to public order and stability through the effects
of unemployment and industrial dislocation, the Duke was privately
searching for some practical way of illustrating that friendship and
common interests could flourish between people from completely
different class backgrounds.

In March 1921, an event occurred which helped him to develop his
ideas further. The welfare officer of the Briton Ferry Steel Company of
South Wales wrote to the Industrial Welfare Society, asking them to
arrange football fixtures for a team of boys from the works who had
saved up enough money to make a visit to London. Subsequently,
three games were arranged for the visitors from Wales. The last of
these, which was played on 10 March 1921, was against Westminster
School. The Duke of York was present at this game, as was Robert
Hyde of the Industrial Welfare Society, and Sir Alexander Grant,
chairman and managing director of McVitie and Price Biscuits Ltd,
against whose boys' club the Welsh visitors had played their second
football match. Everyone who saw the match was impressed by the
boys' spirit of sportsmanship and, on leaving the game, Sir Alexander
Grant spoke to the Duke, saying that in his view much good would be
done if boys from industry and the public schools could be brought
together on terms of equality.

This was exactly the sort of prompting the Duke of York needed. A few days later he invited Robert Hyde and Commander B. T. Coote, a pioneer of physical training in the Navy, to Buckingham Palace to discuss Sir Alexander Grant's idea. Several ideas were tossed about, but none of them seemed to appeal to the Duke. The sporting fixture, though useful in itself, was not sufficient. It was necessary, he argued, that people should live together if they were to get to know each other better. Perhaps a group of public schoolboys and young workers from industry could spend a week together somewhere. Then the final idea struck him. "Let's have a camp."

Preparations went ahead quickly. Robert Hyde agreed to approach various industrial firms with the idea; Dr David of Rugby School, then chairman of the Public Schools Headmasters' Conference, was also consulted and responded enthusiastically; Sir Alexander Grant agreed to handle the finances of the first camp; and Commander Coote was put in charge of overall organization. The site of the camp was to be at New Romney, near Hythe on the Kentish coast. Here, a disused aerodrome offered ideal facilities: there were substantial huts with modern sanitation and electric lighting, adequate kitchen facilities, and a large dining hall. Around the huts were a hundred acres of playing fields, and the proximity of the sea would make bathing a possibility at any time of day.

As George VI's official biographer has pointed out, "There was nothing, of course, intrinsically novel about the idea of a holiday camp. School missions and university settlements had organized them for boys from the East End of London and elsewhere for many years. The Scout Movement, the Boys' Brigade, Cadet Corps and Boys' Clubs had done likewise."[1] What was experimental about the camp was the social mix. One hundred public schools and one hundred industrial firms were each invited to send two boys between the ages of seventeen and nineteen to the first camp. There they would stay as the Duke of York's guests for a week – working and playing together on terms of absolute equality. Two boys had been invited from each institution in the hope that this would help to lessen their initial shyness and embarrassment.

The idea of the Duke of York's camp was not greeted on all sides with rapturous enthusiasm: both in the public schools and in industry there were those who viewed the venture with suspicion, but the fact that the Duke of York, who was generally well regarded by the public, was the patron and moving spirit behind the camp, was obviously a fact in its favour. Robert Hyde, in his rather hearty account of the experiment, *The Camp Book*, summed it up when he said, "If anybody but a member of the Royal Family had started this Camp, I have no doubt that the average parent of the public schoolboy would have been a little timorous about the advisability of allowing Claude to associate with Bill, lest he should 'catch' something detrimental to his health, or, far worse, to his manners. On the other hand, the camp would certainly have been regarded as a trap to tame young Bolshevists."[2]

The opening day of the first camp was Saturday 30 July 1921. Although the right quota of boys turned up, there had not exactly been a rush to take part, and few of those arriving at the opening meeting had any clear idea as to what was going to happen. Some evidently believed that they were going to take part in an experiment in social engineering. Others, playing safe, as is so often the case when members of the public have to come into contact with royalty, arrived at the riding school in the Royal Mews at Buckingham Palace dressed in "gents' natty suitings" or wearing bowler hats and carrying tightly furled umbrellas.

Having been welcomed informally by the Duke of York, the four hundred boys then sat down to lunch. Captain J. G. Paterson, who ultimately succeeded Commander Coote as Camp Chief in 1926, has recalled how tense the atmosphere was at lunch, and how it was touch-and-go whether the experiment would succeed. "Let it be confessed that there was an almost ominous quiet about the atmosphere when they all sat down to lunch. It required complete confidence in the ultimate success of the experiment to preserve the morale of the staff at that stage of the proceedings, and I think that many of the boys themselves would have 'deserted' if they could have summoned up the courage to do so." After this rather frosty lunch, the four hundred boys and their leaders caught a special train provided by the Southern Railway at Cannon Street, and were taken to Dymchurch, from where they were required to walk three miles to the camp site at New Romney. There was no spontaneous co-mingling during the walk, and the public schoolboys and the young workers tended to stick together in peer groups.

Once at the camp site, however, things began to warm up. Perhaps the fact that each boy was required to put on the camp uniform of shirts and shorts had something to do with it – certainly it must have been a relief to get rid of bowler hats and off-the-peg suits. Also, the boys were divided up into twenty groups of twenty each, in which the social classes were intermingled. Each group, or section, competed against the others in the camp games, thus encouraging the boy's loyalty to his section rather than to any other grouping. It is interesting that in the games, cricket and football were ruled out as giving the public schoolboys too great an advantage. Instead, games were devised which, according to one participant, were ". . . perfectly novel and unorthodox, and had probably never been seen, much less played, by anyone before . . . It was a work of genius to have devised games which were so fair to all, and these games struck the key-note of the Camp – an equal chance for all, with the individual, whether schoolboy or factory hand, working for his side and not for himself."[3]

On 3 August the Duke of York came down to visit his guests at the first camp. Prone as he was to anxious introspection, he must have felt some qualms as he motored towards New Romney. He was very conscious that his scheme had many critics, and he could not have failed to notice that the press had been generally unenthusiastic. The few hours of his visit, however, completely reassured him. From all sides he received spontaneous tributes to the success of the experiment. Captain Paterson recalled:

He was no longer vulnerable. He could now go on with confidence. He had four hundred staunch supporters. He had found the perfect means of exposing some of the nonsense that was talked about class relationships, and placed the seal of his influence and leadership on a venture destined to go from strength to strength during the difficult years between the wars, and there can be no doubt of his contribution to strengthening the ties between the Crown and the people.[4]

Other participants were to wax equally enthusiastic. Robert Hyde was to claim, "the Camp is playing a part in oiling the wheels of industry with good fellowship and understanding." One of the original participants later wrote, "in this short week, a great end was achieved – the public schoolboy came to know his brother, the factory hand (and vice versa) – came to know him as a keen sportsman and a staunch comrade; in fact this camp came at a time when it was much needed, when men are striving after a false shadow of democracy which tends towards Bolshevism, when the two classes are at loggerheads." Another boy wrote later in his school magazine, "few of us can have held the slightest expectation that a camaraderie so spontaneous, natural and far-reaching would exist in so short a time between boys drawn from spheres so diverse."

At the most obvious level, these tributes meant that the vast majority of participants in the Duke of York's camps enjoyed their experience greatly. Certainly, there was never again to be a lack of response to the Duke of York's invitation to attend – indeed, a rule had to be imposed that no boy could attend a camp twice. On the other hand, it is difficult to accept the rosy-tinted view of some of the early pioneers that the Duke of York's camps somehow contributed to a greater understanding between the classes. Class antagonism did not melt away during the nineteen-twenties, nor even during the nineteen-thirties. Even at the moment of writing it would be impossible to claim that Britain is a society untroubled by conflict between different sections of the population, whether these differences are based upon class, race, or upon conflicting roles and needs within the prevailing economic system. The decade in which the Duke of York's camp experiment was at its height was marked by episodes of bitter class conflict, especially in industry. In 1924, and again in 1929, the Labour Party, representing organized labour, was able to form a minority government. That a national government, backed by an overwhelming Conservative majority in the House of Commons, was in power for almost the whole of the nineteen-thirties, owed much more to the growth of national prosperity, particularly in the South of England and the Midlands, than to any fundamental reconciliation between the classes.

The Duke of York's camps, therefore, can be seen as rather isolated and artificial events, and could have been part of the Fabian tactics employed so successfully by the British ruling order in the face of the rise of international and domestic Socialism and egalitarianism. Did it really matter that a public schoolboy could appreciate the sporting skills of a factory hand? Did it really alter the attitudes of future generations that a young worker was able to spend a week in the company of public schoolboys, and enjoy the experience? Nonetheless, it is impossible to read accounts of the Duke of York's camps, or to see photographs taken at them, without admitting that a great deal of fun was had. Judged by the more sophisticated and cynical standards of today, the fun was of a rather obvious and hearty kind. Dressing in shorts, taking part in obstacle races, and joining in the communal singing of "Under the Spreading Chestnut Tree" had a straightforward and rather unimaginative appeal. It is symptomatic of the spirit that prevailed that Chapter Five of Robert Hyde's book describing the experiment was entitled "Some Camp Japes".

But, within their limitations, the camps worked. At any rate, from

1921 to 1939 there were eighteen camps in all. In 1930 however, there was no camp. This was because the site at New Romney had become something of a tourist attraction, holiday-makers tending to flock into the area, partly in the hope of seeing the Duke of York himself. This infiltration was a serious encroachment upon the privacy of the camp, and threatened the desired atmosphere of spontaneous freedom. The Duke told Sir Alexander Grant, who continued to give invaluable financial support to the camp, of his decision not to hold a camp in 1930 in the following words:

> As you know, I have decided, owing to the unsuitability of the site & the accommodation at New Romney, not to hold another Camp there again. The place is already over-crowded, & I dare not run risks of any kind with the boys who come to Camp as my guests. The Camp, I have always felt, is my own private enterprise, & I do not want people to look on it as a yearly institution, in the same way as they look upon others of a similar character.
>
> For this reason, & for others with which I will not burden you, I have decided not to hold a Camp at all this year. I am very sorry that this decision has had to be made, and I hope that by next year a suitable site will have been found, & that the Camp will continue to play as valuable a part in the National life as it has in the past.[5]

In 1931, the camp was re-established at Southwold Common in Suffolk, where it continued for the next eight years. Although Sir John Wheeler-Bennett has claimed that the camp's privacy was "scrupulously respected by both townspeople and visitors", the camps still attracted considerable publicity. For example, in August 1937, the *News Review* reported that the camp's patron, now King George VI, had been very angry that the *Star* had revealed the date of his visit to the camp at Southwold, "At first, the King threatened not to go to the Camp again." On the King's instructions, the national press was asked not to follow up the story in the *Star*. George VI, it was made clear, did not want thousands of holiday-makers to crowd round the camp at Southwold.[6]

Apart from problems like these, the camps continued to flourish, and the one day a year which the Duke of York spent at his camps came to be the centre-piece of the ritual. Robert Hyde has left a vivid account of what the Duke's Days were like. Although he tried to arrive with as little fuss and ceremony as possible, this was never quite achieved. As Hyde noted, "little time elapses before the boys are aware of his presence; an awareness that synchronizes with the production of hundreds of cameras, which the Duke good-humouredly faces. He first meets the whole camp at the mid-day meal, and on more than one occasion he has delighted a section by leaving the Camp Chief's table and joining their mess."[7]

The Duke quickly realized that it was impossible for him to arrive unheralded and unnoticed. To remedy this he once, ". . . proposed quite seriously . . . that he should arrive down at midnight, dress in Camp kit in the morning, and wander about unrecognized and free; but he was told that the love of the public for a story of this kind would bring around him all the forces of modern publicity."[8] So, as a general rule, the Duke travelled down by train, reaching the camp a little before midday.

Although the Duke was supposed to partake of the same food as the campers, this was not always the case. For example, once:

He was not too well . . . and his doctor had insisted that if he came to Camp he must eat nothing but white flesh, but this information did not reach us until about half-past ten on the morning of his arrival.

There were no chickens within range of the Camp, but luckily a strange visitor with his car was nearby. We told him of our need, and implored him to scour the country for a young bird. Our plea met with such success that he returned within half-an-hour with a chicken ready for the pot. This was handed to the caterer with instructions to cook it very carefully for the Duke's lunch. Other matters occupied us during the day, so we took no further interest in the bird's career, but at any rate we felt that the doctor's orders had been carried out.

Two or three years afterwards I told the Duke of all the difficulties we had had in getting the chicken – not half of which are related here – and of the pleasure we had felt at having procured for him an invalid diet. To my chagrin, he replied: "I remember it to this day. It was as tough as leather, and we couldn't eat a bite of it."[9]

In the afternoons, the Duke spent his time watching and participating in games. These normally took the form of:

. . . a display of Camp competitions or a water carnival or land sport, and in all this the Duke himself is the first to lead any rag that happens to arise. Last year one of the hazards in the obstacle race was a pond improvised by using a large tarpaulin, and in which many of the Camp leaders were ducked, the chief instigator being the Duke himself, and many of us know to our cost the penalty for coming within his range of vision while bathing.

One year we had arranged a push-ball match, and he was asked if he would referee the game. "Referee be damned" said he, "I'm going to play." Shortly afterwards a lusty young Harlequin was burrowing his shoulder into the ribs of the man in front of him shouting, "Now push like Hell!" In a flash came the Duke's retort: "I *am* pushing like Hell!"[10]

The Duke of York generally liked to bring down about a dozen guests to see the camp. The typical visiting party would have included a cabinet minister, two or three public schoolmasters, some prominent employers or labour leaders, and a few other public figures. The Duchess accompanied him one year. These guests often had to undergo something of an ordeal during the evening's entertainment, as it became a tradition to invite them to make a three-minute speech to the assembled boys, the end of the three minutes being signalled by the discharge of a blank cartridge from a revolver. The speech-makers, however, were not told this. "The Duke took particular and impish delight in the efforts of great orators, accustomed to developing their views at length, confining themselves to the three-minute limit, and their chagrin at being cut short in mid-peroration." Perhaps the Duke took some pleasure in seeing some practised public speakers put under pressure. Certainly he seems to have encouraged the boys to alternately cheer and barrack the speechmakers. Not that all visitors had to make a speech. Colonel David Davies, the industrialist and Liberal MP for Montgomeryshire, once declined to make a speech, saying instead that he would not mind singing a song. Perhaps he was merely being evasive for he said, "I would do this willingly, if I had a piano and music." Miraculously, the door of the hall opened – piano, music and pianist appeared, and the Colonel was obliged to go ahead and sing "D'Ye Ken John Peel?".

Rather oddly, for it must have created a sense of anti-climax, the Duke normally ended his day by leaving the evening entertainment before the finish. Before leaving, however, he would stand up and make a short impromptu speech. According to Robert Hyde, "Those of us who have heard him on these occasions have often wished that a record might be made of his speeches, which come straight from his heart, and meet a response in theirs; but indeed no record could ever convey the impression he makes on his hearers." As the Duke made his departure, the boys used to flock out to line the road leading to the camp gate. Each boy was "armed with a flare, and at a given signal these are lighted, and amid a blaze and a burst of cheering, the Duke takes leave of his guests".

1939 saw the final Duke of York's Camp. Only two hundred boys were invited, and it was held in the grounds of Abergeldie Castle, where the Duke had spent a good many happy days as a child. By now George VI, he played a very active part in this camp, was Camp Chief, and took charge of a different party of boys each day. He outwalked them during a day's tramping over the hills, and was pleased that he had enjoyed more contact with them, telling his mother, "I saw much more of the boys as I went on their walks with them on the hill, & was able to talk to them." During this last camp, the boys went to tea at nearby Balmoral Castle, and Queen Elizabeth and the two princesses, Elizabeth and Margaret Rose, were invited to take supper with them.

The King was apparently in his element amid countryside he loved so deeply, and a rapport developed between him and the boys which had not emerged at earlier camps:

> They listened to him with rapt attention while he described interesting features of the surrounding country, or pointed out activity going on around them which their inexperienced eyes failed to see. Herds of deer; birds of all kinds as they got up from the heather and bracken; the sparrowhawk hovering in the sky. These were all unfamiliar sights to the majority of them, and they created a firm bond between the King and his young guests. They told him of their work and experience in the more crowded parts of his Kingdom, and were not a little surprised by his own knowledge of their everyday world. It was a delightful experience, and typified all that is grand and good in our democratic way of life, and in the contemporary relationship between the Throne and People.[11]

Within a few weeks of this final camp, the Second World War had broken out, and many of the young men who had attended it were destined to be members of the King's Armed Services. During the war, the King met many of them when he made his tours of inspection of the Royal Navy or of his land and air forces in various theatres of war. He was nearly always able to remember at which camp he had first met them. Captain Paterson has left a moving account of the final night of the final camp, with a great bonfire blazing in the background, the Balmoral pipers playing, and, at the finish, the King waving to the boys as they were driven off in the coaches towards Aberdeen and their return home. Captain Paterson wrote:

This was symbolic. It was the end. It was his own conception, and with the willing help of others, his own achievement. It was fitting that these two hundred young men, representing the seven thousand who had enjoyed the unique privilege of meeting the King in such intimate circumstances, should take their leave of him from his own home, because what he had started as an experiment had become an integral part of His Majesty's personal interest.[12]

9

WIDER RESPONSIBILITIES, LIONEL LOGUE, AND THE WORLD TOUR

1924–1927

He was the pluckiest and most determined patient I ever had.
Lionel Logue

I return a thorough optimist. When one has travelled over the vast extent of the Empire . . . it is impossible to despair of the future of the British race.
The Duke of York, 1927

IN 1924, A YEAR AFTER HIS MARRIAGE, the Duke of York was expressing dissatisfaction with his home at White Lodge in Richmond Park. Both he and the Duchess wanted a home in London, but this, however, did not prove easy to arrange. For one thing, if the Duke and Duchess moved out of White Lodge, some other occupants would have to be found to take their place, and the regulations governing the royal residences in the parks of Richmond and Windsor made the finding of suitable replacement occupants a complicated business. Eventually, in 1927, White Lodge was leased to Lord Lee of Fareham, the man who gave Chequers to the nation. (Much later, in 1955, White Lodge was granted as a permanent school to the Royal Ballet.) When Lord Lee took the lease of White Lodge, the Duke and Duchess of York were able to move out to their desired London house, 145 Piccadilly, which was to be their home until the Duke's accession to the throne in 1936.

While the Duke was negotiating to move out of White Lodge, some drastic alterations were made in the composition of his household. Since 1918 Wing Commander Louis Greig had been closely associated with him, first as equerry, and then, from 1920, as Comptroller. With the Duke's marriage, however, his close association with Greig came to an end. Of this change, the King's official biographer simply says, "With the Duke's marriage . . . and the setting up of an independent *ménage*, it was natural that a change should come, and both realized the necessity of this." Accordingly, Greig retired from the Duke's household at the beginning of 1924. His departure symbolized the Duke's new status as a married man and head of a household that would have far different needs from those of his bachelor days. Although officially detached from the Duke's service, Louis Greig was to remain one of his small circle of friends. The new Comptroller of the Duke's household was Captain Basil Brooke, a recently retired naval officer; and Lieutenant Colin Buist, an old friend and fellow term-mate from the Duke's days as a naval cadet, took up the post of equerry.

The newly married Duke and Duchess were soon undertaking official duties on behalf of the Crown. At the end of October 1923, they attended a double royal event in Belgrade, the christening of the son of King Alexander of Yugoslavia, and the wedding of Prince Paul of Yugoslavia to Princess Olga of Greece. Since these two ceremonies were to take place on succeeding days, it seemed sensible that the Duke and Duchess of York should both appear as godparents at the christening and that later the Duke could officially represent King George V at the wedding. For some time, it was not clear whether the Duke and Duchess would be required to attend these two ceremonies, and indeed they had arranged to take a holiday at Holwick Hall, in County Durham. The Foreign Secretary, Lord Curzon, suddenly changed his mind as to the advisability of the Duke and Duchess's visit to Belgrade and, on 23 September, King George V was advised to telegraph his son asking him to leave almost at once.

The Duke showed an understandable exasperation at this abrupt change of plans, which would disrupt his proposed holiday, and he wrote to Louis Greig on 24 September, "Curzon should be drowned for giving me such short notice . . . he must know things are different now." There was, of course, now no escape from the obligations and, after a short period of preparation, the Duke and Duchess of York left London for Belgrade on 18 October 1923. In this way the Duchess of York experienced for the first time the melodrama, mixed with archaic and splendid ceremonial, that tended to characterize Balkan royal occasions.

All the Balkan royal families were there, many of them connected by ties of blood and marriage to the House of Windsor. As the Duke of York told his father in a letter, "we were quite a large family party & how we all lived in the Palace is a mystery. We were not too comfortable, & there was no hot water!!" At both the christening and the wedding the Duchess met some of the more colourful of her new royal relatives, including Queen Marie of Yugoslavia, known to the family as "Missy". Missy had been a high-spirited and ebullient Romanian princess, and was now an equally high-spirited and ebullient Queen of Yugoslavia. The Duke wrote, "Cousin Missy as usual was in great form."

Faced with this extraordinary assortment of Balkan royalty, both in power and in exile, the Duchess of York was her usual charming and accommodating self. As her husband wrote to his father with evident satisfaction, "they were all enchanted with Elizabeth, especially Cousin Missy. She was wonderful with all of them & they were all strangers except two Paul & Olga."

On 19 July 1924, the Duke and Duchess began an official visit to Northern Ireland. The week's visit was the first royal occasion in the province since King George V had opened the Northern Irish Parliament on 22 June 1921. Having achieved the partition of Ireland that the vast majority of them wanted, the Loyalist Protestants of Ulster turned out to give the Duke and Duchess a wildly enthusiastic reception. The Duke gave an account of this demonstration of loyalty in a letter written to his father, which also clearly illustrated his wife's popular appeal:

> Our reception has been quite astounding. There is no other word to describe the wonderful enthusiasm of the people of Belfast. They turned out in the streets at any time of the day & night, & the noise they made cheering was quite deafening. One could feel all the time that they were really genuine about it, & that they were pleased to see us . . . we were received the same wonderful way wherever we went even in the poorest parts, which shows how very loyal they all are to you . . . Elizabeth has been marvellous as usual & the people simply love her already. I am very lucky indeed to have her to help me as she knows exactly what to do & say to all the people we meet . . .[1]

In the winter of 1924, the Duke and Duchess undertook a far more extensive tour. For some time the Duke had very much wanted to visit parts of the Empire, and he was delighted when the King gave his consent for him to visit East Africa and the Sudan. Some official duties were to be carried out, but the trip was also to be a holiday, and was to include some of the big game hunting for which the Duke craved. So on

5 December 1924, the Duke and Duchess, accompanied by a small party, sailed from Marseilles in the P & O Liner *Mulbera*. Arriving at Port Said five days later, after a cold and stormy passage, they found British warships anchored there, among which the Duke was delighted to see his old ship the *Malaya*. Passing through the Suez Canal, *Mulbera* stopped off at Aden, and then sailed south, "crossing the Line", and anchoring at Mombasa on 22 December.

Once landed in the colony of Kenya, the Duke and Duchess were soon immersed in an atmosphere totally new to them. After being received by the Governor, Sir Robert Coryndon, at a garden party given at Government House, they went to see a native dance festival, a *ngoma*, held in a large open space and comprising some five thousand African men and women. The Duke wrote his own account of this extraordinary spectacle: "Representatives of all the different tribes had been collected & they danced their own particular dances, some of which were very weird. The music was also very odd, & it consisted of numerous tom toms & a special kind of horn which they blew through & the noise at times was quite deafening. It was most interesting to have seen."[2] Before leaving Mombasa, the Duke had a lengthy talk with the Governor, whom he described in a letter to his father as "a very nice man & very alive to his responsibilities out here". He went on, "I had a talk with him last night & he told me what a wonderful future this Colony has before it . . . There is a very good type of settler out here & most of them are gentlemen in the true sense of the word."

After spending Christmas at Government House, Nairobi, the Duke and Duchess of York then went on a six-week safari. Both the Duke and the Duchess proceeded to slaughter a large number of animals. The Duchess, perhaps surprisingly for one who had a reputation for both sensitivity and warmth, bagged rhinoceros, buffalo, waterbuck, oryx, Grant gazelle, dik-dik, Kenya hartebeeste, steinbuck, water-hog and jackal.

It was perhaps only appropriate that there should have been at least one act of retaliation. The British press were soon reporting that the Duke had been charged by a rhinoceros, and it was suggested that he was perhaps taking unnecessary risks. As it happened, the Duke had not been charged by a rhinoceros, and an account of the incident in the diaries he kept during his East African tour both explained what exactly happened, and also what it was like to pursue and kill animals:

We found one Oryx alone shortly afterwards & we got up to him within 200 yds by keeping a tree between us & him. I took a rest off the tree & fired & hit him. He was facing me. He went off & we followed & I hit him 3 more times when he lay down. I was going to finish him off when we saw a Rhino on the edge of a thick patch of bush. We forgot about the Oryx, & went after the Rhino. We followed him into the bush & suddenly came upon not one but 2 Rhinos, lying down in the thickest part of the bush 8 yds away. One got up towards us & Anderson fired & killed it. I did not fire as I could not see him properly. It was most exciting. The other one ran away. After this we went back & finished off the Oryx. It was very hot by now at 11.30 & we were glad of the mules to ride home on. Elizabeth came out with us in the afternoon after tea to look at the Rhino.

This is the Rhino the papers said had charged me.[3]

Kenya cast a magic spell over the Duke and Duchess of York. They fell in love with it, particularly cherishing their experiences on safari. The Duke developed a strong and perhaps simplistic sympathy with the colony's white establishment, writing to Queen Mary, "We are both so impressed with this wonderful country, & it has certainly come up to & passed our expectations. I am certain people at home have no idea what its possibilities are & what its future one day is going to be. Everything is so new & utterly different to other parts of the Empire, & being so young it should be made gradually by the best people we can produce from home. By this I don't mean the settlers, who are a very nice lot & for the most part real gentlemen, but the official side of the life of Kenya."

The Duke accepted the Governor's view that, "things are not quite as they should be owing to lack of first hand & personal knowledge of the officials at home . . . I feel it is an important thing for this vast country to be better understood." In fact, successive British governments were indeed struggling hard to understand Kenya; in particular they were much exercised as to whether to accede to the demands of the white settlers for full self-government. Would the interests of the overwhelming, black majority of the population be safeguarded if power was handed over to the whites? Although the nineteen-twenties Conservative governments tended to be more sympathetic to the demands of the white settlers than did Labour governments, in the end, the doctrines of trusteeship prevailed over those of settler self-interest.

[91]

The Duke's obvious enthusiasm for Kenya led to the remarkable offer of a farm there as a gift. Whether there was any political motivation behind the offer is not clear. What is clear is that King George V forbade his son to accept the gift, writing, "Of course it was kind of the Governor to have offered you the gift of a farm on behalf of the Colony. I at once consulted the Colonial Office & I entirely agreed with them that it would *not* be possible to accept it, (as I have telegraphed to you). It would create a precedent, which would mean that other members of the family might be offered farms in other Colonies when they visited them. What would you do if the farm didn't pay? The only way would be to buy a farm yrself (& you have no ready money) like David did in Canada & I thought that was a mistake."

The Duke and Duchess's visit to Kenya was cut short by the unexpected death of the Governor, Sir Robert Coryndon, after an emergency operation. The Duke, who was 250 miles up-country from Nairobi, at once hastened back to attend the funeral, after which the Duke and Duchess now left for Uganda, from where they set off to Nimule on the borders of the Sudan, which they reached on 5 March, 1925. The Duke noted, "The country is so different to Kenya, & much more tropical & much hotter. Uganda is not so attractive as Kenya in any way." Much of the royal couple's journey from Uganda to the borders of the Sudan was either on the great lakes Victoria and Albert, or along the White Nile, and the Duke managed to indulge his passion for hunting as he travelled:

> We landed at Katengeri & made our camp & in the afternoon I went out with Salmon, the game ranger, & in the evening I shot a very good elephant, whose tusks weighed 90 lb. each. It was very lucky as there are not very many big ones left. I got a smaller one 2 days later. Brooke got a 70-pounder & a 45-pounder & Buist also got an elephant the last day. So we did well in the home of the elephant. The next day, March 3rd, we reached Rhino Camp, & I went out & shot a White Rhino with a horn 33" long, which is quite good.[4]

After crossing the Sudan border, the royal party travelled down the White Nile until they reached Khartoum. There they were entertained by the new Governor-General, Sir Geoffrey Archer, and were taken on a tour of the battlefield of Omdurman where Kitchener's Anglo-Egyptian army had broken the Dervish forces sent against them in

1898. On 9 April the Duke and Duchess of York boarded the P & O liner *Maloja* at Port Sudan. Ten days later they were back in London, and in time to greet King George and Queen Mary on 25 April when they returned from their Mediterranean cruise, which had been undertaken to help the King convalesce after a serious attack of bronchitis.

No sooner was the Duke of York back from his Imperial adventure than he turned with enthusiasm towards another Imperial duty. He had succeeded his elder brother as President of the British Empire Exhibition. The great Empire Exhibition was meant to be both a tribute to the Imperial Idea and an inspiration to all the people of the Empire. In this respect, it was ironic that it was mounted at the time when the Empire was slowly and visibly disintegrating: Indian nationalists were pressing hard for a speedy grant of independence; the Southern Irish counties had but recently left the Union; and the British Dominions, particularly South Africa and Canada, wished to assert themselves as independent nations upon the international scene. Despite this, or perhaps because of it, the Empire Exhibition at Wembley was designed to whip up and to consolidate enthusiasm for the Empire. A few days after he had arrived back in London, the Duke of York published a message in *The Times* which was meant to focus public attention on the second opening of the Exhibition, to take place on 10 May 1925. The message read, "The British Empire Exhibition aims to complete in 1925 the educational work for Empire unity and Empire trade so well begun in 1924. The task of showing fresh aspects of our great heritage has been taken up with vigour and enthusiasm, and the new picture of the Empire will be even more vivid than the old. I ask for it the fullest measure of public support."

Despite these brave sentiments, the Duke approached the task of opening the Exhibition with dread. Although he had to make only a brief speech, his stammer was still a grievous handicap, and his anxieties were undoubtedly increased by the knowledge that he would have to make the speech in front of his father – the first time that this had happened – and that radio listeners would also be tuned in. He wrote frankly to his father, "I do hope I shall do it well. But I shall be frightened as you have never heard me speak & the loud-speakers are apt to put one off as well. So I hope you will understand that I am bound to be more nervous than I usually am."

When it came to making the speech, the Duke experienced quite considerable difficulty. He did, however, keep on resolutely, and to many of his listeners, painfully, until the end. His father summed it up in a letter written to his youngest son, Prince George, the following day, "Bertie got through his speech all right, but there were some rather long pauses." For how much longer he could continue to struggle through these public ordeals was, however, another matter. So far, none of the specialists that he had consulted had been able to offer him even a partial cure.

In November 1925, the Royal Family suffered a major bereavement with the death of Queen Alexandra, widow of Edward VII. All of King George and Queen Mary's children were saddened by the passing of a grandmother who had indulged and cherished them during their childhood.

This death in the family was shortly followed by a birth. On 21 April 1926, the Duchess of York gave birth to her first child, a daughter. The British public were not totally unprepared for this event, but the royal pregnancy had certainly been discreetly handled by the press. In fact, the only indication that anything special was about to happen lay in the large number of photographs which Britain's picture magazines suddenly started publishing early in 1926. Even so, there had been no hint in the accompanying captions as to why the young couple should suddenly be so topical. On 21 April, the reason became clear.

The baby was born at 17 Bruton Street, the home of the Duchess of York's parents. The birth was not a straightforward one. "The future Queen Elizabeth II had, in fact, come into the world feet first by Caesarian section."[5] King George and Queen Mary had been awoken at 4.00 am on the morning of 21 April to be told the news. Queen Mary wrote in her diary, "Such a relief and joy . . . at 2.30 we went to London to 17 Bruton Street to congratulate Bertie & . . . saw the baby, who is a little darling with a lovely complexion & pretty fair hair." Another early visitor described the baby as possessing fair hair, "large dark-lashed blue eyes" and "tiny ears set close to a well-shaped head".

The Duke of York expressed both his happiness and feeling of wonder in a letter he wrote on the day after the birth to Queen Mary:

You don't know what a tremendous joy it is to Elizabeth and me to have our little girl. We always wanted a child to make our happiness complete, & now that it has at last happened it seems so wonderful & strange. I am so proud of Elizabeth at this moment after all that she has gone through during the last few days, and I am so thankful that everything has happened as it should and so successfully. I do hope that you and Papa are as delighted as we are, to have a grand-daughter, or would you have sooner had another grandson? I know Elizabeth wanted a daughter. May I say I hope you won't spoil her when she gets a bit older.[6]

Although the British public reacted with appropriate pleasure to the announcement of the birth, there seemed no need to imbue the event with any great significance. There was no reason to suppose, in 1926, that the little girl would one day ascend to the throne. The Prince of Wales was still expected to marry in the near future, and to father children. Even if this did not occur, it was more than likely that in the course of their marriage the Duke and Duchess of York would produce a son. The King and Queen now had a second grandchild, their first having been born more than three years before in February 1923 to Lord Lascelles and Princess Mary.

The choosing of names within the Royal Family had always been a delicate business from the time of Victoria and Albert. After appropriate consideration, the new parents made their choice. The Duke of York wrote to his father:

Elizabeth and I have been thinking over names for our little girl and we should like to call her
Elizabeth Alexandra Mary
I hope you will approve of these names, & I am assured there will be no muddle over two Elizabeths in the family. We are so anxious for her first name to be Elizabeth as it is such a nice name & there has been no one of that name in your family for a long time.
Elizabeth of York sounds so nice too.[7]

The king approved of these names, commenting to his wife, "I have heard from Bertie about the names. He mentions Elizabeth, Alexandra, Mary. I quite approve, & will tell him so, he says nothing about Victoria. I hardly think that necessary." On 29 May, 1926, the baby was christened by the Archbishop of York in the private chapel at Buckingham Palace. Her godparents were the King and Queen, Princess Mary, the Duke of Connaught, Lady Elphinstone, and Lord Strathmore. 'Of course poor baby cried,' Queen Mary recorded in her diary that night.

By a cruel quirk of fate, the new parents had hardly adjusted to their transformed roles, when they were obliged to uproot themselves. In June 1926, Stanley Bruce, the Prime Minister of Australia, formally requested George V to send one of his elder sons to perform the opening ceremony of the new parliament building in Canberra. The day fixed for the opening was 9 May 1927. Although the Duke had earlier expressed his keen desire to be sent on an Empire-wide tour, neither he nor the Duchess welcomed the timing of their mission. The main problem was that the infant would have to be left at home in England. Such separations, though commonplace in the Royal Family and among the classes that governed the Empire, were painful to contemplate. Nonetheless, royal duty had to be done, and the Duke and Duchess set about preparing for the visit.

Quite apart from their reluctance to be separated from their new daughter, another shadow fell, dark and impenetrable, across their path. How could the Duke possibly cope with the heavy programme of speeches which would inevitably form part of the world tour? It was the question that the Australian Prime Minister, Stanley Bruce, had been anxiously contemplating ever since he had been informed that the Duke of York, and not the Prince of Wales, would undertake the visit. According to George VI's official biographer, "Mr Bruce, who had heard the Duke speak on several occasions during the period of the Imperial Conference of 1926, was appalled at the prospect of the King's representative being so gravely inhibited."

No one was more conscious of the problem than the Duke himself:

He was now thirty years old, and, notwithstanding the courage with which he had stubbornly faced his ordeals of public speaking, and in spite of the understanding, the encouragement, and the compassion which he received so unstintingly from the Duchess, the disillusion-ment caused by the failures of previous specialists to effect a cure had begun to breed within him the inconsolable despair of the chronic stammerer, and the secret dread that the hidden root of the affliction lay in the mind rather than in the body.[8]

Writing in December 1950, the journalist Hannen Swaffer recalled that on one occasion, in the early nineteen-twenties, the Duke of York had been, ". . . so nervous that, trying to address an open air gathering of Midland farmers from a cart, he could utter nothing but a painful, wordless mumble for several minutes. Meanwhile, his equerry, with the speech in his hand, wondered what on earth to do."[9] As recently as 31 October 1925, during the closing ceremony on the last day of the Empire Exhibition, the Duke of York had struggled through his speech. One authority described the scene as follows, "The eyes of 100,000 people were on the slim young man in top hat and frock coat. Amplifiers carried his words across the vast stadium. His voice was clear and distinct, but his phrases came awkwardly, with long, unnatural pauses. Sometimes there was an agonizing silence as he stumbled over some difficult word."[10]

But help was at hand: "One man in that huge crowd listened to the Duke's brave efforts with special sympathy and understanding. He turned to his son and said, 'He's too old for me to manage a complete cure. But I could very nearly do it. I'm sure of that.'"[11]

The man in the crowd was Lionel Logue. Logue had been born in South Australia in 1880. As a youth he had wanted to become a doctor, but had abandoned his training because the sight of blood distressed him. He then worked for a time for an electrical engineering firm in Australia. When he had built up some capital, he set up an elocution school in Perth, Western Australia, making his name during the First World War by affecting dramatic cures upon soldiers who had returned from the fighting with speech defects resulting from their grim war experiences.

In 1924, Logue came to London with his wife and three sons. Although he had originally merely intended to take a lengthy holiday in Britain, once in London he began to think of the possibilities of establishing a practice there. He had no medical qualifications, and very little capital, but he was confident, or rash, enough to rent a second-floor room at 146 Harley Street, which he redecorated in smoky grey and pale blue. Patients did not, at first, flock to his door, but gradually word spread, and in the late summer of 1926 he was put in touch with the Duke's Private Secretary, Patrick Hodgson.

The Duke of York's first response to the suggestion that he should consult Logue was unfavourable. None of his previous consultations had worked any miracles, and he saw no reason to trust in yet another speech therapist. The Duchess of York, however, who had already suffered much anguish while listening to her husband struggling to speak in public, persuaded him to make one more attempt to cure his disability. So on 19 October 1926, the Duke consulted Lionel Logue. "He entered my consulting room at three o'clock in the afternoon," Logue later recorded, "a slim, quiet man with tired eyes and all the outward symptoms of the man upon whom habitual speech defect has begun to set the sign. When he left at five o'clock, you could see that there was hope once more in his heart."

Lionel Logue's methods were neither extravagant nor particularly controversial. He had an exceptionally pleasant speaking voice himself, and a simplicity and sincerity of manner which soon put his patients at their ease. His self-evident belief in his own powers of healing not only caused his patients to believe in him, but gave them similar faith in their own capacity to cure themselves. Logue set out to convince his patients that stammerers were not freaks, but were, rather, perfectly ordinary people with a curable disability. He also inspired his patients, very early on, to believe that they *could* be cured. He was fond of saying to his patients, "There is only one person who can cure you, and that is yourself." Or, "I can tell you what to do, but only you can do it."

However, Logue's approach was not purely psychological, and many of his patients must have been reassured to know that he believed that their difficulties could be partly caused by incorrect breathing. He encouraged them to develop their lungs through regular physical exercises, and to control their diaphragmatical rhythm. He required his patients to undertake daily breathing exercises which he had devised, to gargle regularly with warm water, and to stand by an open window intoning the vowels in a fairly loud voice, each sound to last fifteen seconds.

The Duke of York's first consultation with Lionel Logue was a great success. Before agreeing to undertake the consultation, Logue had insisted that the Duke should call on him at 146 Harley Street rather than the other way round, and he further stipulated that they must meet on equal terms, because he regarded a free-and-easy personal relationship as an important part of his treatment. For the next two and a half months the Duke visited Logue's consulting room almost daily, and zealously followed the system of exercises that had been prescribed. It was typical of her close involvement in all that concerned her husband that the Duchess of York was also a frequent visitor to Logue's Harley Street consulting room, making herself familiar with the details of his treatment so that she could render him the greatest possible assistance.

Tracing his royal patient's case history, Logue discovered that, "one of his focal memories was of a day when, as an Osborne cadet, the boy Prince Albert . . . was 'struck dumb' by a question, peremptorily put to him by a tutor who was unaware of his speech impediment: 'What is the half of one-half?'" The boy could have answered as promptly as any other but for his fear of uttering the word "quarter". Logue found that a similar fear overcame him when he had to say "King" or "Queen". As often as was feasible, he used the formula "their Majesties".[12]

Within a month of first consulting Logue, the Duke of York was writing optimistically to his father:

> I have been seeing Logue every day & I have noticed a great improvement in my talking & also in making speeches which I did this week. I am sure I am going to get quite all right in time, but 24 years of talking in the wrong way cannot be cured in a month.
>
> I wish I could have found him before, but now that I know the right way to breathe my fear of talking will vanish.[13]

As the time approached for the Duke to leave for his Australian tour, Queen Mary became insistent that Logue should accompany the Duke, but the specialist firmly declined to do so. He argued, with some justification, that the major speech the Duke had to deliver at the opening of the new Australian parliament was a decisive moment in his life. "The Duke had to learn to stand on his own feet. If Logue went with him, the Duke would rely on him for the rest of his life. So Logue did not go."[14] He must also have known that he did not need to accompany the Duke of York on his tour. The progress which his patient had made within a few weeks of consulting him was clear to both parties. The Duke of York certainly considered that he was well on the way to being cured, now that he knew the right way to breathe.[15] This measure of fresh confidence gained by the Duke is evident in a letter he wrote to Logue on the eve of his departure for Australia, "I must send you a line to tell you how grateful I am to you for all that you have done in helping me with my speech defect. I really do think you have given me a real good start in the way of getting over it, & I am sure if I carry on your exercises and instructions that I shall not go back. I am full of confidence for this trip now."

The Duke kept in touch with Lionel Logue throughout the royal tour. On 25 January 1927, he wrote from aboard HMS *Renown*, "Your teaching, I must say, has given me a tremendous amount of confidence." Later on in the tour, at Sydney, he wrote, "I have ever so much more confidence in myself, and don't brood over a speech as in the old days. I know what to do now, the knowledge has helped me over and over again."[16] There was good cause for the Duke's self-confidence. In general, his speeches in Australia and New Zealand, and in particular one delivered at Canberra, were perfectly satisfactory, even on occasion highly successful. The stammer had not yet been entirely eliminated. No set speech was entirely free of it, and particularly when the Duke was over-tired it could still be a burdensome problem. There was, however, no comparison between the hesitant public speaker the Duke had been before his first consultation with Logue, and the far more assured performer who had emerged as a result of their joint efforts.

Quite apart from being better able to cope with public speaking, the Duke of York was freed from much of the anxiety which had so often beset him in private conversations. Since, whenever the Duke met other individuals, it was the convention that he must open the conversation, inhibitions over his speech defect had sometimes meant that the conversation had not begun at all. The Duke also found that he was able to converse with far more confidence with his father. Whereas before he had often been tongue-tied in King George's presence, he was now able to speak with greater fluency and to express himself more coherently and forcefully. In 1927, after his return from Australia, he wrote to Lionel Logue from Balmoral, saying, "Up here I have been talking a lot with the King, & I have had no trouble at all. Also, I can make him listen & I don't have to repeat everything over again." The King was perhaps equally relieved at his son's new assurance in conversation, writing to Queen Mary at the end of August 1927, "Delighted to have Bertie with me, he came yesterday evening, have had several talks with him & find him very sensible, very different to D[avid]."

Regular consultations between Logue and the Duke were still necessary and continued intensively. Logue did not stand on ceremony during these meetings. He gave the Duke tongue-twisters to practise on, and both men laughed over the patient's variable success with, "Let's go gathering healthy heather with the gay brigade of grand dragoons." Or with, "She sifted seven thick-stalked thistles through a strong, thick sieve." An affectionate friendship developed between the two, and Logue was able to write to his patient, both as Duke of York and King, using the second-person pronoun "you" with a freedom which would have offended any sticklers for royal etiquette. Despite the tremendous progress which the Duke of York had made after two years of treatment, he still spoke slowly and deliberately, sometimes hesitating before difficult words. To counteract these remaining problems, Logue advised his patient to stop pausing between individual words, and to pause instead between groups of words. Although further improvement followed, the Duke of York was still prone to hesitate before certain words, but, as a journalist observed in 1934, "His pauses used to be disturbing. Now they add solemnity to great occasions."

Lionel Logue's work with the Duke of York had not ended by the time the latter acceded to the throne in 1936. Indeed, the extra demands for public speaking that were bound to be made upon the new King were potentially disruptive to all the good work so far done. Logue was particularly exasperated by a reference made by the Archbishop of Canterbury, Dr Lang, when he said in a broadcast on 13 December 1936, two days after the Duke of York had become King George VI, "When his people listen to him, they will notice an occasional and momentary hesitation in his speech." Logue was dismayed lest these well-meant but essentially tactless remarks might undermine the King's confidence. He was, therefore, much relieved to witness the King unveiling the memorial to his late father at Windsor on 25 April 1937. It was an occasion on which he might well have faltered. As it happened, the new King spoke with considerable assurance, and Logue was satisfied to hear a fellow witness of the ceremony remark, "But I thought the King had a speech impediment – the Archbishop said so!"

The coronation was bound to be a particularly severe test, as the words of the service, the King's responses and his oath could not be amended to eliminate difficult passages or words. Logue was still working hard with the King, rehearsing the service, on the very eve of the coronation. They were both tired by their efforts. As Logue got up to leave, the King handed him a small package, and said, "Logue, wear this when you come to the Abbey tomorrow." When Logue opened the package, he found it contained the ribbon of the Royal Victorian Order.

Next day, from a special seat in the Abbey, Logue followed the progress of his patient with increasing satisfaction. When the King completed the complicated Accession Declaration, he flashed a look of relief and triumph at Logue. Later that day, when the King made his Coronation broadcast to the peoples of his Empire and the rest of the world, the only awkward hesitation that the huge audience could have noticed came right at the beginning of the speech, when the King arrived a few seconds late at the microphone.

During the Second World War, Lionel Logue frequently attended the King at Buckingham Palace and Windsor Castle before most of his speech-making engagements, and invariably before he was obliged to make a broadcast. The King, in fact, never mastered his dislike of the microphone, and on more than one occasion said that he hated it.

Logue left several accounts of the work they did together. For example, on 23 September 1940, the King made a broadcast announcing the creation of a new award, the George Cross. Logue's notes read as follows:

At 5.40 we went down to the dugout for another run-through, very good. As we were waiting the last few minutes, he suddenly began to laugh, and said, "I must write a book called *Places I Have Broadcast From*."

One minute to six, and he is in his armchair, just waiting – always the hardest part of the whole thing. Six o'clock, three red lights, and he steps up to the microphone, gives a little smile, and begins.

After the first paragraph, the All Clear can just be heard – a most dramatic moment. Despite the unpleasant conditions he spoke splendidly – in a dugout, with an air-raid warning on, after having been bombed the week before – a stout effort. He was very tired and pleased when he left for Windsor with the Queen at 6.30.[17]

Logue was again called to the Palace for the VE-Day broadcast on 5 May 1945. There were rehearsals of the speech both before and after dinner. Just before the broadcast was about to be made the Queen came into the room where the King sat with Lionel Logue:

She turns at the door, and says: "*in your growly voice*". I followed the Queen into the technical room, where Wood of the BBC and his men are altering lights and turning knobs.

The Queen in her white dress stands at one window, and I at another, and we both stand rigid for the first two sentences, but the King's voice is gathering strength and power and we glance at one another and smile, and so we stand until the end. I know the Queen was praying. I was too.

At the finish of the broadcast I shake the King by both hands, and say my heartiest congratulations, and then his wife quietly kisses him, and says: "Well done, Bertie!"[18]

The King's Christmas Day broadcasts also required Logue's attendance until the broadcast of 1945. After that speech had been rehearsed, the King suddenly said, "Logue, I think the time has come when I can do a broadcast by myself, and you can have a Christmas dinner with your family."

Logue later remarked to the Queen, "You know, Ma'am, I feel like a father who is sending his boy to his first public school." The Queen responded by putting her hand on Logue's arm and patting it, saying "I know just how you feel."

So, in 1945, Logue listened to the King's Christmas broadcast at home. He later declared that he was, ". . . astonished when the King's voice came through, how firm and resonant it was, and what a lovely tone, and I realized that we had builded better than we knew. All the three-word breaks had disappeared, and he was speaking confidently and with good inflection and emphasis. Only one stop, at the word God." As soon as his broadcast had finished, Logue telephoned Windsor Castle. He recalled, "When I said 'My job is over, Sir', he said, 'Not at all. It is the preliminary work that counts, and that is where you are indispensable.' He thanked me, and two days later wrote a very beautiful letter, which I hope will be treasured by my dependants."[19]

Logue continued to advise the King until the latter's death in February 1952. Even when the King underwent surgery for lung cancer in 1951, the breathing techniques which Logue had taught him caused Price Thomas, the surgeon in charge, to ask him if he had always breathed in that manner. The King replied to that question, "No, I was taught to breathe that way in 1926, and I've gone on doing so." Relating this incident to Logue in a letter, the King added, "Another feather in your cap, you see!" The King also believed that, "all the exercises I've done since the operation have come very easily to me, due to right breathing, I find."[20]

But for Logue, it is possible that the Duke of York would have made a far less impressive and competent monarch than turned out to be the case. Perhaps some would have tried to keep him from succeeding his brother. Apart from handsome fees for his services, Logue received only the Royal Victorian Order. In the circumstances, it seems strange that he was never knighted. Apparently, "To one of his closest friends,

Logue confided his hope of receiving a knighthood. That it was not fulfilled never became a grievance."²¹ At least Logue, and the King, knew the full extent of his triumph.

The Duke of York had various preparations to make before sailing from Portsmouth on 6 January 1927 in the battle-cruiser *Renown*, for Australia and his world tour. In particular, both the Duke and the Duchess were deeply saddened to be leaving their baby daughter behind. "I felt very much leaving on Thursday, and the baby was so sweet playing with the buttons on Bertie's uniform it quite broke me up," the Duchess of York later wrote to Queen Mary. As it happened, the King and Queen were fond and doting grandparents, and the King wrote, with a tenderness that had been untypical of his relationship with his own children, "I am glad to be able to give you the most excellent accounts of your sweet little daughter, who is growing daily. She has 4 teeth now, which is quite good at 11 months old, she is very happy & drives in a carriage every afternoon, which amuses her."²²

The itinerary of the royal tour had not been arrived at without some controversy, since when the Duke of York had accepted the invitation to visit Australia, the New Zealand government had also been prompt with an invitation. Which country was he to visit first? The Australian government was in no doubt that the opening of the Commonwealth Parliament in Canberra on 9 May was the main purpose of the Duke's voyage, and that therefore he should arrive in that country first. In the end, after much thought, it was decided that the royal party should go out by way of the Pacific, visit New Zealand first, and then conclude their tour with the opening ceremony at Canberra. The Australian government showed resentment at this decision, but it was adhered to all the same.

The Duke and Duchess sailed via Las Palmas and Jamaica, through the Panama Canal, and into the Pacific Ocean on 20 January 1927. Four days later they "crossed the Line", and both were initiated in traditional fashion. Press photographs show the Duke of York being lathered and shaved before being ducked, as part of the ceremonies aboard the *Renown*. For her part, the Duchess of York was invested with the Most Maritime Order of the Golden Mermaid.

On 22 February the *Renown* anchored at the port of Auckland, and within a few hours the royal tour of New Zealand had officially begun. It was an undoubted success. The Duke coped well with the demands of public speech-making, and wherever they went the young couple were received with demonstrations of the most tremendous enthusiasm and loyalty. New Zealand was, with Australia, the most loyal and patriotic of the British Dominions. The charm and vitality of the Duchess of York was an important ingredient in the success of the tour. Where the Duke tended to be shy, she, according to one observer, "shines and warms like sunlight." Although, on 12 March, the Duchess went down with an attack of tonsillitis, and the Duke at first anxiously thought of cutting short his programme, he managed to carry on without her. In fact, the warmth of the reception he received alone was a boost to his self-confidence. The crowds, it seemed, came to cheer him as much as they had come to greet his wife.

The Duke certainly needed all the self-esteem he could muster as his father observed his progress, through the Press, with an eagle eye. Having studied the photographs of the Duke's arrival at Las Palmas, the King wrote, "I send you a picture of you inspecting Gd. of Honour. (I don't think much of their dressing) with yr. Equerry walking on yr. right next to the Gd. & you ignoring the Officer entirely. Yr. Equerry should be outside & behind, it certainly doesn't look well." The Duke made a placating reply, saying, "I noticed the same thing about the photograph you sent me . . . It was an unfortunate moment for the photograph to be taken . . ."[23]

On 26 March 1927, in perfect weather, the *Renown*, with her escort of destroyers from the Royal Australian Navy, entered Sydney Harbour. If the New Zealand tour had been a success, the visit to Australia was a triumph on an even larger scale. In the words of one authority, "the Duke and Duchess of York passed from State to State of the Colony in a blaze of eager ecstasy, which evoked an equally eager response." The Duke of York wrote contentedly to his father, "The people here have got a most wonderful spirit of loyalty to you & the Empire. No one can understand it until they have been out here. It is such a wonderful thing, & we are so glad to be able to stimulate it by coming here for you."

The large crowds of spectators not only showed a keen interest in the Duke and Duchess, but also in their daughter. The Duke wrote to his mother, "It is extraordinary how her arrival is so popular out here. Wherever we go, cheers are given for her as well, & the children write to us about her." The royal couple's post-bag was full of letters containing expressions of goodwill and welcome. Some of these letters had been allegedly written by children, and contained opening phrases like, "I am four and a half months old, and I should like a photograph of Princess Betty." Another letter writer wanted to show her varicose veins to the Duke and Duchess.

On 25 April, the Duke took the salute at the ANZAC Day ceremonies at Melbourne. Twenty-five thousand ex-servicemen, among them twenty-nine holders of the Victoria Cross, marched past the saluting base. At a special veterans' service after the parade, the Duke, in an emotional speech, paid tribute to the sacrifices of Australian and New Zealand troops during the First World War, asserting, "That great feat of arms and the heroic deeds of all who shared in it will be remembered so long as the Empire lasts. They gave their all for the King and Empire, and their sacrifice will remain forever a shining example of what human will and endurance can accomplish."

On 9 May the Duke of York performed the opening ceremony at the new Houses of Parliament in Canberra. He had been apprehensive the night before, particularly at the prospect of making two speeches, one of which was to be delivered, at his own suggestion, on the steps which led to the Parliament buildings, and before a crowd of some twenty thousand onlookers. However, the Duke of York's speech on the steps, after he had unlocked the doors of the Parliament with a golden key, was judged to be "a tremendous success" and was broadcast by radio throughout Australia. The speech included the inevitable references to the ending of one epoch and the beginning of another, and closed with an appeal which seems rather mannered by today's standards:

> On Anzac Day, we commemorated those gallant men and women who laid down their lives in the War. Though they have passed into the Great Beyond, they are still speaking to those who choose to listen. And if Australia listens to the Voices of the Noble Army of the Dead, and if the Great Army of those Living, and those yet Unborn is determined to march in step with them towards the ideals for which they died, then the glorious destiny of this country will be assured for all time.[24]

Next, the Duke entered the Senate chamber, and read the King's message and commission to both Houses of Parliament. The Duke later recalled his experiences in a letter to his father:

> The members of both Houses were the only ones present at that ceremony. It was a very small room, & not a very easy one in which

to speak. I was not very nervous when I made the Speech, because the one I made outside went off without a hitch, & I did not hesitate once. I was so relieved, as making speeches still rather frightens me, though Logue's teaching has really done wonders for me, and I now know how to prevent & get over any difficulty. I have so much more confidence in myself now, which I am sure comes from being able to speak properly at last.[25]

On 23 May 1927, HMS *Renown* sailed from Fremantle for home. The Duke and Duchess must have been confident that they had left behind an extremely favourable impression. The Governor of South Australia, Sir Tom Bridges, summed it up when he wrote to George V, "His Royal Highness has touched people profoundly by his youth, his simplicity and natural bearing, while the Duchess has had a tremendous ovation, and leaves us with the responsibility of having a Continent in love with her. The visit has done untold good, and has certainly put back the clock of disunion and disloyalty twenty-five years as far as this State is concerned."

The *Renown*'s voyage home was not entirely smooth, for on 26 May, the vessel hit storms in the Indian Ocean and oil fuel overflowed below decks, causing a serious fire in one of the boiler-rooms. For a while there was a chance that the ship might be completely destroyed. The fire, however, was put out before the blazing fuel could reach the main oil tanks, and on 27 June the Duke and Duchess landed in Britain. The Duke's three brothers greeted them at Portsmouth, and at Victoria Station King George V and Queen Mary were waiting to welcome them. The King had issued typically precise instructions as to the uniforms to be worn by the Duke and his staff on the occasion, and had even issued the instructions, "We will not embrace at the station before so many people. When you kiss Mama, take yr. hat off."

His experiences in the Antipodes had inspired and stimulated the Duke, and on 15 July he spoke of his feelings before an audience assembled at Guildhall to formally welcome him home:

I return a thorough optimist. When one has travelled over the vast extent of the Empire; when one has witnessed what our fathers have accomplished; when one has seen how the grit and creative purpose of our kinsmen have triumphed over the most tremendous difficulties, it is impossible to despair of the future of the British race. The same qualities which carried us successfully through the war will, I am convinced, so long as we remain united as members of one family, enable us to surmount all difficulties that may beset us, however formidable or however perplexing. If we hold together we shall win through . . .[26]

Once back in Britain, the Duke continued to be associated both with his Boys' Camps and with the cause of industrial welfare. In the light of his recent triumphant tour of New Zealand and Australia, however, it was time for him to become acquainted with the inner workings of international and Imperial affairs. Members of his household and some of the King's advisers were certainly in favour of the idea, but King George proved resistant to such suggestions. Rather like his grandmother, half a century before, he did not wish his heir or his second son to be present at audiences granted to ministers, or to examine the contents of the despatch boxes from government departments. It was only after some pressure that the King reluctantly agreed to allow the Prince of Wales and the Duke of York to see a very limited selection of Foreign Office and Dominion Office telegrams.

The relationship between the Duke and his father was dramatically affected by the King's serious illness in the winter of 1928–29. At the end of November 1928, the King developed acute septicemia, with a dangerous centre of infection at the base of the right lung. His condition continued to deteriorate, and on 1 December 1928 the bulletin from Buckingham Palace referred to "a decline in the strength of the heart". The Prince of Wales was undertaking a tour of East Africa at the time, where he was warned that there "was cause for anxiety". He decided to return home, but was not expected to arrive before 11 December. So serious had matters become by 4 December that a meeting of the Privy Council was summoned to enable the King to assent to the transfer of power to the hands of six Councillors: these were the Queen, the Prince of Wales, the Duke of York, the Archbishop of Canterbury, Lord Hailsham (the Lord Chancellor), and the Prime Minister, Stanley Baldwin. The King was at least able to approve these arrangements.

The Duke of York wrote two letters to the Prince of Wales, who was then travelling home as fast as possible. In the second letter, the Duke wrote wryly, "There is a lovely story going about which emanated from the East End, that the reason of your rushing home is that in the event of anything happening to Papa I am going to bag the Throne in your absence!!!! Just like the Middle Ages . . ."

Once the Prince of Wales arrived in Britain, the Duke of York, having met him at Victoria Station, prepared him for what he would find at Buckingham Palace. As Duke of Windsor, the Prince recalled in his memoirs what his brother had told him:

> He prepared me for the shock that my father's appearance would bring. "You will find him greatly changed", he said, "and now Dawson says an operation will be necessary in a day or two." Then he spoke admiringly of my mother. "Through all the anxiety she has never once revealed her feelings to any of us." This seemed to trouble him, for he quickly added, "She is really far too reserved; she keeps too much locked up inside of her. I fear a breakdown if anything awful happens. She has been wonderful."[27]

Soon after the Prince of Wales returned, the King was operated on successfully and slowly began to recover strength. Early in February 1929, he was taken to Bognor Regis to convalesce, and returned to Windsor in May. On 7 July 1929, accompanied by his wife and children, the King drove in State to Westminster Abbey for a service of thanksgiving, which was broadcast throughout the world. Relieved as he was at his father's recovery, the Duke could find almost equal pleasure at the way in which he had coped with the crisis. Despite the considerable stress which had been felt throughout the Royal Family, he had remained calm and in control. He wrote, with evident self-satisfaction to Lionel Logue, "Through all this nervous strain my speech has *not* been affected one atom." There could be no clearer indication that the shy, hesitant, and rather unsure young man had become a valuable and mature member of the House of Windsor.

10

FAMILY MAN

1926–1936

It was obvious that they were devoted to each other and very much in love, and I remember thinking they looked just as a Duke and Duchess ought to look, but often don't.

The Duke was immensely proud of [Princess Elizabeth]. He had a way of looking at her that was touching. But Margaret brought delight into his life. She was a plaything. She was warm and demonstrative, made to be cuddled and played with.

Marion Crawford, The Little Princesses

IN THE DECADE BETWEEN the birth of their first daughter and King Edward VIII's abdication, the Duke and Duchess of York led a life that must have appeared idyllic to most observers. They had a guaranteed income, plenty of servants, free accommodation in a variety of houses in different parts of the United Kingdom, lengthy holidays in which to indulge their love of outdoor life and other interests, and, above all, an apparently secure future. The Depression of the early thirties hardly touched them – the Duke did not join the nation's three million unemployed, although he did make a sacrifice which he felt keenly – he gave up hunting and his stable of horses. Ramsay MacDonald's first National Government of 1931 had imposed ten per cent cuts in the wages of public servants, and it had seemed appropriate for leading members of the Royal Family to make economies as well. George V decided to give up the shooting at Windsor Park, the Prince of Wales contributed £50,000 to the National Exchequer, and the Duke of York sacrificed his hunting. Like all acts of genuine self-denial, it hurt. Writing to the Master of the Pytchley Hunt, the Duke said, "It has come as a great shock to me that with the economy cuts, I have had to make my hunting one of the things I must do without. And I must sell my horses too. This is the worst part of it all, and the parting with them will be terrible." Instructing his Equerry, Commander Colin Buist, to superintend the sale of his horses, he wrote sadly, "the horses are looking so well, too". In 1929 he took up the office of Lord High Commissioner to the General Assembly of the Church of Scotland. He held this office from the end of March 1929 until the end of May. The Duke's work as Lord High Commissioner was not arduous: he opened and closed the sessions of the General Assembly, and attended its daily meetings. The main work of this assembly was to bring about a union between the Church of Scotland and the United Free Church of Scotland. This was successfully accomplished, and the Union was formally inaugurated on 2 October 1929. The Duke had no effect on the Assembly's deliberations one way or the other, but at least his appearance in Edinburgh to take up a brief official residence in the Palace of Holyrood House, with a Scottish wife at his side, provoked a warm and patriotic reception in Scotland.

There followed, between 1930 and 1936, what his official biographer has described as "Six Quiet Years". In January 1930, the Duke travelled to Rome as King George's representative at the wedding of the Crown Prince of Italy and Princess Marie-José of Belgium, but he seems not to have enjoyed this visit. For one thing, his wife was unable to accompany him due to a severe attack of bronchitis, and for another, the wedding ceremony was marked by an organizational chaos quite unknown in Britain. The Duke, who set great store by ceremonial precision, could not have been pleased that amid the confusion the ex-King of Afghanistan was accorded precedence over all other royalty.

A year later, there was some discussion in government circles as to the advisability of the Duke of York being proposed as the new Governor-General of Canada. Lord Willingdon was about to retire, and the Conservative Prime Minister of Canada, R. B. Bennett, was not averse to the Duke's name being put forward. J. H. Thomas, Dominions Secretary in the minority Labour government, however, ". . . was not very keen about the Duke of York . . . he said that they did not want a Royal in Canada as it was too close to the USA and the Canadians prided themselves on being as democratic as the Americans."[1] Although George V was apparently sympathetic to the idea of his son being appointed Governor-General, nothing came of the idea, and Lord Bessborough eventually took up the post.

Although the Duke of York would undoubtedly have accepted the post in the line of duty, he was doubtless relieved for one major reason, to be able to stay in the United Kingdom. The birth of the Duke and Duchess's second daughter on 21 August 1930 had both brought great joy and increased his domestic responsibilities. Although it was not clear at the time, the arrival of the second baby completed the Duke and Duchess's family, and they were now immersed in a close and loving domestic circle.

The birth of the second daughter took place at Glamis, after a labour that was far more straightforward than that which had ended in a Caesarian section four years earlier. The only complication attending the birth was provided by the Home Secretary, J. R. Clynes. It was then traditional that Home Secretaries should attend royal confinements, a practice dating back to the time of James II's reign, when there had been fears of a plot to kidnap any male heir at birth. In keeping with this antiquated and eccentric tradition, J. R. Clynes had sped post-haste to Glamis on 5 August 1930. His arrival was premature, that of the baby was not, and one of the leading ministers of Ramsay MacDonald's government was detained until 21 August. This fiasco was not repeated, and when Prince Charles was born in November 1948, the Home Secretary of the day was merely informed of the fact by telephone.

The new daughter was soon visited by her royal grandparents, who had travelled from Sandringham to Balmoral the day after the birth. When they arrived at Glamis on 30 August, Queen Mary found, "E. looking very well, and the baby a darling."

Negotiations over the new child's name soon began in earnest. The Duchess of York wrote to Queen Mary, "I am very anxious to call her Ann Margaret, as I think that Ann of York sounds pretty, & Elizabeth and Ann go so well together. I wonder what you think? Lots of people have suggested Margaret, but it has no family links really on either side."[2] The King, however, did not like the name Ann – perhaps faint echoes from the unhappy history of the House of Stuart influenced his attitude. At any rate, his view prevailed, and the Duchess of York wrote to Queen Mary, "Bertie & I have decided now to call our little daughter 'Margaret Rose' instead of M. Ann, as Papa does not like Ann – I hope that you like it. I think that it is very pretty together."

In a little over a year, the Duke and Duchess were given a new house: in September 1931 the King offered them Royal Lodge, in Windsor Great Park, as their country home. Owned and altered at various times by George III's son the Duke of Cumberland (the "Butcher of Culloden"), the Prince Regent, and various members of the Royal Family, their friends and retainers, Royal Lodge was not an ideal home, neither was it ready to be occupied. "Inconvenience and dilapidation were the keynotes of the house when the Duke and Duchess first visited it in September 1931, and it is a tribute both to their perspicacity and courage that they saw the possibilities of the place, and, having done so, were not daunted by the difficulties of realizing them."[3] The Duke wrote, perhaps optimistically, to his father, "It is too kind of you to have offered us Royal Lodge, & now having seen it, I think it will suit us admirably." As the economic crisis eased, slowly the Duke and Duchess were able to turn Royal Lodge into the home that they wanted:

> Restoring the grand saloon to its pristine magnificence, they added brand-new wings to each flank, had the whole exterior wing washed in a shade of warm rose, and designed two fine bedrooms for themselves on the ground floor. The Duchess's room was carpeted in her favourite colour, grey-blue, the large double bed having blue silk covers with lemon pleatings and her furniture white apple wood, boasting lights fitted inside, which switched on automatically when the doors were opened: the Duke's more austere room had the character of a sailor's cabin – hard-looking bed, a simple dressing-table and just one bookcase, with only a few personal knick-knacks laid out as if awaiting the arrival of the inspecting officer. . . .[4]

> They concentrated all their efforts on making this their real home – to which they could retire and relax from the eternal programme of official and semi-official engagements, the home that they could make for themselves, of which the keynote was to be gaiety and love and laughter; above all, a home where their children might grow up with the boon and the blessing of a family life replete with affection and understanding, such as the Duchess had enjoyed and the Duke had never known . . .
>
> No two people – not even Queen Victoria and Prince Albert – could have been happier in their home-making than were the Duke and Duchess of York.[5]

Until the birth of Princess Margaret Rose, the Duke and Duchess's parental energies had been entirely devoted to their firstborn, Elizabeth. The Duchess had breast-fed her until she was just over a month old; after that her feeding was shared with Mrs Knight, who was Elizabeth's nanny during the first months of her life at 17 Bruton Street.

> She was an old-fashioned nanny, a family retainer in the traditional style, whose whole life was her work, welcoming the role of surrogate mother put on her by her employers, delighting in the challenge of coping with everything, and scarcely ever taking a

[113]

holiday or even a day off. With the help of a nurserymaid she fed, dressed and exercised the new baby Princess and, twice a day, presented her in a clean dress to her adoring parents. When the little girl woke up crying in the night, it was the nursery staff who went to comfort her. Mrs Knight's Christian name was Clara, but this defeated most of her charges, who could only manage "Alla" – and this remained the name by which Princess Elizabeth knew her.[6]

Earlier, in August 1926, the Duke and Duchess of York had been to Scotland to stay with the Bowes-Lyons at Glamis. Here, it is recorded, the baby slept very contentedly: "Her nursery was in the modern wing of the castle, built in the nineteenth century overlooking Lady Strathmore's Dutch garden, and in the afternoon her pram would be wheeled out for her to sleep amid the clipped yews to the sound of water splashing round a little stone Cupid in a blue-tiled pool. Her grandmother and her nurse saw most of her."[7] Elizabeth was to spend all of the summers of her childhood at Glamis. "It was to shape her as significantly as the more obvious influence of her royal grandfather. If her father's family moulded her formal public identity, her mother's gave her the warmth with which she has brought up her own children, and the gaiety she has kept for her private life."[8]

When her parents had departed for the royal tour of New Zealand and Australia on 6 January 1927, it was arranged that the care of the infant should be shared between both sets of grandparents. She went first to the Bowes-Lyons' home in the Hertfordshire countryside – St Paul's Walden Bury: "a warm old red-brick house in the style of Queen Anne, overgrown with magnolia and honeysuckle, its garden alive with chickens, ponies, kittens, tortoises and dogs. The Strathmores had two chows, fat furry beasts, one chocolate-brown and one sooty, and the baby was soon burying her fists in their fur with great pleasure."[9] In February 1927 she was taken back to London to be with her royal grandparents. George V wrote fondly in his diary, "our sweet little grandchild, Elizabeth, arrived here yesterday, & came to see us after tea." A warm and affectionate bonding was to result from this intimate contact between the baby and her grandparents, and Queen Mary, though painfully shy and reserved herself, set out to play an active grandmotherly role in her upbringing. One of her chief influences was to be in Elizabeth's education, for Queen Mary believed firmly in the value of reading history books and studying genealogical trees, in visits to museums and art galleries, and in lecturing members of her family on the heritage of the artistic treasures that they possessed. Her artistic tastes were certainly not avant-garde, and her preferred paintings were usually those of her own relatives, but she nonetheless had firm views as to what was desirable in furniture, decorations, miniatures, and works of art generally. Queen Mary played an important part in forming her grand-daughter's character. According to Queen Elizabeth II's biographer:

> She has been afflicted by a similar blend of shyness and severity and has cultivated the same devastating reaction as Queen Mary to observations by which she is not amused – totally ignoring the remark while looking its perpetrator full in the face. Many of her deepest instincts reflect her kinship and also a closeness to her grandmother that extended throughout her youth, for when Queen Mary died at the age of eighty-five in March 1953, Elizabeth II had already been on the throne for more than a year.[10]

For one who had been so severe with his own children, King George V doted on his first grand-daughter. The adoration was reciprocated, and Elizabeth gave an indication of her feelings when she heard carol singers on Christmas Eve 1928, sing "Glad tidings of great joy I bring to you and all mankind", climbing on to her grandfather's knee and saying, "I know who is that old man, kind. He is you, Grandpapa, and I does love you!"[11]

Such displays of affection must have touched the King deeply during the serious illness he suffered from the end of November 1928 until the New Year. When the crisis passed and he was sent to convalesce in the sea air at Bognor, a sandpit was dug for his favourite grand-child in the corner of the garden of the mansion which the King had taken there. Elizabeth arrived at Bognor in March 1929 with her nurse to visit her grandparents. "G delighted to see her," Queen Mary recorded in her diary. "I played . . . in the garden making sandpies!" When King George later made his first public appearance after the illness, on the seafront at Bognor, he did so with the three-year-old girl at his side, waving to the crowd.

When he returned to London, George V insisted that he needed regular contact with his grand-daughter in order to complete his convalescence. Intimate little rituals developed between them:

> The young princess took to drawing back the curtains in the front windows of 145 Piccadilly. She would wave across the park in front

of the house soon after her breakfast every morning, and her grandfather would look out of Buckingham Palace at the same time and wave back. He called her "Lilibet", for as she learned to talk, and attempted her own name, she could only lisp "Lillibeth". The name stuck. She was Lilibet to her family from then onwards.[12]

George V continued to follow Elizabeth's progress with affectionate interest. When, for Christmas 1929, she was given a pony of her own, he was delighted to observe that soon she could ride well. The King set great store by the virtue of riding proficiently, telling the Prince of Wales, "English people like riding, and it would make you very unpopular if you couldn't do so. If you can't ride, you know, I'm afraid people would call you a duffer."[13] When Elizabeth's fourth birthday in April 1930 coincided with Easter Monday, it was spent at Windsor, Queen Mary giving her a birthday present of a set of building blocks made from fifty different woods from various parts of the Empire – an example of the Queen's consistent desire to combine learning and pleasure. For his part, the King was as devoted to her as ever, ". . . letting her sweep the food off his plate to feed a pet, or going down on his hands and knees to search for her hair-slide under the sofa."[14]

The little girl had a great many toys apart from building blocks. Too many, in fact, for every post seemed to bring a gift from some part of the world. It was estimated, for example, that during her parents' tour of Australia and New Zealand they had been presented with something like three tons of toys for her. Such adulation made nonsense of her mother's desire to bring her up like any other little girl born into a good family. On the other hand, she did not live amid great luxury at 145 Piccadilly:

> Her nursery . . . was up at the top of the house, stocked with dark, polished grown-up furniture, complete with a clock and a glass-fronted display case for delicate toys. The night nursery in which she slept was unplumbed, with a large jug and basin holding water to wash her hands. On the landing outside, the Princess took to collecting toy horses, which she could ride around the house on wheels. Every evening she would change their saddles and harness before she went to bed.[15]

Whether Princess Elizabeth was jealous of the arrival of her baby sister, is not recorded, although it would be unusual if she had not experienced some sense of displacement. What is known is her reaction to her new sister's name. She told Lady Cynthia Asquith, "I've got a baby sister, Margaret Rose, and I'm going to call her Bud." "Why Bud?" Lady Cynthia asked. The four-and-a-half-year-old replied, "well, she's not a real Rose, yet, is she? She's only a bud."[16]

One consequence of Margaret's birth was that her elder sister began to spend more time in the company of Margaret MacDonald, who had worked as under-nurse to Mrs Knight. Since Mrs Knight was inevitably closely involved with the new baby, Elizabeth began to develop with Miss MacDonald a relationship which "over the years, became one of the closest friendships of her life". In 1977, the year of the Queen's Silver Jubilee, Robert Lacey was to write, "Miss MacDonald is today, after nearly half a century of personal service, dresser to the Queen, with a suite of her own in Buckingham Palace. She helps to choose the Queen's clothes and travels with her everywhere. Elizabeth II acknowledges her as one of her most trusted confidantes. She calls her Bobo."[17]

In the spring of 1932 Miss Marion Crawford arrived at Royal Lodge to begin a month's trial as governess. Miss Crawford, soon nicknamed "Crawfie", stayed in her post for seventeen years. After she left the royal service in the late nineteen-forties she started writing books and articles which are an invaluable source to those interested in the private lives of the Royal Family. It should be said that Miss Crawford's literary activities were neither authorized nor approved of by the House of Windsor. She has, however, left some vivid descriptions of the Duke and Duchess of York's home life. She recorded her first impressions of the royal couple:

I was quite enchanted, as people always were, by the little Duchess. She was petite, as her daughter Margaret is today. She had the nicest, easiest, most friendly of manners, and a merry laugh. It was impossible to feel shy in her presence.

The Duke was extraordinarily handsome, but I recall thinking he did not look very strong. He was slight, and looked like a boy of eighteen, though he was considerably older than I. He had a diffident manner and a slight impediment in his speech, that was not so much a stutter in the ordinary sense as a slight nervous constriction of the throat, I thought.[18]

There had been opposition in some quarters to Miss Crawford's youth, but the Duke and Duchess, ". . . were anxious that the little girls should have someone with them young enough to enjoy playing games and running about with them. The Duke, I gathered, had throughout his own childhood been hampered by somewhat immobile pastors and masters. He wanted someone energetic with his children, and had been impressed with the amount of walking I did!"[19] It is certainly true that the Duke of York had admired Miss Crawford's energetic walking, first hearing of her when she was walking several dozen miles a week through the hills around Dunfermline between her various pupils scattered in the houses of Scottish aristocracy there. Among the homes she visited was that of Lady Rose Leveson-Gower, an elder sister of the Duchess of York.

Marion Crawford was much more than energetic – she was also spirited, carefree, intelligent, interested in child psychology and a fine teacher. When she was first offered the post of governess she took two weeks to decide whether to give the job even a trial, realizing that she would not "be able to go on with what I intended to be my life's work – child psychology". The month's trial period that followed her decision to join the Duke and Duchess's household, therefore, was not simply a case of the employers trying out the governess; the governess was also scrutinizing her employers. However, the relaxed attitude of the Duke, and particularly the Duchess, towards the upbringing of their children must have encouraged Miss Crawford to stay. She later wrote:

> No one ever had employers who interfered so little. I had the feeling that the Duke and Duchess, most happy in their own married life, were not over-concerned with the higher education of their daughters. They wanted most for them a really happy childhood, with lots of pleasant memories stored up against the days that might come out and, later, happy marriages.[20]

There was little stuffiness and formality in the York household. The Duchess had broken away, as her mother had done before her, from the conventions of child-rearing that characterized her class. "Princess Elizabeth and later Princess Margaret knew no barrier between the nursery and the rest of the house . . . as they grew up, their ease and freedom in adult society was a constant source of wonder to their father."[21] Since both the Duke and Duchess did a large amount of their work from home, the girls saw a good deal of them. In the morning they would go down to their parents' room from the nursery. They took lunch with their parents if both or either were at home, and at tea-time they would be joined sometimes by guests of their own age, like their cousins, the two Harewood boys, and sometimes by the Prince of Wales, Uncle David, who enjoyed joining in the games his nieces played after tea – Snap, Happy Families or Rummy. When the two sisters had been undressed and were in their baths, their parents, ". . . would go upstairs and join in the fun, and then the party would move onto the bedroom, with pillow fights, squeaks and giggles – Alla rather desperately pleading for the children not to be made too excited."[22] "Arm in arm, the young parents would go downstairs heated and dishevelled and frequently rather damp . . . The children called to them as they went until the final door closed, 'Goodnight, Mummie, goodnight, Papa!' "[23]

There was serious schooling as well. Shortly after she joined the family, Marion Crawford discovered that Elizabeth could already read, having been taught to do so by her mother. Miss Crawford built on this promising beginning by taking out a subscription for the *Children's Newspaper*, which offered its young readers samples of adult literature, especially adapted for their tastes. When Elizabeth reached the age of six, she was given a properly drawn-up school curriculum, consisting of a timetable running over a six-day week, in which the mornings were filled with half-hour lessons, and the afternoons given over to a traditional training in the arts of singing, drawing, music and dancing. It is interesting that Queen Mary, when given a draft of the curriculum to peruse, considered that insufficient time had been allotted to history, geography and Bible-reading. Although such subjects reflected her own interests, there was something in the argument that, as leading members of the Royal Family, the little girls would benefit from a greater knowledge of the world and its history.

It soon became apparent that the two children had strikingly different personalities. Elizabeth tended to be more solemn and shy, gravely aware of the need to maintain her poise in public; she needed "drawing out". When, after her father's accession to the throne in 1936, it slowly dawned upon Princess Elizabeth that she was the heir, and what the nature of her future role would be, this accentuated characteristics that had already been bestowed upon her by heredity and environment, and Marion Crawford noted that:

Lilibet was far more strictly disciplined than Margaret ever was. Margaret was having quite a lot of social life from the age of ten onwards. But the King set a very high standard for Lilibet, perhaps because she is heir to the throne. Margaret was a great joy and a diversion, but Lilibet had a kind of natural grace all her own. The King had great pride in her, and she in turn had an inborn desire to do what was expected of her.[24]

Lady Airlie also observed, at first hand, the differences between the two sisters:

In that family setting [Elizabeth] seemed to me one of the most unselfish girls I had ever met, always the first to give way in the small issues that arrive in every home. I thought that no two sisters could have been less alike than the Princesses, the elder with her quiet simplicity, the younger with her puckish expression and irrepressible high spirits – often liberated in mimicry.[25]

According to Marion Crawford, the Duke was immensely proud of Elizabeth:

He had a way of looking at her that was touching. But Margaret brought delight into his life. She was a plaything. She was warm and demonstrative, made to be cuddled and played with. At one time he would be almost embarrassed, yet at the same time most touched and pleased, when she wound her arms around his neck, nestled against him and cuddled and caressed him. He was not a demonstrative man.[26]

There is no doubt that the Duke of York was a devoted father to both his daughters, but at the same time, the tensions beneath the surface of his personality sometimes showed themselves. Marion Crawford quotes an interesting example of his irritability. Elizabeth apparently greatly admired Owen, the groom, and looked upon him as something of an oracle. On one occasion, when she asked her father a question, he replied a trifle testily, "Don't ask me, ask Owen. Who am I to make suggestions?"[27]

As his two daughters grew up, their wellbeing remained central to their father's happiness. Perhaps his devotion was a little claustrophobic, but neither of his daughters seems to have complained. Lady Airlie noticed that the personality differences that had marked their childhood were still there in 1946: "The King . . . spoiled Princess

Margaret and still continued to treat her as an *enfant terrible*, though Princess Elizabeth was his constant companion in shooting, walking, riding – in fact in everything. His affection for her was touching."[28] In a way, the contrasting qualities of his two daughters could not fail to increase their appeal. Princess Elizabeth's serious high-mindedness coincided with his own sober approach to public duties and responsibilities. Princess Margaret, on the other hand, with her early gifts for music and mimicry, was a tonic to the repressed side of her father's personality – he encouraged her mimicry and her sense of fun, and even licensed a childish naughtiness. Courtiers were heard to murmur, "What a good job Margaret is the *younger* one!"

Apart from his family, the Duke of York's chief interests in these years centred on field sports, riding, stamp collecting and gardening. He was a crack shot, and bagged enormous numbers of animals and birds during his lifetime. His interest in stamp collecting, a hobby he shared with his father, appealed to his almost obsessional preference for symmetry, order and minute detail, and gardening, especially after the family moved to Royal Lodge, became one of his greatest passions. He had, apparently:

> . . . a genius for landscape gardening, which soon gained him an acknowledged position as an authority in this field, for he combined considerable horticultural lore with a gift for design and display, and the priceless possession of a "green finger". He was no fair-weather gardener, who merely liked to stroll among his lawns and flower-beds on a pleasant day . . . he created at Royal Lodge one of the most beautiful smaller gardens in the country, distinguished alike for its display of colour and its perfection of arrangement.[29]

In his book *The Royal Gardeners*, W. E. Shewell-Cooper confirms that the Duke was "the expert on gardening with vistas and views . . . his best subjects were undoubtedly rhododendrons and azaleas". Apart from this, both before and after he ascended the throne, the Duke seems to have had few firm views: "As far as plants were concerned, he had no real dislikes, except perhaps in the greenhouse, where he had little or no use for the Coleus, and especially the type with maroon-coloured leaves. These he did not consider attractive or beautiful . . ."[30] Nor could he say which royal garden he preferred. Whereas his wife was an expert on the colour and scent of blooms, and excelled at creating the typical British flower border, her husband, ". . . was extremely interested in meteorological records – weather, in fact, was quite one of his absorbing interests. . . . Woe betide any head gardener who was not able to provide the necessary data at the determined time and day!"[31] At Royal Lodge he had the latest clock-like machine for recording temperature fixed outside his bedroom window, and would note its reading as soon as he got up in the morning. Perhaps the physical activity of gardening also helped to rid the Duke of some of the inner tensions that he felt: certainly, later on, Prince Philip recalled coming across his future father-in-law in the middle of a rhododendron bush, hacking away and swearing.

By 1936 the Duke had every reason to be contented with his life. He was the head of a happy home, he had carved out a clear and sympathetic public identity, and he had gone a long way towards conquering his speech impediment. But the death of King George V on 20 January 1936, at five minutes before midnight, set in train a sequence of events which, within a year, were to completely transform the Duke's status and prospects.

I I

THE ABDICATION:

THE MONARCHY IN CRISIS

1936

After I am dead, the boy will ruin himself in twelve months.

George V

The whole affair has lasted since 16 November, and is very painful. It is a terrible blow to us all, and particularly to poor Bertie.

Queen Mary, December 1936

ALTHOUGH HE WAS ILL, KING GEORGE V had managed to deliver his Christmas Day radio broadcast to his people in 1935. He did not, however, feel fit enough to indulge his passion for shooting on the Sandringham Estate. During the first days of the New Year, he went for a few rides upon Jock, his white pony, but on 17 January 1936 he wrote in his diary for the last time, "A little snow & wind. Dawson arrived. I saw him and feel rotten." The Prince of Wales, who was shooting at Windsor, was summoned to Sandringham by Queen Mary. He arrived by aeroplane – a symbolic contrast between the life-style of the old, failing monarch and the heir to the throne.

On 19 January, the Prince of Wales motored to London to inform the Prime Minister, Stanley Baldwin, that the King was dying. During these last few days of his life, King George sat in front of a bright fire in his bedroom at Sandringham, wearing a Tibetan dressing-gown brought back from one of his visits to his beloved India. The BBC issued a series of medical bulletins to the nation. Eventually, the people heard, "The King's life is moving peacefully to its close."

King George died tranquilly, on 20 January, in the presence of his wife and children, and after struggling, with his customary sense of duty, to sign the proclamation setting up a Council of State. Queen Mary wrote in her diary, "Am *heartbroken* . . . at 5 to 12 my darling husband passed peacefully away – my children were angelic . . ."

On 23 January the coffin of the dead King was taken to Wolferton Station for the journey to London; its procession wound for two and a half miles along the muddy Norfolk roads. The new King, Edward

VIII, walked bare-headed with his brothers, then came Jock the white pony, led by his groom, and finally Queen Mary, her daughter and her daughters-in-law in closed carriages. The King's body was taken to lie in state at Westminster Hall for four days, while 809,182 mourners filed past. On 28 January, King George was taken from London to the Chapel of the Knights of the Garter at Windsor Castle to be buried.

While millions throughout Britain and the Empire mourned the passing of George V, there were those who hoped that the new King would breathe fresh life into the institution of monarchy. King George had privately disapproved of many of the developments of the modern world; his successor seemed to exemplify them. As Prince of Wales, Edward VIII had managed to endear himself to his people through his dash, his lack of formal airs, and his apparent willingness to grapple with some of the more pressing problems of his times. "Prince Charming he had been justly termed; to the men and women of his generation he typified all that was best in the twentieth century, and they looked forward to the promise of a modern monarch, cognizant of the problems of his people, and closely identified with their interests and aspirations."[1]

That the new King believed himself to be an effective and necessary agent for change is indicated by his own words:

> I was, after all, the first King of the twentieth century who had not spent at least half his life under the strict authority of Queen Victoria. My father was already half-way through his life span when his grandmother died; and by the gravity of his temperament it was to her, rather than to the livelier example of his own father, that he looked for a model of the Sovereign's deportment. His Court retained a Victorian flavour to the end; and I had come to look upon it as at least sexagenarian in composition and outlook.[2]

There is no doubt that Edward VIII had wanted to accede to the throne and was determined to be a successful monarch. In 1957, looking back upon the momentous year of his accession, he vehemently denied that he did not want to be King: "This is a lie. I say it now and for all time: all my life I was trained for the job, and for 24 years as Prince of Wales I served my country and the Commonwealth devotedly. For a year as King I worked as hard and selflessly as I knew how. Of course I wished to be King. More, I wished to *remain* King."[3] His wife was to confirm this, writing, "He was excited and challenged by what he took to be his mission to modernize the monarchy within its traditional glory and strength."[4]

King Edward's deportment in the immediate aftermath of his accession to the throne, however, caused disquiet in some circles. Although it was natural that King George's children should grieve for him, his eldest son's reaction to the death, seemed, in the eyes of Lady Hardinge, whose husband was soon to become the King's Private Secretary, to be "frantic and unreasonable", and she thought it odd that his display of suffering "far exceeded that of his mother and three brothers".[5]

A bizarre and somewhat distasteful incident that had occurred while the old King lay dying at Sandringham also illustrates the tremendous pressures that were affecting his heir's behaviour. At Sandringham the clocks had always been kept half an hour fast, since the time of Edward VII, who had deemed it necessary to make the arrangement in order to ensure that his guests assembled punctually for shooting expeditions. George V, who valued punctuality and tradition even more than had his father, had maintained the practice. During the long hours while his family waited for the King's death, some small mistake had occurred due to the discrepancy between Sandringham time and real time, and the Prince of Wales had exclaimed angrily "I'll fix those bloody clocks." The Sandringham clockmaker was immediately summoned, and was obliged to toil through the night of George V's death until the early hours of the morning, resetting the household clocks to Greenwich Mean Time.

A conventional explanation of the new King's excessive grief, and his apparently callous altering of the Sandringham clocks, would be that he was deeply disturbed and momentarily thrown off balance by his father's death. However, there are other ways of looking at it. For one thing, the Prince of Wales had not resolved his fundamentally unhappy relationship with his father before he died. Their lifestyles and views of the world had differed almost as markedly as those of the Hanoverian monarchs of the eighteenth century and their heirs. Shortly before he died, according to Lady Airlie, George V had said, "I pray to God that my eldest son will never marry and have children, and that nothing will come between Bertie and Lilibet and the Throne." He had also once said to Lady Airlie, "Bertie has more guts than the rest of his brothers put together."[6] The Prince of Wales knew of his father's disapproval, yet at the same time he loved – and more than a little feared – the old King. Death removed any final opportunity of a reconciliation between the two. Edward VIII's almost hysterical grief, therefore, probably owed a good deal to feelings of guilt that his father had gone to his grave still disapproving of him, and that nothing could now be done to remedy matters.

But there was another explanation for Edward VIII's rather unbalanced behaviour. Since 1934, he had been obsessively in love with the American wife of a naturalized Englishman, Ernest Simpson. Mrs Wallis Warfield Simpson had first met the Prince of Wales in 1930. She had been born in Baltimore in 1896, and had divorced her first husband, a Lieutenant in the United States navy, in 1927. She had been presented to King George and Queen Mary at Buckingham Palace during 1934, amid rumours that she was involved in a secret relationship with the Prince of Wales. King George V had not been reassured by this meeting, and there is no doubt that his last months were darkened by anxieties over his son's relationship with this brassy American divorcee.

The Prince of Wales had had various sexual relationships hitherto. Among the most recent of these were his love affairs with Thelma, Lady Furness, and with Mrs Dudley Ward, who had fallen from favour when he became obsessed with Mrs Simpson. The Prince's love affairs followed an irregular but predictable course: he was attracted to, and found satisfaction with, reasonably mature and experienced married women. Having been brought up in a repressed and inhibited household, displaying a whole range of nervous tics and mannerisms, it was unlikely that the Prince of Wales would have turned out to be a confident and accomplished lover, but whatever inadequacies he felt on this score were reduced by the ministrations of experienced women.

None of his mistresses, apparently, had ever satisfied him as fully as Mrs Simpson. Society gossips speculated that her hold over the Prince was primarily sexual in nature, and that she was able to use techniques which led him to experience physical love to the full for the first time. The Prince of Wales' youngest brother, Prince George, Duke of Kent, whose playboy image mirrored that of the heir to the throne "ascribed her enchantment to something approaching sorcery", and he passed his interpretations on to the rest of the family. Certainly, the romance did not give the impression of Prince Charming sweeping Cinderella off her feet. There is, in any case, some doubt as to whether the Prince of Wales deserved such a title. Frances Donaldson, in her research for her authoritative biography of Edward VIII, asked one of her women friends about the alleged magnetic charm of the Prince of Wales. Her friend replied, "I didn't think of him like that. I thought him rather pathetic." It seems, therefore, that if either of the two lovers was the more charming, it was Mrs Simpson.

From the time of his accession, Edward VIII tried to ingratiate Mrs Simpson with his family and with society at large. In the spring, for example, he drove her over to Royal Lodge to show a new American station wagon to his brother and sister-in-law. Later, as Duchess of Windsor, Mrs Simpson left a record of this meeting:

> The Duke and Duchess of York met David at the door. David insisted they inspect the station-wagon. It was amusing to observe the contrast between the two brothers – David all enthusiasm and volubility as he explained the finer points of the machine, the Duke of York quiet, shy, obviously dubious of this newfangled American contrivance. It was not until David pointed out its advantages as a shooting brake that his younger brother showed any real interest.

> After a few minutes they returned, and we all walked through the garden. I had seen the Duchess of York before on several occasions at the Fort [Belvedere] and at York House. Her justly famous charm was highly evident. I was also aware of the beauty of her complexion and the almost startling blueness of her eyes. Our conversation, I remember, was largely a discussion of the merits of the garden at the Fort and at Royal Lodge. We returned to the house for tea, which was served in the drawing-room. In a few moments the two little Princesses joined us. Princess Elizabeth, now Queen, was then 10, and Princess Margaret Rose was nearly 6. They were both so blonde, so beautifully mannered, so brightly scrubbed, that they might have stepped straight from the pages of a picture book. Along with the tea things on a large table was a big jug of orange juice for the little girls. David and his sister-in-law carried on a conversation with his brother throwing in only an occasional word. It was a pleasant hour; but I left with the distinct impression that while the Duke of York was sold on the American station wagon, the Duchess was not sold on David's other American interest.[8]

There was no doubt at all that the Duchess of York disliked Mrs Simpson with a vehemence that was uncharacteristic of her. In July 1936, when Edward VIII had broken the British press's self-imposed embargo on reporting his liaison with Mrs Simpson by insisting on publishing her name in the court circulars which announced the guests at his evening dinner parties, the Duke and Duchess of York attended a dinner which was to produce an interesting conversational exchange. Among the guests, apart from the King and Mrs Simpson, were Winston Churchill and his wife. During the dinner party, Churchill, rather indiscreetly, raised the uncomfortable subject of George IV's unconstitutional marriage while Prince Regent to Mrs Fitzherbert. The Duchess of York replied steadily to this point, "That was a long time ago." Churchill then mischievously turned the conversation to the historic confrontation between the houses of York and Lancaster during the Wars of the Roses. (It was known to a small circle that the King was about to take a summer cruise with Mrs Simpson under the pseudonym of "The Duke of Lancaster".) "Oh, that was a very long time ago," the Duchess firmly replied.

It was not merely the Duchess of York who disliked Mrs Simpson intensely. Queen Mary, now the custodian of her husband's view of royal duty and appropriate behaviour, was equally disapproving, feeling that the American's effect upon the King was taking him further and further from his family. Princess Marina of Greece, who had married George, Duke of Kent on 29 November 1934, also resented Mrs Simpson's influence. There was no reason to suppose that King Edward VIII's second brother, Prince Henry, Duke of Gloucester, felt any more kindly disposed towards her.

Perhaps the Royal Family also resented Mrs Simpson's influence at a time when it had weathered a number of storms and seemed to be pressing confidently ahead in relatively tranquil seas. The Duke and Duchess of York's marriage had been a triumphant success, and the birth of their two daughters completed an apparently ideal family structure. The Duke of Kent's marriage had proved a stabilizing factor for a prince who had been "prone on occasions to black depressions, and after one unhappy love affair . . . had been drawn towards drugs. He had suffered a breakdown as he had tried to crack the addiction . . ."[9] Prince Henry of Gloucester's marriage in November 1935 to Lady Alice Montagu-Douglas-Scott, daughter of the seventh Duke of Buccleuch, had confirmed the prevailing pattern of marital stability that the House of Windsor regarded so highly.

It was the twin pillars of monogamy and royal duty which under-pinned the magnificent structure of the House of Windsor, but, in 1936, Edward VIII seemed to threaten its security. That he remained unmarried was an uncomfortable deviation from the family norm; that he now seemed to be enslaved by an American divorcee compounded the discomfort tenfold. Not that Mrs Simpson's American origins necessarily counted against her, although her divorce undoubtedly did. The upper reaches of British society were littered with American wives, and in the mid nineteen-thirties both Nancy Astor and Emerald Cunard were fully accepted by society, despite being American and proud of it. Nor had Victorian and Edwardian statesmen shown any unwillingness to take American wives: Lord Randolph Churchill, Joseph Chamberlain, Lord Curzon, and Lewis Harcourt, son of the Liberal Party leader, were among those who had married American women. Nor, according to one authority, ". . . need Mrs Simpson's track record with men have proved an insuperable obstacle. That was a trait accommodated in others at that level of society."[10] Mrs Simpson was unacceptable for other reasons:

The more basic problem was that she had no idea how to behave in the circle to which she so nakedly aspired. Her brassy repartee jarred on ladies of high birth. She would run her finger along the top of the mantelpiece and call for the housekeeper if she found dust. King Edward VIII had never come across this domesticity before and found it entrancing. But in a royal household such bourgeois habits were absolutely fatal.[11]

She was also starting to behave with proprietorial airs towards the King. On her visit to Royal Lodge with the King, Mrs Simpson, while looking out of the drawing-room window, had been tactless enough to suggest to the King that certain improvements might be made in the trees if some of them were felled. Later, in September 1936, the King had held a house-party at Balmoral for Mrs Simpson and some of her American friends. Invited over to Balmoral from nearby Birkhall, the Duchess of York was not pleased to find herself effectively the guest of Mrs Simpson, as it was Mrs Simpson who came forward to receive her when she arrived, she who was playing the part of hostess, and she who was even sleeping in the bedroom formerly used by Queen Mary. As if this was not enough, the American behaved with considerable high-handedness. For example, she "insisted on going into the kitchens to show the cooks how to prepare double-decker sandwiches, a speciality of which she was particularly proud, and insisted that these be made and served fresh to guests at midnight or even later, long past the hour when the servants were normally allowed to retire."[12]

The King seemed to the diarist "Chips" Channon to be "Mrs Simpson's absolute slave". It was noticed that if she broke a fingernail he was apt to dash off to find her the means to repair it, or that at the theatre she was capable of plucking the cigar out of his mouth to prevent him smoking at an inappropriate moment. It was her dominating personality that held a particular appeal:

All his life the Prince of Wales had sought "a woman with a strong male inclination", and one of the most enduring links between these two was that, in the context of this relationship, although apparently in no other, he was made for domination, while she was made to dominate. He and Wallis Simpson were quite unusually suited to each other, two parts of a whole, and it was her misfortune as well as his that, when two complementary natures join, it is not really the best in each that finds completion. The time might come in the crisis that was to follow – although even here the evidence is not strong – when she would temporarily lose her power to influence his behaviour, like someone who, having whipped up a sensitive horse, momentarily loses control of it, but she must bear a large responsibility for everything that follows, because his greatest happiness in life was to obey her slightest wish."[13]

The King's behaviour became more and more indiscreet, and in August 1936 he hired a yacht, the *Nahlin*, and sailed with Mrs Simpson and a few close friends down the Dalmatian coast and into the Mediterranean. Often dressed only in the skimpiest of clothes, the couple made no secret of their affection for each other, and it was not long before photographs and gossip about the voyage were appearing in the American press. At home, the British press, due to a self-denying ordinance between the two press barons, Beaverbrook and Rothermere, still made no mention of the "King's affair".

Tempted into the indiscretion of this summer cruise, Edward VIII soon committed a second act of folly, nearer at home. Although he had spent a fortnight in September at Balmoral with Mrs Simpson, he had earlier refused an invitation from the Lord Provost of Aberdeen to open new hospital buildings in that city, giving the excuse that the Court was still in mourning. It had not escaped notice, however, that he had publicly enjoyed Ascot Week during June, nor that he delegated the duty in Aberdeen to the Duke of York. Worse was to follow. On the day when he should have been opening the new hospital buildings in Aberdeen, Mrs Simpson arrived at Aberdeen Station, and the King, in an act of monumental tactlessness, drove himself into the city to collect her from the station. There were no signs of mourning here, and this act of self-indulgence shocked many people.

In October, the intensity of the King's relationship with Mrs Simpson precipitated the crisis which was to end a few months later in his abdication. On 20 October 1936, he told Stanley Baldwin that Mrs Simpson was set on divorcing her husband. On 27 October Mrs Simpson obtained her divorce *nisi* on the grounds of her husband's adultery with a married woman called Mary Kirk Raffray. It was at this point that the King's Private Secretary, Alexander Hardinge, paid a visit to 145 Piccadilly to warn the Duke of York that he must consider the possibility of his elder brother's abdication.

Mrs Simpson's *decree nisi* would become final on 27 April 1937, making her completely free to marry the King. A tempting sequence of events now presented themselves to Edward VIII. His coronation had been fixed for 12 May 1937, and between Mrs Simpson's final divorce and the coronation there was a fortnight – just enough time in which to get married and take his new wife to Westminster Abbey to be crowned at his side. Such a prospect was unacceptable to the Royal Family, to the Prime Minister and the Government, and to most leading members of the British establishment.

Since Baldwin found it difficult to talk openly with the King about his plans, it was left to Alexander Hardinge, to write, with the Prime Minister's approval, a frank and necessary letter to Edward VIII. Hardinge's letter of 13 November 1936 warned the King that the silence of the British press on the subject of his affair with Mrs Simpson was not going to be maintained, and that the Government were meeting urgently to discuss what action should be taken to deal with the developing situation. If the Government were to resign, Hardinge doubted whether the King would:

> ... find someone else capable of forming a Government which would receive the support of the present House of Commons. I have reason to know that, in view of the feeling prevalent among members of the House of Commons of all parties, this is hardly within the bounds of possibility. The only alternative remaining is a dissolution and a general election in which Your Majesty's personal affairs would be the chief issue, I cannot but help feeling that even those who would sympathize with Your Majesty as an individual

would deeply resent the damage which would inevitably be done to the Crown – the corner-stone on which the whole Empire rests.

If Your Majesty will permit me to say so, there is only one step which holds out any prospect of avoiding this dangerous situation, and that is for Mrs Simpson to go abroad *without further delay* – and I would *beg* Your Majesty to give this proposal your earnest consideration before the position has become irretrievable. Owing to the changing attitude of the Press, the matter has become one of great urgency.[14]

The King was "shocked and angry" at Hardinge's letter. But at least it made him determined to clarify his position with the Prime Minister. On 16 November Baldwin was summoned to Buckingham Palace, where the King told him unequivocally that he intended to marry Mrs Simpson as soon as she was free to marry him. He informed the Prime Minister that although he wanted to marry Mrs Simpson as King, if this proved impossible, he was prepared to abdicate. Baldwin was so shaken by the interview that, having informed his senior Cabinet colleagues as to the content of his audience with the King, he told the government Chief Whip, Captain David Margesson, "I have heard such things from my King tonight that I never thought to hear. I am going to bed."

The crisis now approached its climax at breakneck speed. On the same evening as his fateful interview with Baldwin, the King saw his mother, and informed her of his intentions. Queen Mary, though sympathetic to his personal needs, baulked at the prospect of abdication. According to the Duke of Windsor's memoirs, "To my mother, the monarchy was something sacred, and the Sovereign a personage apart. The word 'duty' fell between us."

The next morning, Edward VIII told his brothers that he was prepared to abdicate if that proved the price of his marrying Mrs Simpson. The three princes reacted in a similar way to their mother, although the news affected them in different ways:

The Duke of York, literally dumbfounded by what it meant for his own life and that of his daughter Elizabeth, could not say anything at all. Trying to come to terms with the shock in the arrangement of details, Harry, the Duke of Gloucester, talked about the practical difficulties of abdication for himself, the next brother in line – since if anything happened to Bertie, he would have to act as Regent for

Lilibet. And the Duke of Kent was consumed with anger. " 'Besot-
ted'. That was what the Duke of Kent called it over and over again,"
Stanley Baldwin remembered. " 'He is besotted on the woman . . .
One can't get a word of sense out of him.' "[15]

The Duke of York viewed his brother's abdication with a mixture of
dread and resolution. He has been described as being "in an agony of
apprehension" as he "watched the gradual but unrelenting approach
of that dreaded moment when he would have to take up the burdens
and responsibilities of kingship". He put on a brave front to his Private
Secretary, Godfrey Thomas, telling him on 25 November, "if the
worst happens & I have to take over, you can be assured that I will do
my best to clear up the inevitable mess, if the whole fabric does not
crumble under the shock and strain of it all."

On 3 December the news of the King's determination to marry Mrs
Simpson was made public for the first time, commanding banner
headlines in the nation's newspapers. A week of feverish speculation
and some uncertainty ensued. That same day Mrs Simpson went
abroad; in Britain there was talk of the formation of a "King's Party",
and the Beaverbrook and Rothermere press lent open support to the
King; the possibility of a morganatic marriage was touted; Winston
Churchill made a plea for time and patience. For a while, indeed, it was
not clear what the outcome would be.

There was also a curious lack of communication between Edward
VIII and the Duke of York, especially between 3 and 7 December.
Although the King had invited his brother to see him on Thursday 3
December, it was not until the following Monday that the meeting
eventually took place, and the Duke of York learnt that he was to
succeed to the throne. Yet the Prime Minister had been informed on
Saturday 5 December of the King's definite decision to abdicate. In his
journal, the Duke of York recorded what looks to have been the
sequence of rebuffs and evasions between these dates:

He told me to come & see him at the Fort the next morning [Friday 4
December]. I rang him up but he would not see me & put me off till
Saturday. I told him I would be at Royal Lodge on Saturday by
12.30 pm. I rang him up Saturday. "Come & see me on Sunday"
was his answer. "I will see you & tell you my decision when I have
made up my mind." Sunday evening I rang up. "The King has a
conference & will speak to you later" was the answer. But he did not

ring up. Monday morning [December] came. I rang up at 1.0 pm & my brother told me he might be able to see me that evening. I told him, "I must go to London, but would come to the Fort when he wanted me". I did not go to London but waited. I sent a telephone message to the Fort to say that if I was wanted I would be at Royal Lodge. My brother rang me up at 10 minutes to 7.0 pm to say "Come & see me after dinner". I said, "No, I will come and see you at once." I was with him at 7.0 pm. The awful & ghastly suspense of waiting was over. I found him pacing up & down the room, & he told me his decision that he would go. I went back to Royal Lodge for dinner, and returned to the Fort later. I felt having once got there I was not going to leave. As he is my eldest brother I have to be there to try & help him in his hour of need.[16]

Frances Donaldson attributes Edward VIII's behaviour to his lack of consideration:

> During the whole of the abdication crisis Edward VIII behaved to his family, lovers and friends with a cold and childish lack of feeling reminiscent of an Evelyn Waugh heroine, Brenda Last or Lady Metroland.
>
> For weeks at a time, he did not communicate with his mother, he was unavailable to his brothers and he allowed his family to learn, as everyone else did, his intentions from the Press.
>
> [His brother] if he abdicated, would inherit the Crown, but he neither consulted him nor took him into his confidence, merely allowing him to await an increasingly inevitable outcome.[17]

There are, however, at least two other explanations of the hiatus which occurred between 3 and 7 December. One was that the King was gripped by a panic-stricken fatigue during these days. Winston Churchill, who dined at Fort Belvedere on 4 and 5 December, recalled, "He had two marked and prolonged blackouts, in which he completely lost the thread of his conversation . . ."[18] Then there was the time consumed by long telephone conversations with Mrs Simpson, now in Cannes, "painful, naked, nagging calls".

There is a further, more ominous, explanation. It seems that in the highest circles there may have been some doubt as to whether the Duke of York would make an adequate monarch. Compared superficially to his elder brother, the Duke of York certainly had far fewer of the attributes associated with successful kingship. There was not a Duke of York's Party, as there had been a prospective King's Party during the abdication crisis. According to King George VI's official biographer, as the time of his coronation approached in 1937:

> Coming from none knew where, passed from mouth to mouth, in some cases unheedingly, in others with malignant intent, there swept through London a wave of idle and malicious gossip which embraced not only the general health of the King and the Royal Family, but also his ability to discharge his functions as a Sovereign . . . there was the crowning calumny that, even if he succeeded in getting through the ordeal of the Coronation, the King would never be able to undertake all the arduous duties which would fall to him, that he would never be able to speak in public, and that he would be a recluse or, at best, a "rubber stamp".[19]

It is possible that serious consideration was given to the prospect of by-passing the Duke of York and offering the Crown to his apparently more able and eligible brother the Duke of Kent. King Edward VIII's failure to keep his successor fully informed of events between 3 and 7 December may have been part of this plot. It may be that, "on hearing from Edward VIII that he wished to abdicate, Stanley Baldwin asked the King not to talk straight away to his family, but to give the Government a few days to decide whether the accession of Prince Albert – and subsequently Princess Elizabeth – would really provide personalities dynamic enough to win back the lustre of the monarchy after abdication".[20] In his book, *Princess Elizabeth, Duchess of Edinburgh*, published in 1950, Dermot Morrah wrote, "It was certainly seriously considered at this time, whether by agreement among the Royal Family, the Crown might not be settled on the Duke of Kent, the only one of the abdicating king's brothers who at that time had a son to become Prince of Wales, and so avoid laying so heavy a future burden upon the shoulders of any woman."[21] That the Duke of York was appalled at the prospect of succeeding to the throne is well documented. At the same time, it is unlikely that the British establishment would have found the Duke of Kent, with his recent problem of drug addiction, a more acceptable future king than the Duke of York. Prince Henry of Gloucester, an uninspiring figure, was even less acceptable than either the Duke of Kent or the Duke of York.

But on 7 December the suspense was over. The Duke of York now knew, barring a miracle, that he would succeed his brother as King. Even so, he seems to have hoped that such a miracle would occur. On 8 December, after dining at Fort Belvedere with Edward VIII, Baldwin, the Duke of Kent and Walter Monckton (who throughout the crisis had been the King's closest adviser), the Duke recorded, "my brother was the life & soul of the party . . . I whispered to W.M. '& this is the man we are going to lose.' One couldn't, nobody could believe it."[22] The next day, 9 December, the Duke met his brother again, and seems to have tried to persuade him not to abdicate. "I then had a long talk with D, but I could see that nothing I said would alter his decision. His mind was made up." The Duke of York later motored back to London where, "I went to see Queen Mary, & when I told her what had happened I broke down & sobbed like a child."[23]

There was now no turning back. On 10 December the Duke of York, ". . . was present at the fateful moment which made me D's successor to the Throne. Perfectly calm, D signed 5 or 6 copies of the instrument [of abdication] and then 5 copies of his message to Parliament, one for each Dominion Parliament. It was a dreadful moment, & one never to be forgotten by those present."[24]

Lord Louis Mountbatten, however, recalling the last moments of Edward VIII's reign in the BBC Television programme "Lord Mountbatten Remembers" broadcast in November 1980, saw his cousin and friend at that moment rather like a high-spirited schoolboy at the end of term, as "gay as a lark". At the very least, the King seemed unperturbed. In Lord Mountbatten's words: "It was absolutely incredible. In the great downstairs bedroom, a vast big double bed was covered with telegrams and cables from every part of the Commonwealth to a depth of several inches with appeals from governors-general, prime ministers, cabinets, mayors and just ordinary people: 'For God's sake, don't abdicate, don't give up the Empire.' He sat in an armchair with his foot upon a footstool while Mr Mock, his personal chiropodist, cut his corns for the last time".

At 2 am on Saturday 12 December, having delivered his abdication message to his people, the ex-King left Portsmouth on the destroyer *Fury* for Boulogne. At eleven on the same morning, King George VI attended his Accession Council at St James's Palace. The abdication crisis was over.

Quite apart from his determination to marry Mrs Simpson, were there other reasons why King Edward VIII was driven from the throne?

There were certainly grounds upon which the Government, after the initial honeymoon of his accession, had become disillusioned with him by December 1936. Although Edward VIII had begun his reign by enthusiastically reading through all the official papers sent to him, and even scribbling comments of his own in the margin, he was unable to sustain this interest, and after a few months it was clear that highly confidential documents were being returned to the Cabinet office unread, sometimes even bearing the marks of spilled cocktails and the rings of wet glass-bottoms. There were often long delays before the King returned the red boxes which contained Cabinet papers, and it was discovered that these were frequently left unattended at Fort Belvedere while the house was thronged with guests. A disinclination to read the official documents sent to him was not, of course, a characteristic unprecedented in the history of the British monarchy: Edward VII had been equally unenthusiastic for paperwork, and his ministers had known it.

If Edward VIII was slipshod in his treatment of the red dispatch boxes, he was even more indiscreet in giving vent to his views on foreign affairs. In particular, the King was notoriously sympathetic towards the fascist dictatorships of Germany and Italy. That the King should have found the tyrannies of Mussolini or Hitler attractive is difficult to accept, but it is not impossible to understand. Horrified at the examples of poverty which he had seen at first hand in his own country and believing that "something must be done", Edward VIII was not sure what could *actually* be done. Certainly, the liberal democracy of the United Kingdom had apparently provided no solution. Perhaps the strong centralized governments of Germany and Italy were a better model? Disliking and fearing Bolshevism like so many other members of Britain's ruling class, Edward VIII was prepared to flirt with fascism.

There is a good deal of evidence to support this view of the King. Shortly after Edward had acceded to the throne, von Hoesch, the German ambassador in London, sent a dispatch back to Berlin dated 21 January 1936 in which he said, "you are aware from my reports that King Edward, quite generally, feels warm sympathy for Germany. I have become convinced during frequent, often quite lengthy, talks with him that his sympathies are deep-rooted and strong enough to withstand the contrary influences to which they are not seldom exposed."[25]

King Edward had no desire to oppose German and Italian expansion. On the contrary, when German troops reoccupied the Rhineland in March 1936, thus raising the possibility that Britain might intervene, he made it clear to the German government that he was opposed to British intervention. When, in the same year, Italy invaded Abyssinia, "he worked to undermine any government attempt to stand up to Fascist aggression, with force or with bluff. He was reported as assuring Mussolini's ambassador in May 1936 that the League of Nations, which was trying to enforce economic sanctions against Italy, and to which the British government had pledged its support, could be considered dead and that for peace in Europe it was absolutely essential that two great nations, Germany and Italy, should be afforded full satisfaction by granting them, with full realization of their needs, the necessary colonial markets."[26]

So plain had the King's sympathy for Nazi Germany become by December 1936, and so strenuously had he tried to influence the British Government, that "Chips" Channon, writing in his diary, said, "He, too, is going the dictator way, and is pro-German, against Russia and against too much slipshod democracy. I shouldn't be surprised if he aimed at making himself a mild dictator, a difficult task enough for an English King."[27] Mrs Simpson was also thought to be pro-Nazi, indeed Lord Mountbatten later claimed that she encouraged the King in his anti-democratic tendencies.

The King was not, of course, alone in his tendency to sympathize with fascist dictatorships. The policy of appeasement which characterized the late nineteen-thirties was, after all, based on the desire to accommodate arguably legitimate German territorial demands. There were also many members of the Conservative Party who were prepared to overlook Hitler's reign of terror, so long as the victims were Jewish or Communist or Socialist. It was not until Britain went to war with Germany in 1939 that revulsion at Nazi bestiality, encouraged by the wartime propaganda machine, became a widespread and commonplace response. All the same, apart from some indiscreet meddling, what did Edward VIII achieve in his support for Germany and Italy? One judgement is that:

The dictators may have miscalculated the power which the monarch possessed in the British political system. But they were right in supposing that they had a friend sitting on the throne of England, and this was one reason for the German decision to send von Ribbentrop to London as ambassador in 1936. In his memoirs, he explains his feelings that he could be more use at the Court of St James than actually directing foreign policy in Berlin, because Hitler's main intention at this time was to neutralize Britain, if possible with an Anglo-German alliance. Some thought it unlikely that such an alliance could be concluded, but "because of Edward VIII, it seemed that a final attempt should be made".[28]

Certainly Baldwin decided to withhold from the King certain sensitive and confidential documents. Since there was no way of restricting the King's tendency to speak spontaneously and freely to foreign ambassadors, it seemed sensible to restrict his access to certain confidential material. In fact, the Prime Minister had no right, according to constitutional practice, to withhold any government documents from the King, but by the time this decision had been taken, Edward VIII's scrutiny of his official papers had become so intermittent that he did not notice.

Despite Edward VIII's sympathy for the fascist dictatorships, there is no sound evidence to suggest that the Government wished to get rid of him on that account. It was inconvenient to have a monarch who considered it his right to interfere in foreign affairs, but on the other hand, it was normally possible to neutralize such interference. The problem was never discussed at Cabinet level, and the King's indiscretions in the field of foreign policy simply compounded his indiscretions over Mrs Simpson. On both counts, Baldwin was glad to see him go.

THE NEW KING

1936–1939

[Stanley Baldwin] thought the new King would have a great deal to contend with. "There's a lot of prejudice against him. He's had no chance to capture the public imagination as his brother did. I'm afraid he won't find it easy going for the first year or two."

Lady Airlie

KING GEORGE VI ASCENDED THE THRONE with the greatest reluctance, and was beset with doubts over whether he could cope adequately with his new role. According to his official biographer:

> From every aspect his new dignity was unwelcome to him; the sudden and tragic circumstances of its coming, his personal dislike of publicity and limelight, and his practical unpreparedness, all tended at first to overwhelm him.
>
> Now was displayed the fallacy of King George V's policy of refusing to allow his second son to be initiated even into the ordinary everyday working of government. The new King stood appalled at the volume and the nature of the business which emerged day by day from those leather-clad dispatch boxes, which inexorably dog the life of every British sovereign. He was, moreover, more than ever conscious now of his physical disability, and of what he believed to be his inferiority in comparison with his brother.[1]

There is abundant evidence of George VI's anxieties on assuming the kingship. On the first night of his reign, as he waited at Fort Belvedere while his elder brother made preparations for his departure, the new King said with much emotion to his cousin, Lord Louis Mountbatten, "Dickie, this is absolutely terrible. I never wanted this to happen: I'm quite unprepared for it. David has been trained for this all his life. I've never even seen a State Paper. I'm only a Naval Officer, it's the only thing I know about." Lord Louis' reply could have hardly been bettered, reminding his cousin that the new King's father had himself never expected to succeed to the throne: "This is a very curious coincidence. My father once told me that, when the Duke of Clarence died, your father came to him and said almost the same thing that you have said to me now, and my father answered: 'George, you're wrong. There is no more fitting preparation for a King than to have been trained in the Navy.'"[2]

Despite these encouraging words, King George was weighed down with the responsibilities that now descended upon him. An eye witness observed his return to 145 Piccadilly by car on the evening of his brother's abdication: "His face was deathly serious. . . . For once the Duke made no attempt to recognize the good-humoured tribute of the crowd. He did not see it. His eyes were looking into a world of their own, a world of endless crowds and cruel loneliness, a world of pomp in which the slave would play the Emperor, a world from which there could be no release save for a few hours at a time."[3]

George VI also knew that there was a lack of enthusiasm for his succession in certain circles. Lady Airlie recalled a conversation with the Prime Minister in January 1937:

> Stan thought that the new King would have a great deal to contend with. "There's a lot of prejudice against him. He's had no chance to capture the popular imagination as his brother did. I'm afraid he won't find it easy going for the first year or two."
>
> I answered that King George V had said to me long ago, "Bertie has more guts than the rest of his brothers put together," and that I had always found him an unerring judge of character.[4]

To emphasize the links with the father whom he had admired so much, and who had been pushed, like him, into an unexpected occupancy of the throne, the new King chose to be officially known by the last of his four christian names, George. Thus was continuity symbolized – a point not missed by Baldwin, who said on 14 December 1936, "What will endear him to his people is that more than any of his brothers he resembles in character and mind his father."[5] Queen Mary provided another link with the past and was a valuable symbol of continuity. Lady Airlie recalls that she ". . . was a tower of strength in those days, drawing as she always did when others depended on her on some inner force within her own personality. In the past year she had undergone strain which would have caused a weaker character to crumple up. Grief for her beloved husband had been followed by anxiety, suspense and bitter humiliation. But her son, who was now the Sovereign, and his wife facing a colossal task needed her courage to sustain them."[6]

[141]

The new King's anxieties at his changed circumstances were also felt by his wife and family. The Duchess of York had been prostrated with influenza during the final phase of the abdication crisis, and she wrote, shortly after becoming Queen, to the Archbishop of Canterbury, "I can hardly now believe that we have been called to this tremendous task, and (I am writing to you quite intimately) the curious thing is that we aren't afraid. I feel that God has enabled us to face the situation calmly." Certainly, as Queen, Elizabeth Bowes-Lyon exhibited even more of the resourcefulness and creative purpose that she had shown as Duchess of York. Lady Airlie noticed, "When I first had tea with her in her sitting-room at Buckingham Palace a few weeks after King George's Accession, I saw that the room was already beginning to show the traces of her own personality – the little feminine touches which I have always associated with her. 'It looks homelike already,' I said spontaneously. The King, who had come in for a few minutes, smiled proudly . . . 'Elizabeth could make a home anywhere.'"[8]

Lady Airlie was also fully sensitive to what their changed circumstances meant in practical terms to the Yorks:

They had been completely happy in the simplicity of their private life; that would be forfeited forever. The cosy house – 145 Piccadilly – where they had entertained informally and had got their own supper when they came in late from a theatre – had to be exchanged for the cold magnificence of Buckingham Palace.

I pitied most of all the new Queen. In the fourteen years of her marriage she had remained completely unspoiled, still at heart the simple unaffected girl I had known at Glamis, carrying out her public duties with an efficiency that won Queen Mary's admiration, but finding her true happiness in her home and her own family circle.[9]

However, half of that family circle were excited rather than depressed by their change of status. On 11 December 1936, the day of Edward VIII's abdication, Lady Cynthia Asquith was invited to 145 Piccadilly, where she found the Princesses Elizabeth and Margaret Rose intrigued by the changes that were taking place. Princess Elizabeth noticed a letter lying on the hall table which was addressed to Her Majesty the Queen, and she said to Lady Cynthia, "That's *Mummy*, now, isn't it?" Princess Margaret, who was just learning to write, grumbled, "I had only just learned to spell York – YORK – and now I'm not

25 A sombre Duke and Duchess of York at the 1926 Welsh National Eisteddfod at Swansea

26 The Duke and Duchess being greeted at Suva in the Fiji Islands, 1927

26

25

ROYAL VISITS

27 Arriving at Sydney in May 1927 during the tour of Australia

27

28 The Prince of Wales and Mrs Simpso[n] at Ascot, 1935

29 Funeral of George V, 1936. His fo[ur] sons follow the coffin.

2[9]

30 December 1936. His face drawn and strained, the new King George VI at the climax of the Abdication Crisis arriving at 145 Piccadilly.

31 King George VI during the ordeal of his coronation, May 1937

31

32 The newly crowned King and Queen, with the Princesses Elizabeth and Margaret Rose, and a thoughtful Queen Mary on the balcony of Buckingham Palace, May 1937

33 Lionel Logue, the speech therapist who cured King George VI's stammer and gave him the confidence to face public occasions

33

ANGLO-AMERICAN ACCORD

34 A laughing George VI with President Roosevelt during the 1939 royal visit to the United States   35 Eleanor Roosevelt on her way to the wartime austerities of life at Buckingham Palace during her 1942 visit

35

GEORGE VI's THREE PRIME MINISTERS

36 Winston Churchill, shortly before taking over as wartime Prime Minister in 1940
37 The King leaves 10 Downing Street in 1939 having visited Neville Chamberlain
38 A donnish Clement Attlee, Labour Prime Minister, 1945–51

THE HUMAN TOUCH

39 The King and Queen standing amid the bo
damage to Buckingham Palace, 1940   40 Talkin
workmen demolishing damaged buildings in west Lon
in September 1940 and   (41) to the victims of Gern
raids on Sheffield in 1941

42

42 With the Allied forces. George VI with Field-Marshals Alanbrooke (left), Alexander, and General Dwight D. Eisenhower in North Africa in 1943

43 The King scrutinising air reconnaissance photographs of the damage caused by the famous 'Dambuster' raids on Germany

45

ιe Princesses doing their bit for victory. 44
ιying War Savings Certificates in 1943, and (45)
ghteen-year-old Second Subaltern Elizabeth Alex-
dra Mary Windsor pausing in her investigations
ɔo the internal combustion engine while serving in
ɛ ATS

46

46 The Royal Family flank Winston Churchill as they acknowledge the cheering crowds on VE-Day, May 1945   47 Victory Parade, June 1946. The King takes the salute, watched by Churchill (now the leader of the Opposition) far right, and Labour Cabinet ministers including Herbert Morrison and Ernest Bevin in the row behind him.

47

to use it any more. I'm to sign myself Margaret all alone."[10] When George VI's accession was publicly proclaimed the next day, Marion Crawford observed how the Princesses behaved towards their father before and after the ceremony:

> Lilibet and Margaret had run as usual to give their father a final hug as he went off, looking very grave, dressed as an Admiral of the Fleet. . . . When the king returned, both little girls swept him a beautiful curtsey. I think perhaps nothing that had occurred had brought the change in his condition to him as clearly as this did. He stood for a moment touched and taken aback. Then he stooped and kissed them both warmly.[11]

The King had been far less at ease at the Accession Council held at St James's Palace, looking pale and haggard as he faced his Privy Councillors. When he addressed them, although he spoke "in a low, clear voice", it was noticeable that there were many hesitations in his speech. He said:

> Your Royal Highnesses, My Lords, Gentlemen,
> I meet you to-day in circumstances which are without parallel in the history of our Country. Now that the duties of Sovereignty have fallen upon me, I declare to you My adherence to the strict principles of constitutional government, and My resolve to work before all else for the welfare of the British Commonwealth of Nations.
> With My wife and helpmeet by My side, I take up the heavy task which lies before Me. In it, I look for the support of all My people.
> Furthermore, My first act on succeeding My brother will be to confer on him a Dukedom, and he will henceforth be known as His Royal Highness the Duke of Windsor.[12]

George VI's accession speech carried a striking example of the new monarch's capacity to assert himself. The typewritten speech, headed "Declaration to be made at the Accession Council", was formally typed only down to the sentence, "In it I look for the support of all My people." The paragraph announcing the conferring of the Dukedom of Windsor upon the abdicated King was written on the bottom of the sheet of paper in pencil, in George VI's own handwriting. The extra paragraph seems to have been written in some haste, with several phrases crossed out. (This interesting document aroused a furore in

December 1979, when an anonymous seller proposed to auction it at Sotheby's, who put its value at between £4000 and £6000.)[13] This handwritten part at the end of King George VI's speech was a significant indication that, amid his understandable anxieties and confusion, the new monarch could be firm and decisive. On 11 December 1936, Lord Wigram (George VI's Private Secretary from 1931–35) and Sir Claud Schuster (Clerk of the Crown and Permanent Secretary to the Lord Chancellor from 1914–44) had come to see the Duke of York for advice as to the future style and titles of King Edward VIII, who was going to announce his abdication that evening. King George VI left a revealing account of the interview and his part in it in a memorandum:

> Lord Wigram & Sir Claud Schuster (as representative of the Lord Chancellor) came to see me in the forenoon, as Schuster wanted to ask me what my brother, King Edward VIII, was going to be known as after his abdication. The question was an urgent one, as Sir John Reith (Director of the BBC) was going to introduce him on the air that night as Mr Edward Windsor. I replied: – That is quite wrong. Before going any further, I would ask what has he given up on his abdication, S. said I'm not sure. I said, It would be quite a good thing to find out before coming to me. Now as to his name, I suggest HRH D. of W[indsor]. He cannot be Mr E.W. as he was born the son of a Duke. That makes him Ld. E.W. anyhow. If he ever comes back to this country, he can stand & and be elected to the H of C. Would you like that? S. replied No.
>
> As D of W he can sit & vote in the H of L. Would you like that? S replied No. Well, if he becomes a royal duke he cannot speak or vote in the H of L, & he is not being deprived of his rank in the Navy, Army or R. Air Force. This gave Schuster a new lease of life & he went off quite happy.[14]

That night Sir John Reith introduced Edward VIII as His Royal Highness Prince Edward, before the King made his abdication broadcast, and the next morning the new King announced his intention of creating his brother Duke of Windsor at his speech delivered to the Accession Council.

For one who had lived for so long in his elder brother's shadow, King George VI was able to adjust to the changed relationship between them with remarkable swiftness: perhaps the rivalry which had been noted between them as young men, and which had largely expressed itself in sport, was a helpful factor during the first part of the new king's reign. It was George VI who had now to decide what financial provision should be made for his brother in his self-imposed exile, and since, under the wills of Queen Victoria and King George V, Edward VIII was a life tenant of the royal houses of Balmoral and Sandringham, the transfer of these rights to his brother provided the basis of the financial settlement between them. How much was the settlement worth? According to one authority, "Naturally no one but their financial and legal advisers was a party to the settlement, but informed guesses put the figure for Sandringham and Balmoral at one million pounds, and the yearly income paid by George VI to his brother at £60,000. Over and beyond this the Duke of Windsor is believed to have taken substantial sums out of the country from other sources."[15]

It was also George VI who decided that when, in June 1937, his brother married Mrs Simpson, his wife, though becoming the Duchess of Windsor, should not hold the title of Her Royal Highness. The Duke of Windsor was affronted by this decision, exclaiming, "What a *damnable* wedding-present!" The refusal to allow Mrs Simpson the style and title of Her Royal Highness probably owed a good deal to Queen Mary's implacable hostility towards her – Queen Mary intended never to receive Mrs Simpson if she could help it. If she had been created Her Royal Highness and had returned to Britain, Queen Mary might have felt obliged to pay her the courtesy due to her title. As it was, the Duke of Windsor solved the dilemma by announcing, "No HRH for Wallis, no home-coming for me."

As it happened, the effect of the Duke of Windsor's ultimatum was beneficial to both parties. The Windsors did not return to the United Kingdom, which meant that the new King and Queen had a chance to establish themselves in the affections of the British public without any competition from the once widely popular "Prince Charming" and his bride. Elizabeth Longford has said, "During the first three years of their reign, the new King and Queen felt a real sense of insecurity. How would the country take *us*? they asked themselves. No prince had ever been more popular than Edward, and their own style by comparison was quiet and unassuming. It was not beyond the bounds of possibility that the Windsors could stage a comeback – or so it seemed in those troubled early days."[16] Queen Elizabeth was as firm as Queen Mary in insisting that there was no place for the Duke and Duchess of Windsor in her husband's kingdom. She knew how often the King talked of his exiled brother; she knew how deeply he had suffered during the abdication crisis, and that perhaps at one level he felt he had somehow usurped his more brilliant elder brother. "In the interests of her family, her husband and his people, the firm line taken by the Queen was justified, and any other wife of equal character would have hoped to do likewise."[17]

For the Windsors, too, the withholding of the title of HRH for the Duchess proved to be something of a blessing, though at the time a heavily disguised one. Since they were eventually offered tax-free hospitality by the French public, and were thus enabled to live in far greater luxury than would have been the case in Britain, the slight suffered by the Duchess provided them with the justification of staying abroad. "It enabled the Windsors to keep up what amounted to a bluff of martyrdom, while living sophisticated and prosperous lives in Paris. And it provided a shield behind which the new royal line could develop in undisturbed harmony."[18]

What inspired the harsh decision which created such an irreparable breach between the Duke of Windsor and his family? Would the British public allow no more generous a treatment? Was it resentment of the role which the Duchess had played in precipitating the abdication crisis? Was it simply due to the animosity from other members of the Royal Family, particularly Queen Mary? Or did it arise from King George VI's belief that rules should invariably be obeyed, by himself and his family as much as by others? A. J. P. Taylor believes, "Certainly this was his deep-rooted conviction. He would continue the tradition of duty which his father had inherited from Queen Victoria."[19]

The Duke of Windsor's behaviour after the abdication did a great deal to widen the breach between himself and his brother. Although no longer King, he continued for some time to behave as if he were still sitting on the throne. One of the Duke's oldest and closest friends, "Fruity" Metcalfe, staying with the Windsors in their first refuge of Schloss Enzesfeld, a house belonging to Baron Eugene de Rothschild near Vienna, observed some of the friction between the two brothers. For example, on 21 January 1937:

Tonight [the Duke of Windsor] was told at dinner that H.M. wanted to talk on the phone to him. He said he couldn't take the call, but asked it to be put through at 10 pm. The answer to this was that H.M. said *he would talk at 6.45 pm tomorrow* as he was *too busy to talk any other time.* It was pathetic to see HRH's face. He couldn't believe it! He has been so used to having everything done as he wishes. I'm afraid he is going to have many more shocks like this.[20]

So difficult did the Duke of Windsor find it to adjust to his new station, and perhaps so low was his opinion of the new King's judgement, that he also continued to ring up his brother regularly to advise him on questions of the day. Walter Monckton, who remained a close and trusted adviser of the Duke of Windsor during this time, later wrote, "This advice often ran counter to the advice that the King was getting from his responsible ministers in the government. This caused him trouble which no one would understand who did not know the extent to which before the Abdication the Duke of Windsor's brothers admired and looked up to him." These telephone conversations between the two brothers proved particularly hard for George VI, since they tended to exacerbate his speech impediment, particularly when some question arose affecting Mrs Simpson. Apart from advising his brother how to conduct himself as monarch, the Duke of Windsor also used the telephone to protract the wrangle of the legal and financial settlement following the abdication. The Duke of Windsor was later to recall in a series of articles published in the *New York Daily News* in 1966 that his brother found these discussions over his property rights irksome, but that to him they were a matter of life and death. In the end, it was left to Walter Monckton to advise the Duke of Windsor that the telephone calls must cease. The bitterness which the Duke felt at being forbidden to contact his brother frequently was felt long after the King's death.

The Duke of Windsor also felt ill-used by his family at the time of his wedding to Mrs Simpson. It was George VI who was finally responsible for the choice of the Chateau de Candé, near Tours, for his brother's wedding, and although the Duke had no objections to the choice of the chateau, he naïvely expected that his family would in some way attend the ceremony. The Duchess of Windsor was later to write, "David longed to have his sister and brothers, and most of all his mother, near him at his marriage . . . But . . . the unspoken order had gone out; Buckingham Palace would ignore our wedding. There would be no reconciliation, no gesture of recognition. That also meant that many of the friends with whom David had made his life would find it awkward to come to Candé."[21] Among those friends who found it impossible to attend the wedding was Lord Louis Mountbatten – the

Duke of Windsor had earlier expected him to be best man. However, the Duke may have gained some comfort from the fact that when he married Mrs Simpson on 3 June 1937, he received "a very nice telegram" from King George VI and Queen Elizabeth. A telegram also arrived from Queen Mary.

The rift between the Windsors and the Royal Family was not helped by the newly married couple's visit to Nazi Germany in the summer of 1937. The Nazi propaganda machine was quick to make capital out of the visit, and the Windsors met many leading Nazis, including Goering, Himmler, Hess, Goebbels, and finally the *Führer* himself. Both the Duke and the Duchess waxed enthusiastic at what they saw in Nazi Germany, particularly praising workers' houses and conditions in the factories, hospitals and youth camps. Wherever they went they were given an unexpectedly enthusiastic welcome by the German people. In return, the Duke was reported as having given the full Hitler salute on at least two occasions.[22]

In the circumstances, it is not surprising that relations between the House of Windsor and the ex-King remained decidedly cool. Although during the Second World War, and after desperate appeals to his brother and the British Government, the Duke of Windsor was allowed to become Governor of the Bahamas from 1940–45, the post could hardly be described as of first-rate importance in the war effort. Perhaps this was just as well, for the Duke's governorship was not without controversy; indeed, he sometimes expressed blatant colour prejudice, insisting, for example, that a white man be given the job of liaison officer between the Bahamians and the American contractors who were to build airfields on the island. Many years later, Lord Louis Mountbatten asked the Duke, ". . . if the stories circulating there that in his day coloured men were not permitted to enter through the front door were true. The Duke freely admitted it and said that it was important for the successful administration of the government that coloured people should be kept in their right place when visiting Government House."[23] Shortly afterwards, Nassau had its first riot.

If the Duke was tactless and narrow-minded, the Duchess was even more unpopular. She seemed inordinately preoccupied with her appearance, and her displays of jewellery and fine clothes were judged unsuitable to the role of a governor's wife of a small group of islands. The American press were soon reporting that she needed to visit Miami every week to have her hair done, and that while in Nassau she bought on average a hundred dresses a year from New York at approximately 250 dollars each.

After the war the Windsors remained estranged from the Royal Family, and although the Duke of Windsor came to the funeral of George VI in 1952, he came alone; he was also alone when he came to bury his mother a year later. After her accession to the throne, however, Queen Elizabeth II set about achieving a reconciliation with the Windsors. When the Duke came to London for an operation on his eye, and was accompanied by the Duchess, Queen Elizabeth II went to visit them, and in 1964 she was careful to send him a telegram congratulating him on his seventieth birthday. Although these personal gestures of reconciliation were not welcomed by Elizabeth the Queen Mother, who had come to believe that her husband's premature death was partly the result of the great burdens that had been passed on to him after the abdication. Elizabeth II went further in 1966. In that year she invited both the Duke and Duchess of Windsor to the unveiling of a commemorative plaque to Queen Mary. The Windsors rode in the official procession, and the public saw photographs of them meeting and talking with the Queen and with the Queen Mother – this was the first time that the Duchess of Windsor had been publicly recognized by the British monarch. When, in May 1972, the Queen paid a state visit to France, she visited her uncle's house in the Bois de Boulogne, where he was desperately ill with cancer of the throat. The Queen was accompanied by the Duke of Edinburgh and by the Prince of Wales. All three were photographed greeting the Duchess before going up to see the dying man.

When the Duke of Windsor died, eight days later, his body was flown to London and his widow was invited to stay at Buckingham Palace as the Queen's personal guest. The Duchess was treated with sympathetic courtesy by the Royal Family, and the Prince of Wales and Lord Louis Mountbatten accompanied her when she went to see her husband lying in state in the chapel at Windsor. The Duke was buried privately in the royal burial place at Frogmore, and it was understood that the Duchess would in due time lie beside him in a space reserved for her.

This tardy and gradual reconciliation could not have been achieved during George VI's reign. Quite apart from any personal resentment felt towards the Duke and the Duchess of Windsor over the abdication crisis, the new King had been obliged to work hard to restore public faith in the stability of the monarchy. There had even been some voices raised calling for the establishment of a republic. In the debate in the House of Commons on the Abdication Bill, James Maxton, Chairman of the Independent Labour Party, moved an amendment calling upon the House to reject the bill ". . . which has been necessitated by circumstances which show clearly the danger to this country and the British Commonwealth of Nations inherent in an hereditary monarchy, at a time when the peace and prosperity of the people require a more stable and dignified form of government of a republican kind, in close contact with, and more responsive to, the will of the mass of the people, and which fails to give effect to the principle of popular election."[24] Maxton's amendment was defeated by 403 votes to 5, but that it had been put at all indicates the bitter feelings aroused by the abdication crisis, and the serious political consequences which might have flowed from it.

George VI was fully aware of the gravity of the position, and realized that the whole fabric of the monarchy might crumble under the weight of the crisis. He wrote to Stanley Baldwin soon after his accession, hoping "that time will be allowed to me to make amends for what has happened". For one who set great store by order, the uncertainty and stress that accompanied his brother's abdication were particularly unpleasant, making it impossible for George VI to stretch out the hand of friendship and forgiveness to the Duke and Duchess of Windsor. The malicious rumours and speculation that had abounded at the time of the abdication, Maxton's amendment to the Abdication Bill, the crowds around Buckingham Palace shouting "Down with Baldwin, we want the King", all indicated that unprecedented forces were at work. Above all, would the new King be able to cope adequately with the demands of his great office?

Published to coincide with the new King's coronation in May 1937, a book written by an "American Resident" and entitled *The Twilight of the British Monarchy* reflected the mood of introspection and doubt. The author pointed out the contradiction that the British monarchy, though almost completely devoid of political power (evidently the King could not even choose a wife without the consent of the Prime Minister of the day), at the same time had "a vaster influence over the minds and social life of a great portion of the people than that of any Dictatorship in Europe". But, "In no other western monarchist country in Europe is Royalty less democratic, so widely separated from the people, so aloof, so profoundly snobbish socially as in this politically most democratic of all countries."[25] Turning to the traumatic events of December 1936, the author claimed:

> The abdication of Edward was not the revolt of a king against his ministers or parliament, but something greater – the revolt of a king against his own institution, the Monarchy. No more original revolt has been known in English history than that of the king who rebelled against himself and the symbol he stood for. If English society was not so hopelessly and stolidly Tory, even to its Labour Party, an act of this kind might have fired the imagination of the people, and have led to many profound social and spiritual changes.[26]

What of the aftermath of the abdication? The author believed that there had been no substantial growth in republicanism, though, "It is true that Republicanism is at the moment probably stronger in England than at any time since the days of Joseph Chamberlain . . ." At least the crisis, in the view of the author, had broken some taboos: people were now talking more frankly of the Royal Family, seeing them clearly as human beings with problems and desires like their own. "The genuine modesty and reticence of the new King may help to consolidate the new, less glamorous position of the Monarchy, and make it a position as quiet and unassuming socially as it is politically." On the other hand, the Coronation in May 1937 could be seen as the swan song of the British monarchy. The author dismissed it as "the finishing touch of the Act of Abdication" – Baldwin's final flourish to his greatest masterpiece. It was bound to be "more a sad than a gorgeous affair", and was only being mounted on a large scale to disguise the "conspicuous absence of real glamour and jollity . . ."[27]

In the five months between the King's accession and his coronation in May 1937, the royal couple struggled to adjust to their new roles, and the new Queen, with her usual aplomb, set about transforming Buckingham Palace into a more homely place. This was no easy task. The vast building, with its antiquated services and facilities, and its six hundred rooms, had been basically neglected by Edward VIII, who had preferred to put his money into his home at Fort Belvedere. After some effort, "Queen Elizabeth succeeded in dragging at least part of Buckingham Palace into the twentieth century, with a minimum of new carpets and curtains in the rooms they actually used, and the maximum of flowers . . . A family atmosphere costs nothing; and in

Queen Elizabeth the Royal Family at last acquired a creative artist in home life. Perhaps for the first time since the Stuarts, the Royal Family were now completely united and at ease with one another."[28]

The Queen's informality and her dislike of stuffy protocol meant that, as one of her first acts, she scrapped the traditional custom of children of the monarch curtseying or bowing to their parents, so that the two Princesses could now rush to greet their parents as they had always done. Significantly though, and as a tactful recognition of other standards, the two Princesses still curtseyed to their grandmother, Queen Mary. For her part, "Queen Mary drew nearer to her son and daughter-in-law in those weeks before the Coronation than in her husband's lifetime. She had been ill in the winter of the Abdication — she had actually lost two stones in weight — but the thought that they depended on her for help and advice did more to restore her than anything else. She threw herself into the arrangements for the Coronation, with a cheerful concentration on realities that dispelled the nervous tension around her."[29] Both the new King and Queen went out of their way to integrate Queen Mary into their activities. "The King showed the greatest kindness to his mother, and the Queen, with loving intuition, constantly asked her advice, which pleased her very much."[30]

Despite his initial misgivings, George VI became markedly more assured and self-confident as the early months of his reign passed by. An eye witness who came into close contact with him at Aintree during March 1937 later wrote, "I was quite unprepared for the change in him. All diffidence had gone. Those hesitant gestures that had been characteristic of his personality had been replaced by a sureness of movement and an ease of manner that would have marked him out if he had been surrounded by a hundred men."[31]

Uncertainty as to how the King would cope with his new responsibilities, and what effect the strain of the Coronation would have upon him, did lead to the postponement of the proposed Accession Durbar, which was planned for the winter season of 1937–38 at Delhi. In 1911, shortly after being crowned, King George V had gone to his Indian Empire to be acclaimed King-Emperor before his Indian subjects. George VI was anxious to fulfil his obligations towards his Indian Empire in a similar fashion, but his physician, Lord Dawson of Penn, argued that the exhausting programme of a Durbar following so soon after the strain of the Coronation and its preliminaries might prove too much for the King and Queen. It was also considered unwise for the monarch to leave the United Kingdom, necessitating the appointment of Councillors of State, barely a year after the abdication crisis. On the other hand, both the Secretary of State for India, Lord Zetland, and the Viceroy, Lord Linlithgow, were anxious that the King should make the trip to India.

Having weighed the different arguments, the King decided against going to India, and wrote to Lord Zetland, saying, "Much as I should like to meet the wishes of yourself and the Viceroy, I do feel that from a personal point of view it would be better to postpone the visit until the winter of 1938–1939. As the Viceroy himself said in his recent telegram (which you quoted in your letter of January 18), 'I do need time to settle in.' "[32] This commonsense decision, based on a realistic appraisal of his own capacities, unfortunately meant that the King would never see his Indian Empire, for in January 1938 the proposed visit was again postponed, this time indefinitely, due to Britain's continued failure to placate the aspirations of Indian nationalists.

The day of the Coronation was set for 12 May 1937. The Archbishop of Canterbury, Dr Lang, believed that the ceremony in Westminster Abbey should be constructed to emphasize, ". . . to the peoples of the British Commonwealth the real and spiritual significance of the Coronation, to associate them with it in a way never before attempted, and to establish the position of the Sovereign, in Bagehot's phrase, as 'head of our morality'."[33] In order to reach as many people as powerfully as possible, Dr Lang wished the service inside the Abbey to be broadcast by the BBC. Despite his own anxieties over his speech impediment, the King resolutely supported the Archbishop of Canterbury against those who were opposed to broadcasting the service. As a consequence, the Coronation was broadcast to many millions, both throughout the British Empire and beyond.

The King also approved several major changes in the order of the service; the most significant of these alterations was to the form of the oath, where a formula had to be found to satisfy the Dominions who, since the Statute of Westminster of 1931, were kingdoms in their own right. The oath was eventually rephrased, and the question put to the King became, "Do you solemnly promise and swear to govern the peoples of Great Britain, Ireland, Canada, Australia, New Zealand and the Union of South Africa, of your possessions, and the other territories to them belonging or pertaining, and of your Empire of India, according to their respective laws and customs?" These constitutional matters settled, the King approached his Coronation glad to give expression to his sense of service and duty in the beautiful ceremonial at the Abbey. At the same time, he faced a great ordeal, as he well knew that behind the scenes at public ceremonials things could often go wrong. The King's own account of the day illustrates, often wryly, the stresses and unforeseen complications of the great event:

We were woken up very early, about 3.0 am, by the testing of the "loud speakers" which had been placed in Constitution Hill; one of them might have been in our room. Bands & marching troops for lining the streets arrived at 5.0 am so sleep was impossible. I could eat no breakfast & had a sinking feeling inside. I knew that I was to spend a most trying day, & to go through the most important ceremony in my life. The hours of waiting before leaving for Westminster Abbey were the most nerve racking. At last the time came & we drove in the State Coach to the Abbey in our robes.

On our arrival our pages & train bearers met us to carry our robes to our retiring rooms.

Elizabeth's procession started first but a halt was soon called, as it was discovered that one of the Presbyterian chaplains had fainted & there was no place to which he could be taken. He was removed however after some delay & the procession proceeded & arrived in position.

I was kept waiting, it seemed for hours due to this accident, but at last all was ready for my progress into the Abbey. This went off well & my pages & I negotiated the flight of steps going up to the Sacrarium. I bowed to Mamma & the Family in the gallery & took my seat. After the Introduction I removed my Parliamentary Robes & Cap of Maintenance & moved to the Coronation Chair. Here various vestments were placed upon me, the white Colobium Sindonis, a surplice which the Dean of Westminster insisted I should put on inside out, had not my Groom of the Robes come to the rescue. Before this I knelt at the Altar to take the Coronation Oath. I had two Bishops, Durham & Bath & Wells, one on either side to support me & to hold the form of Service for me to follow. When this great moment came neither Bishop could find the words, so the Archbishop held his book down for me to read, but horror of horrors his thumb covered the words of the Oath.

My Lord Great Chamberlain was supposed to dress me but I found his hands fumbled & shook so I had to fix the belt of the sword myself. As it was, he nearly put the hilt of the sword under my chin trying to attach it to the belt. At last all the various vestments were put on & the Archbishop had given me the two sceptres. The supreme moment came when the Archbishop placed the St Edward's Crown on my head. I had taken every precaution as I thought to see that the Crown was put on the right way round, but the Dean & the Archbishop had been juggling with it so much that I never did know whether it was right or not. The St Edward's Crown, the Crown of England, weighs 7 lb, & it had to fit. Then I rose to my feet & walked to the throne in the centre of the amphitheatre. As I turned after leaving the Coronation Chair I was brought up all standing, owing to one of the Bishops treading on my robe. I had to tell him to get off it pretty sharply as I nearly fell down. The Homage of the Bishops & Peers went off successfully.[34]

In the circumstances, King George VI's deportment during his coronation service was a triumph. No one knew better than him that the ceremony required precision and much rehearsing, and he was quoted in *Time* magazine in March 1937 as saying, "Not only must you be letter-perfect with your lips, but with your feet. If you turn left instead of right, or step back instead of forward, you throw the whole show out of gear."[35] *Time* also quoted the King as saying, prior to his coronation, "according to the papers, I am supposed to be unable to speak without stammering, to have fits, and to die in two years. All in all, I seem to be a crock!"[36]

The assured bearing of the King during the service indicated that vital stability and continuity had been restored to the British monarchy. The fact that Queen Mary and the two Princesses – Elizabeth now aged just eleven, and Margaret Rose six and a half – were in the Abbey to watch the King and Queen crowned also emphasized the strong bonds of family unity that now bound the House of Windsor together.

Broadcasting from Westminster Abbey immediately after the conclusion of the Coronation, Howard Marshall recalled some of the highlights of the event:

We shall never forget the moment when the King himself appeared in his crimson Parliament robes, greeted by those thrilling fanfares and the shouts of the Westminster boys, preceded by the shining Swords of State, surrounded by the gorgeous vivid scarlet of his train-bearers – the most brilliant centrepiece of the pageant.

And the Queen in her procession – the Queen alone. As she came, how eagerly Princess Margaret Rose peered round the corner of the Gallery, and Queen Mary raised her lorgnette . . .

The concentration round St Edward's Chair. The slow interweaving of it all – the pattern of purple, crimson and gold, copes and robes – and Queen Elizabeth's crimson train spread out like a fan across the gold carpet; and the King standing alone, looking strangely youthful, during the historic ceremonial of the Recognition. How closely the Princesses watched that ceremony!

. . . And then the wonderful moment when the hymn swelled out from the choir and the Archbishop took the golden ampulla to prepare the King's anointing. And while the hymn was being sung, I remember so vividly His Majesty's intense seriousness as he leant at his crimson faldstool. And behind him in the Royal Gallery, Princess Elizabeth put Princess Margaret Rose's robe straight because it was in danger of wriggling off her shoulders . . .

And so we came to the climax. The King in his long iridescent golden robes under the central light. About him, in those robes, an almost Oriental look somehow . . .

I remember the Archbishop in his long Cope, standing alone in that circle of light before the Coronation chair, still and frail rather, waiting for the moment of crowning . . .

And Princess Margaret couldn't quite see over the head of the Queen's train-bearers, so she stood on tiptoe, and behind the King massed together the Peers and great Officers of State, and the pages carrying the coronets. And then the Archbishop lifting the heavy Crown high above the King's head, holding it there for a moment without sign of strain, and placing it gently in position . . .

And there is the Archbishop, the centre of the great scene again as he addressed the King; and then the extraordinary emotion which swept through the congregation – the unrehearsed effects of acclamation – the cries of "God Save the King"; the pealing of bells outside; those wonderful fanfares; the ripple of colours as the Peers assumed their coronets, and the Kings of Arms their crowns; until the anthem carried us onto the quiet thankfulness of the Benediction; and so to the final gorgeous pattern of the homage . . .[37]

From across the Atlantic, *Time* magazine had its own, less awed, way of describing the service:

It was the Middle Ages in the midst of Modern Times – arc lamps, newsreel cameras, radio microphone hanging high above the chancel, pneumatic tubes to speed copy from the press box to the telegraphs downstairs. The crowd that rose in the Abbey to greet their King was aware of all this. Five months of intensive propaganda had told them what this 1937 Coronation was held for: a gorgeous and expensive pageant of the solidarity of the British Empire, and the permanence of British institutions in a changing world.[38]

After the ceremony, King George VI and Queen Elizabeth, anointed and crowned, drove through miles of streets lined with cheering people who seemed oblivious to the rain that was falling. The next day the King and Queen drove again through the streets of London, concentrating on the East End, and once more received a rapturous reception from the crowds. Within the next six weeks they undertook a strenuous programme, showing themselves to the people, culminating with a visit to Northern Ireland between 27 and 29 July. Despite his new responsibilities, King George VI even insisted on making his annual visit to what was still called the Duke of York's Camp, flying up to Southwold on 3 August.

On 26 October 1937 he opened Parliament in State. Since this meant making his first speech from the throne, the prospect caused him a great deal of anxiety, especially since he believed that the sitting position from which the speech was to be delivered would upset the rhythm of his breathing and that his stammer might return with full force. However, with Lionel Logue's help and lengthy rehearsals, he was able to deliver the speech successfully, though there were some hesitations.

At the end of the year, the King and his family went to Sandringham for Christmas. On Christmas Day he made his first broadcast to the people, though informing them that it was not his intention to follow his father's tradition of an annual broadcast: "But as this is the first Christmas since our Coronation, the Queen and I feel that we want to send to you all a further word of gratitude for the love and loyalty you gave us from every quarter of the Empire during this unforgettable year now drawing to its end."

King George VI could be well pleased with the first year of his reign: he had successfully stepped, not into his brother's shoes, but into his father's. "Into everything that he had had to do, he had thrown himself with an energy, and an ever-ready cheerfulness and amenity."[39] He was doubtless gratified to receive at this time a letter from the Archbishop of Canterbury which, after reminding the King that he was used to meeting "all sorts and conditions of people, from Cabinet Ministers to the man in the street", said:

> At first, the feeling was one of sympathy and hope. It has now become a feeling of admiration and confidence . . . I *know* this to be true.
>
> I notice, all who have in any way come into contact with Your Majesty have noticed, how remarkably and steadily, if I may presume to say so, You have *grown into* Your high office. Thus the courage with which a year ago You accepted the burden of a great responsibility suddenly thrust upon You, has been amply vindicated.[40]

Despite the personal satisfaction which the King could justifiably feel as the second year of his reign opened, his nation and his Empire faced an uncertain future. Although the British economy had recovered from the worst effects of the great depression, the growing strength of the fascist dictatorships of Germany and Italy posed a grave threat to the continuing peace of Europe. At the end of May 1937, having waited for the Coronation to be over, Stanley Baldwin resigned his office of Prime Minister. He was succeeded by Neville Chamberlain, ex-Lord Mayor of Birmingham, and son of Joseph Chamberlain, one of the most controversial of Victorian and Edwardian politicians. Chamberlain was not unlike his father: "Masterful, confident, ruled by an instinct for order, he would give a lead, and perhaps impart an edge, on every question. His approach was ordinarily careful, but his mind, once made up, hard to change; he would make relevance a fundamental, and have the future mapped out and under control, thus asking his departmental ministers to envisage two-year programmes."[41]

Neville Chamberlain was to remain George VI's Prime Minister until his resignation in May 1940. Cold, self-sufficient, obstinate and high-minded, he soon won the admiration of the King – a sympathy perhaps partly based on the recognition by one shy man of another, but also owing a great deal to the Prime Minister's capacity to keep the King fully informed upon every aspect of government policy. One result of the trust established between Prime Minister and monarch was that the King steadfastly supported Neville Chamberlain's attempts to maintain peace in Europe.

In this sense, George VI supported the policy of appeasement. This does not mean that he wished to surrender to the dictators – on the contrary, he conceived it as his duty to preserve the integrity of the British Empire at all costs. Nor had the young naval officer who had fought in HMS *Collingwood* in the Battle of Jutland been transformed into a middle-aged pacifist. Put very simply, Neville Chamberlain's policy of appeasing the axis powers was a creative alternative to forming an alliance against them, and being prepared to go to war sooner rather than later. Chamberlain also believed, rather ingenuously perhaps, that it was possible, through personal diplomacy, to make fruitful contact with fascist dictators who were, after all, "members of the human race". Nor was the country in a position, in 1937, to contemplate war against Germany: although Britain had begun to rearm in a leisurely fashion following Hitler's occupation of the Rhineland in 1936, there was still much leeway to make up before an all-out war could be contemplated. In addition, having so recently experienced the horrors of the First World War, the nation wished to preserve peace. George VI therefore supported the policy of appeasement in the sense that he wished to avoid a precipitate war. His official biographer has summarized his position thus:

> King George was very deeply a man of peace. The prospect of the peoples of his Commonwealth and Empire being plunged into war shocked and appalled him. To him, the counsels of patience and reason were ever more welcome than those of precipitance, and, whereas he viewed with horror the more bestial aspects of the dictatorships, he was at one with his Prime Minister in believing that no reasonable effort must be spared to prevent the dictators from involving the world in a general conflagration.[42]

Not every member of Neville Chamberlain's government, however, was prepared to support the policy of appeasement. In particular, in February 1938 the Foreign Secretary, Anthony Eden, expressed his distaste for Hitler's bullying tactics towards the Austrian Chancellor, Dr Schuschnigg, who had been summoned to a meeting at Berchtesgaden; neither could he believe that Chamberlain's policy of opening negotiations with Mussolini would preserve the integrity of Austria. Rather, he was convinced that Hitler was free to act so aggressively towards Austria because the Italian government had already given him secret assurances that they would not oppose a German occupation of that state. When he discovered, during lengthy Cabinet meetings on 19 and 20 February 1938, that the Prime Minister's desire to open negotiations with Italy had the backing of the vast majority of his colleagues, the Foreign Secretary resigned. The King only learned of this from the headlines in the newspapers on Sunday 21 February, and expressed his annoyance that he had not received prior information.

However, Eden's resignation was no great blow to the King, who had been unable to establish close personal relations with the Foreign Secretary. He felt more at ease with Eden's successor, Lord Halifax, partly because he was on very cordial personal terms with him, and partly because Halifax was a confident exponent of the Prime Minister's policy of appeasement.

A month after Eden's resignation, Nazi Germany annexed Austria. Hardly had Austria been incorporated into the Reich, than Hitler began his campaign to bring the German-speaking areas of Czechoslovakia, the Sudetenland, under German rule. The *Führer's* demands set in train a sequence of diplomatic manoeuvres that were to reach an apparent climax with the Munich agreement of the autumn of 1938, but which did not prevent the German conquest of Czechoslovakia in March 1939.

On 12 September 1938, Hitler, speaking at a rally at Nuremburg, signalled the intensification of Nazi Germany's campaign to annex the Sudetenland. Chamberlain now decided to intercede personally in the crisis, and on 15 September flew to confer with Hitler at Berchtesgaden. There now began a series of highly dramatic meetings between the British Prime Minister and the *Führer*, which ended with the signing of the Munich agreement on 30 September 1938 – a sordid contract which sacrificed the integrity of Czechoslovakia for the fragile prospect of a lasting peace in Europe.

George VI warmly and consistently supported Neville Chamberlain during these negotiations, and when Chamberlain arrived back from his first meeting with Hitler on the evening of 16 September, he found a letter waiting for him at the airport: "My dear Prime Minister, I am sending this letter to meet you on your return, as I had no opportunity of telling you before you left how much I admired your courage and wisdom in going to see Hitler in person. You must have been pleased by the universal approval with which your action was received."[43] When the Prime Minister flew back to Heston Airport on 30 September, waving the piece of paper bearing the text of the agreement for Anglo-German friendship signed by Hitler, he found another letter waiting for him from the King, requesting that he should come straight away to Buckingham Palace "so that I can express to you personally my most heartfelt congratulations on the success of your visit to Munich". Chamberlain and his wife duly appeared on the balcony of Buckingham Palace, at the side of the King and Queen, and received a grateful reception from the crowds below. War seemed to have been averted, and peace with honour achieved. "Yesterday was a great day," the King wrote to Queen Mary. "The Prime Minister was delighted with the result of his mission, as we all are, & he had a great ovation when he came here."[44]

Despite the gratitude with which many British citizens greeted the news of the Munich agreement, voices of criticism were also heard. Among the most notable of these was Winston Churchill, at that time in the political wilderness and demanding rapid re-armament. It was soon evident that even within the Conservative party, Chamberlain's action had not won universal applause. On 2 October 1938 Duff Cooper, First Lord of the Admiralty, resigned from the Cabinet, and the following day a House of Commons debate revealed bitter hostility to appeasement on both sides of the House. The King's reaction to these critics was expressed in a letter he wrote to Queen Mary saying, "I am sure you feel as angry as I do at people croaking as they do at the PM's action, for once I agree with Ly. Oxford, who is said to have exclaimed as she left the H. of Commons yesterday, 'He brought home Peace, why can't they be grateful' – It is always so easy for people to criticize when they do not know the ins and outs of the question."[45]

The King's support of Chamberlain's policy was very much the response of the ordinary, decent-minded man who wanted to preserve peace. If his whole-hearted endorsement of Chamberlain's initiatives was naïve, it was naïvety shared with more sophisticated observers, and there is not a shred of evidence to suggest that George VI supported the fascist dictatorships in the way that Edward VIII had. All the same, it is interesting that, in 1946, H. G. Wells, writing in *Socialist Leader*, asked whether the King was involved in Mussolini's pre-war financial support of Sir Oswald Mosley's fascist movement. If this were the case, Wells said, "there is every reason why the House of Hanover should follow the House of Savoy into exile". In the United States, *Time* magazine, reporting this remarkable outburst, said, "Everyone seemed to agree that this time old H.G. had really put his foot in his gabby mouth. Snorted Mosley: 'Absolute nonsense.' The Keeper of the Privy Purse (treasurer to the King) thought it 'most amusing'. Most Britons ignored it; H. G. Wells simply did not understand a King who was neither tyrant nor snob, who merely served his people as a symbol of their past, their pride and their good manners.''[46]

By March 1939, however, Chamberlain's "peace with honour" was exposed for the illusion that it was. The Czech President, Dr Hácha, was browbeaten into placing the remnant of his country under German protection, and by the evening of 15 March the *Führer* was in Prague. From the Hradschin Castle, the palace of the Kings of Bohemia, he declared, "Czechoslovakia had ceased to exist." George VI was as disillusioned and downcast as Neville Chamberlain by the failure of the Munich agreement, and he consoled his Prime Minister by telling him, "I am sure that your labours have been anything but wasted, for they can have left no doubt in the minds of ordinary people all over the world of our love of peace & of our readiness to discuss with any nation whatever grievances they think they have."

The German dismemberment of Czechoslovakia, and the new demands Hitler made almost immediately against the sovereignty of Poland brought about a diplomatic revolution in Britain. Appeasement had failed. It was now up to the British Government to rearm as rapidly as possible, and to offer guarantees of support for Poland which might finally deter German aggression. On 31 March, Neville Chamberlain announced in the House of Commons that both Britain and France had given guarantees to Poland that they would support her, by going to war if necessary, against any German assault. Exactly how Anglo-French forces were to be deployed to protect Poland's western frontier was not clear, and perhaps did not matter greatly. What was now evident was Britain's determination to stop the rot in Europe, and if necessary to fight Nazi Germany.

As Britain prepared seriously for war at last, the *Daily Mirror* in April 1939 made much of the King's visit to the RAF School for Aircraft Apprentices at Halton in Buckinghamshire. While inspecting the school, George VI met Sergeant-Warden Christian outside a workshop and, with a smile of recognition, said "I remember you. You were at Cranwell with me." The *Daily Mirror* carried a photograph of the King inspecting a classroom at RAF Halton, placing under it a caption which was virtually an advertisement for the RAF: "Well, here's the class. LOT OF EMPTY PLACES ON THE DESKS, AREN'T THERE? One of the best jobs in the Services is the Air Force, and one of the most important. TAUGHT A TRADE YOU ARE, TOO, BOYS. A DARNED GOOD

WAGES TRADE. WHY NOT FILL ONE OF THOSE PLACES?"[47]

If the RAF was to be Britain's first line of defence, it was also necessary to cultivate allies. In the summer of 1938, as Hitler built up his campaign for the "return" of the Sudetenland to the Reich, George VI and Queen Elizabeth went on a state visit to France. The visit was a timely reminder of the common interests of Britain and France, and if it was expedient diplomatically, it was also tremendously successful at a more personal level. Queen Elizabeth in particular, though in mourning for the recent death of her mother and wearing white in remembrance of her, enchanted the Parisian crowds. "We have taken the Queen to our hearts," the French press announced. "She rules over two nations." Lady Diana Cooper remembers, "We saw the King and Queen from a window, coming down the Champs Elysées, with roofs, windows and pavements roaring exultantly, the Queen a radiant *Winterhalter*."

A year later the King and Queen paid similar visits to the United States of America and to Canada. The Prime Minister of Canada, Mackenzie King, had originally broached the subject of a royal visit to Canada in 1937, and with the subsequent worsening of the diplomatic situation in Europe, it seemed more than appropriate to respond favourably to the American invitation to extend the royal visit to include Washington and New York as well. President Roosevelt issued the invitation in order to offer visible proof of the depth of Anglo-American friendship, and Mrs Roosevelt was later to write, "My husband invited them to Washington largely because, believing that we all might soon be engaged in a life and death struggle, in which Great Britain would be our first line of defence, he hoped that the visit would create a bond of friendship between the people of the two countries."[48]

George VI had some misgivings at leaving Britain at a time of grave uncertainty, and partly salved his conscience by refusing to sail to Canada in HMS *Repulse* on the grounds that the battleship could not be spared by the Royal Navy. Before this decision was taken, he had refused to have a gun-mounting removed from the cabin he was to occupy, on the grounds that as a naval man himself he was used to that sort of thing.[49]

The King and Queen eventually sailed in May, aboard the liner *Empress of Australia*. The voyage across the North Atlantic was extremely hazardous, and the *Empress of Australia* was delayed by two days as she negotiated thick fog and icebergs. Eventually, on 17

[163]

May the royal couple landed at Quebec. Thus began the first ever royal visit to Canada by a monarch and his consort, and the success of the tour exceeded all expectations. Huge crowds greeted the royal couple with an outpouring of affection which took many local observers by surprise. If there had been any anxiety that Canada would pursue a neutralist course in future conflict between Britain and Germany, the patriotic response of the country dispelled any such fantasy. The Governor-General, Lord Tweedsmuir (the novelist John Buchan), later wrote to a friend in Scotland, "Our Monarchs are most remarkable young people. I have always been deeply attached to the King, and I realize now more than ever what a wonderful mixture he is of shrewdness, kindliness and humour. As for the Queen, she has a perfect genius for the right kind of publicity." Lord Tweedsmuir was particularly impressed by Queen Elizabeth's spontaneity:

> ... at the unveiling of the War Memorial, where we had some 10,000 veterans, she asked me if it was not possible to get a little closer to them. I suggested that we went right down among them if they were prepared to take the risk, which they gladly did. It was an amazing sight, for we were simply swallowed up. The faces of the Scotland Yard detectives were things I shall never forget! But the veterans made a perfect bodyguard. It was wonderful to see old fellows weeping, and crying, "Ay man, if Hitler could just see this." The American correspondents were simply staggered. They said that no American president would have dared to do that. It was a wonderful example of what true democracy means, and a people's king.[50]

On 9 June King George VI and Queen Elizabeth entered the United States of America. Although both Edward VII and Edward VIII had visited the United States when they were Princes of Wales, this was the first time that a reigning British king had set foot on United States soil. The visit lasted only three full days, and was undertaken amid an intense and humid heat, its progress dogged by the not always friendly attentions of a multitude of reporters. However, it was a tremendous and not altogether expected success.

Interest in the American press at the prospect of a royal visit had been intense. Towards the end of May, Sir Ronald Lindsay, British Ambassador to the United States, had held a press conference to try to satisfy the curiosity of the American reporters. Sir Ronald had to field a number of gauche questions:

Should American men bow from the waist when they meet the King? Sir Ronald thought they might do as he did when meeting the President – "... behave in a simple and respectful manner. I certainly make him a bow. Whether it comes from the waist or not I don't know."

Would the Queen "do something human while she is here, like going shopping?" Sir Ronald almost swallowed his walrus moustache at that one. If shopping became necessary, he thought Her Majesty probably would send her maid.[51]

If the vast American crowds who turned out to see the King and Queen expected a rigid, old-world formality from them, they were soon disabused. The King's youthful appearance, his evident friendliness and good humour, were disarming. To many American observers, "Elizabeth was the perfect Queen: eyes a snapping blue, chin tilted confidently... fingers raised in a greeting as girlish as it was regal. Her long-handled parasol seemed out of a story book."[52]

Washington, "its streets jammed with citizens and soldiery, thundered salutes and applause". At a garden party given at the British Embassy, the King and Queen met a steady stream of American notables. There, according to a contemporary account:

A standard device of the King's was to exclaim about the youth of people he met. Said the King to Under Secretary of the Treasury, John Hanes: "You look very young for such an important post!" Said Hanes: "Your Majesty, I will not grow old in it." When a presentee dropped a coin in confusion, the sweltering King cracked, "Finders keepers!" But he did not pick it up.

He was well coached. When he met South Carolina's senior senator, he said: "Cotton Ed Smith?" ... Of the Queen's lace-trimmed parasol, an old-timer said: "I haven't seen one of those since the Taft Administration."[53]

Perhaps the most valuable part of the royal visit to the United States of America came when the King and Queen spent some informal hours with President and Mrs Roosevelt at their home at Hyde Park, New York. The royal procession had received a rapturous reception as it drove the ninety miles to Hyde Park, and arrived noticeably late. When the royal couple at last arrived, President Roosevelt had a tray of cocktails waiting for them, but said, "My mother thinks you should have a cup of tea; she doesn't approve of cocktails." "Neither does my mother," said the King, and reached out his hand to take one.

At Hyde Park, informality was the rule:

The King shed his necktie, ate hot dogs, drank beer (Ruppert's) at a "dream cottage" picnic, photographed the Indian storyteller and singer who performed. Squire Roosevelt whizzed the Royal pair around in his Ford with manual brakes and gear shift, giving Scotland Yard palpitations. He and the King had another swim. By this time the Roosevelts had developed a father-&-motherly feeling towards this nice young couple ("very, very delightful people" was the President's authorized phrase), who they were quick to entertain at home as no President since Taft could have done.[54]

The twenty-four hours which the King and Queen spent at Hyde Park were not merely passed in fostering affectionate goodwill with the Roosevelts. George VI spent several hours talking, in some depth, with the President about what help the United States would give to Britain in the eventuality of her finding herself at war with the fascist powers. The King made detailed notes of his conversations with the President, and imparted the substance of them to his government when he returned home. Although Roosevelt was over-optimistic as to when the United States could be persuaded to enter such a war – "If London was bombed, the USA would come in" – the conversations "nevertheless contained the germ of the future Bases-for-Destroyers deal, and also of the Lend-Lease Agreement itself".

Alaric Jacob was one of the three newspaper men who travelled in the royal train. In his autobiography, *Scenes from a Bourgeois Life*, Jacob relates an incident when the train stopped at Banff, in the Rockies, which illustrates the diplomatic importance of the visit:

In the hotel there, an American correspondent, who had dined too well, asked the King, who had relaxed over dinner, whether he thought the trip would produce American support for England in the event of war.

To this indiscreet enquiry, the King gave an indiscreet reply. "It's in the bag" he said.

Soon afterwards, the correspondent was found in a befuddled condition in a telephone booth trying to transmit this story to New York.

The rest of us dragged him out of the booth by force, and agreed among ourselves that on no account should the unfortunate aside be published anywhere, since to do so would not only constitute a breach of confidence but would also be dangerous politically.[55]

The significance of the visit to North America was not lost upon the British public. When the King and Queen returned to London on 23 June 1939, more than fifty thousand people crowded round the gates of Buckingham Palace to give them a heartfelt welcome home. According to the *Daily Mirror*, "the roar could be heard in the Strand above the noise of London's traffic." Over a large picture of the welcoming crowd, the *Mirror* proclaimed in banner-headline type, "TO OUR LOVE AND GRATITUDE YOU ENTER ONCE AGAIN YOUR HOME IN THE EMPIRE'S HEART." The paper believed that the King and Queen "have rendered the nation great service . . . and yesterday the nation came to thank them".[56]

Partly as a result of the outstanding success of their North American tour, the King and Queen now realized that they were firmly established as popular and effective heads of state. In the view of King George VI's official biographer:

The North American tour was indeed a climacteric in the King's life. It had taken him out of himself, had opened up for him wider horizons and introduced him to new ideas. It marked the end of his apprenticeship as a monarch, and gave him self-confidence and assurance. No longer was he over-awed by the magnitude of his responsibility, the greatness of his office and the burden of its traditions. Now at last, he felt he could stand on his own feet and trust his own judgement.[57]

Such self-assurance was timely, as within a few weeks of the royal couple's return from North America, the situation in Europe began to deteriorate rapidly. On 22 August, the announcement of the Soviet-German pact of non-aggression opened the way for Hitler's assault on Poland, and despite a desperate flurry of diplomatic activity, on 1 September 1939 the German army crossed the Polish border.

There was now no vacillating on the part of the British Government, as in the immediate past. Both Britain and France stood by their guarantees to Poland. An ultimatum was issued demanding that the Germans should withdraw their troops behind their own frontiers, or face an Anglo-French declaration of war.

No reply from Germany was received, and at 11 am on Sunday 3 September, Great Britain and France went to war with Hitler. George VI wrote that day in the diary that he was to keep for the duration of the war and beyond:

As 11 o'clock struck that fateful morning, I had a certain feeling of relief that those 10 anxious days of intensive negotiation with Germany over Poland, which at moments looked favourable, with Mussolini working for peace as well, were over. Hitler would not & could not draw back from the edge of the Abyss to which he had led us. . . .

At the outbreak of War, at midnight of Aug. 4th–5th, 1914, I was a midshipman, keeping the middle watch on the bridge of HMS 'Collingwood' at sea, somewhere in the North Sea. I was 18 years of age. . . .'

Today we are at War again, & I am no longer a midshipman in the Royal Navy.

For the last year ever since the Munich agreement, Germany, or rather its leaders, have caused us incessant worry in crises of different magnitudes. Hitler marched into Czecho-Slovakia in March this year. Then Memel. We knew the Polish Question would be the next on the list of Hitler's bloodless victories. The whole country knew it, & had been preparing for it, by making arms, aeroplanes & all the engines of war in record time, to withstand the next real Crisis.

So today when the Crisis is over, & the result of the breakdown of negotiations is War, the country is calm, firm & united behind its leaders, resolved to fight until Liberty & Justice are once again safe in the World. . . .[58]

That evening, King George broadcast to his nation and his empire. (The air-raid sirens had already wailed in the afternoon before the King's speech.) In his broadcast, the King asserted that the British Government had declared war against "the mere primitive doctrine that Might is Right". He went on, "If this principle were established throughout the world, the freedom of our own country and of the whole British Commonwealth of Nations would be in danger. But far more than this – the peoples of the world would be kept in the bondage of fear, and all hopes of settled peace and of the security of justice and liberty among nations would be ended." The King concluded with an exhortation which, in its directness and power, foreshadowed the broadcasts which Winston Churchill was later to make during the darkest days of the war:

> It is for this high purpose that I now call my people at home and my peoples across the Seas, who will make our cause their own. I ask them to stand calm and firm and united in this time of trial. The task will be hard. There may be dark days ahead, and War can no longer be confined to the battlefield. But we can only do the right as we see the right, and reverently commit our cause to God. If one and all we keep resolutely faithful to it, ready for whatever service or sacrifice it may demand, then, with God's help, we shall prevail.[59]

For the second time in three decades, Britain was at war with Germany. Whether the outcome would be as successful as before, however, was by no means clear.

13

THEIR FINEST HOURS
1939–1941

I am very worried over the general situation, as everything we do or try to do appears to be wrong, & gets us nowhere.
George VI, March 1940

Personally, I feel happier now that we have no allies to be polite to & to pamper.
George VI to Queen Mary after the fall of France, 1940

GEORGE VI'S BEARING DURING the Second World War, and particularly during the first two years of the conflict when it seemed that Britain might at any moment be invaded and overwhelmed, confirmed his reputation as a monarch of supreme integrity and courage, a people's king. From the outbreak of war he never appeared in public except in uniform, a powerful symbol that he, like the whole of his people, was on active service. When in 1940 France fell and German bombers passed again and again over London, George VI stood in the front line. During these perilous times:

> George VI did not falter. This seems easy and obvious now. It was different at the time. Probably only the united resolve of King and Prime Minister prevented a wholesale scuttle of Court, Government and Parliament into the country. Such plans had been made by the previous Government. George VI and Churchill tore them up. The King and Queen remained steadfastly at Buckingham Palace through the heaviest bombing.[1]

Such kingly resolve was an inspiration to his people, and, by a curious quirk of history, had been forecast nearly two centuries before. In 1763, three years after George III ascended to the throne, a book had been published in England entitled *The Reign of George VI, 1900–1925*. This eighteenth-century prophetic fantasy set the reign of the future King George VI amid a great, and at first disastrous, war against a mighty European power – in this case Russia. The imaginary George VI faced early and catastrophic defeat in the greatest European war in which his country had so far been involved; when Russian warships scattered the British Navy in a battle off the Dutch coast there was confusion and panic in England, with a run on the Bank and stocks and shares plummetting. In these dire circumstances:

> The King . . . was undismayed . . . but it was a clap of thunder to every mortal besides. . . . In this critical moment all eyes were upon the King, as the only pilot in so terrible a storm. It was impossible to be guided by a better; and had not Britain possessed a Sovereign of such singular intrepidity and prudence, she would have seen her last days.[2]

In September 1939, the real George VI was the head of a world-wide empire at war, just as his father had been in August 1914 – but much had changed since those days. Whereas in 1914 the British declaration of war had committed the whole empire automatically to hostilities, in 1939 the Dominions, under the 1931 Statute of Westminster, could decide for themselves whether or not to become belligerent powers. At first sight, the preservation of Poland's sovereignty was not essential to the interests of the British Dominions. Indeed, it was arguable that Hitler was genuine when he claimed that he had no designs on the British Empire. Once Germany had acquired her *Lebensraum* (living space) in Eastern Europe and the Ukraine, it was quite conceivable that her ambitions would not include the acquisition of an empire that was already difficult to govern. To some, Britain's involvement in the conflict seemed a quixotic gesture, lacking real meaning. After all, Britain had co-operated with totalitarian and autocratic governments in the past. It was also difficult, as in 1914, for the British Government to proclaim a crusade for freedom when full political freedoms were simultaneously withheld in large parts of the Empire.

As it happened, reaction to the war was predictably varied. Australia and New Zealand considered themselves bound by the mother country's declaration of war, though no doubt Australasian dependence upon Britain's defence system in South-East Asia and the South Pacific was as potent a factor as traditional loyalty. Canada, as befitted the senior Dominion, availed herself of the right to defer any decision to her own Parliament – though when the Canadian House of Commons met the week after the outbreak of War it declared itself unanimously in favour of entering the hostilities. In South Africa the Nationalist Prime Minister, Hertzog, hoped to remain neutral. A resolution to this effect was put before the Union Parliament at Cape

Town, but an amendment by Smuts, which was pro-British and anti-German, secured a majority of thirteen votes. Failing to secure a dissolution of Parliament from the Governor-General, Hertzog resigned and Smuts, ever eager to don uniform, took over the premiership. Afrikaner opposition to the war, however, was considerable. The "purified" Nationalists led by Malan and Strijdom, were unashamedly pro-Nazi; the Government interned some of these extremists, including three future prime ministers of South Africa.

The Irish Free State proved that the Statute of Westminster was no hollow statement of Dominion sovereignty by declaring itself neutral. It maintained a meticulous official neutrality throughout the conflict, even though there could be little doubt which side the de Valera government wanted to win, and recent evidence suggests that it would have accepted British military assistance in the event of a German invasion. In practical terms, though, the Free State's decision denied the Royal Navy the use of its Southern Irish bases, which would have been useful in containing the U-boats. Official neutrality did not, however, prevent thousands of Southern Irishmen from joining the United Kingdom's forces. Ulster was, of course, part of the United Kingdom, yet the British Government showed itself sensitive to the Republican sympathies of its large Catholic minority by exempting the six northern counties from conscription.

If the Dominions' reaction to the outbreak of war was uneven, so was India's. The Viceroy simply announced that war had broken out between the King-Emperor and Germany. No democratic process was followed. The Muslim League was prepared to accept Britain's decision, but although the Congress Party in general disliked Nazi Germany, the official British attitude to India's involvement in the war rankled. In the Indian provinces, Congress ministries resigned in protest. Nonetheless, the Empire-Commonwealth as a whole rallied to Britain's side. Dominion, British, African, West Indian, Asian and Polynesian troops fought throughout the conflict and in many of the theatres of war. The fact that the Dominions were able to choose whether they entered the conflict or not strengthened their eventual participation. If the war was being fought to make the world safe for democracy, it was at the very least appropriate that the democratic process had been followed in the self-governing portion of the Empire at the outbreak of war. The royal family's practical commitment to the war was soon plainly demonstrated. On 7 September 1939, *News Review* reported that:

Three most striking signs of war at the Palace were: Guards and sentries in khaki and steel helmets, members of the Royal Household in khaki and blue uniforms, and high household officials walking back to their homes at St James's Palace, each carrying a gas-mask in a cardboard box.

Several household officials, like other members of the Royal Family, have already taken up war duties. Captain Michael Adeane, Assistant Private Secretary to the King, who is in the Grenadiers, is acting as a Railway Transport Officer.

Both the Dukes of Gloucester and Kent have joined up for war service. Rear Admiral the Duke of Kent, relinquishing his dearly anticipated plans for the Governor-Generalship of Australia, is at the Admiralty. His brother is at the War Office.

Still at Balmoral are Princesses Elizabeth and Margaret. Daily the elder Princess writes to her mother and father, and when the lines are free the King and Queen have a brief chat to her by telephone.[3]

At the outbreak of war, Neville Chamberlain set about reorganizing his government. It was not possible to form a coalition war cabinet, as both the Liberal and Labour parties declined to become associated with a prime minister whose national reputation was already badly damaged. Chamberlain did, though, manage to bring two rebel Conservatives into his government: to the King's surprise, Winston Churchill went to the Admiralty, and Anthony Eden took the post of Secretary of State for the Dominions.

While George VI was called upon merely to approve these ministerial changes, he set about using still more influence to rally Britain's potential allies to her cause. On 11 September 1939 he had a lengthy interview with Joseph Kennedy, American Ambassador to the United Kingdom, and the father of the future president of the United States. Joseph Kennedy had been a strong supporter of Chamberlain's policy of appeasement, and he apparently expressed to the King his incredulity that Britain should pursue a war which might financially ruin her and which was apparently being fought to protect the territorial integrity of Eastern Europe. The next day, having absorbed what Joseph Kennedy had said to him, and disturbed that such views would be transmitted to Washington, the King wrote the Ambassador a frank letter.

As I see it, the USA, France & the British Empire are the three really

[173]

free peoples in the World, & two of these great democracies are now fighting against all that we three countries hate & detest, Hitler & his Nazi regime and all that it stands for. You were speaking about the loss of prestige of the British Empire under the changed conditions in which we live since the last war.

England, my country, owing to its geographical position in the World, is part of Europe.

She has been expected to act, & has had to act, as the policeman, and has always been the upholder of the rights of smaller nations.

The British Empire has once again shown to the World a united front in this coming struggle . . .

I know that you appreciate things when they are plainly expressed, & that is why I do so now.

And I do it in a very friendly spirit as I have a tremendous admiration for your country, for your President & for yourself.

We stand on the threshold of we know not what. Misery & suffering of War we know. But what of the future? The British Empire's mind is made up. I leave it at that.[4]

George VI also sent a personal message to King Boris of Bulgaria, a ruler for whom he had a genuine liking, and who had won his admiration by his prowess with a gun. Bulgaria had fought on the German side in the First World War, and was more than likely to find herself once more allied with Germany in the second. King Boris received George VI's letter in Sofia on 22 September 1939, and was apparently deeply moved by the King's references to his own efforts for peace in 1938. "How good of him to remember that," he said several times tearfully. Thus encouraged, King Boris threw his weight behind those members of his government who wished to keep Bulgaria neutral. George VI repeated his exhortation to King Boris a little over a year later, when Bulgaria was tempted to join the war on Germany's side and to realize some of her territorial ambitions in the Balkans. This second appeal to King Boris undoubtedly helped to keep Bulgaria out of Hitler's clutches for the time being, although by March 1941 the country succumbed to German pressure and joined the Axis Pact.

In the early weeks of the war, George VI also made a substantial contribution to the conclusion of the Franco-British Treaty of Alliance with Turkey. When General Mehmet Orbay, head of the Turkish military mission, arrived in London in October to negotiate the terms of the treaty, he came demanding a wide range of armaments, many of which were in short supply in both Britain and France. When his demands were not met General Orbay soon showed signs of wishing to return home. On 11 October 1939, however, he was received in a private audience with the King, and in his conversation with the disgruntled general, George VI explained clearly, ". . . that we need all our guns & aircraft here & in France, as the seat of War is now on the Western Front. I did my best to tell him this too." This combination of frankness and personal charm worked wonders with General Orbay, and two days later he was much more accommodating in his conversations with the French and British representatives. On 19 October the Allies' Treaty of Alliance with Turkey was signed.

While George VI was conducting these diplomatic initiatives, all seemed quiet on the Western Front. The British and French armies were positioned behind the Maginot Line awaiting a German attack; but no attack materialized, and the months of curious inactivity were soon nicknamed the Phoney War.

On the Eastern Front, on the other hand, a great deal had happened: Germany had overrun Poland, and the Soviet Union had invaded from the east and also occupied a substantial portion of Poland, including the Galician oilfields. In addition, Russia had occupied the Romanian-Polish and Romanian-Hungarian frontiers to block a German advance into the Balkans. On 24 September the King summarized events in his diary: "After 3 weeks of War, many strange things have taken place. It is all an amazing puzzle." George VI also noted that Mussolini was proclaiming his desire to stop the war, and that it was thought certain that Hitler would offer Britain and France peace terms after the Polish question had been settled. "Germany," the King wrote, "has not interfered with our mobilization in any way, & has not raided us from the air. Why? We must wait and see."[5]

Various peace offers did ensue. On 6 October Hitler spoke of his desire to achieve peace with Britain and France before the Reichstag, and early in November King Leopold of Belgium and Queen Wilhelmina of the Netherlands offered to act as intermediaries between Germany and the governments of Britain and France. George VI was at one with his government in robustly rejecting these proposals, writing in his diary, "We cannot make peace with Hitler, as the whole reason for our being at war with him still holds good."

During these first months of the war, the King made a number of visits to his forces in the field, and in the first week of October he made a trip to visit the fleet at Scapa Flow. The journey to Scapa was undertaken in a special bullet-proof train, leaving from Euston Station. The King boarded the train at platform six in the utmost secrecy, with detectives and policemen guarding all the approaches, and with an engine and empty carriages drawing alongside to screen the number six special from view. When the train eventually steamed out of the station, neither the driver nor the fireman knew their eventual destination: they were informed from halt to halt. In this way the King, often accompanied by Queen Elizabeth, travelled some 52,000 miles during the war, visiting and encouraging the people.

It is symptomatic of King George's commonsense approach that he travelled so much in this bullet-proof train. Insisting that it was out of the question for great landowners or important local officials to meet him and to give him quarters for the night during wartime, the King instead made extensive and effective use of the train. The royal apartments had air-conditioning, coach-to-coach telephones, electric fires, mechanical cushioning to reduce vibrations, and every comfort the experts could devise. The King and Queen each had their own coach, with a lounge, a dining car, sleeping cabins, bathrooms, and accommodation for the King's valet and the Queen's maid. Despite these undoubtedly luxurious conditions, and the maintaining of the Victorian convention that men and women passengers should travel in different ends of the train, separated by the royal coaches in the middle, the King acknowledged the restrictions of wartime by scrapping elaborate menus and ordering the preparation of simple three-course meals to conform with rationing laws. In order to ensure the King's safety, the peacetime practice of printing and distributing in advance royal train timetables was abandoned, and a pilot engine always left the station fifteen minutes in front of the royal train.[6]

In December the King made a visit to the British Expeditionary Force in France, and inspected the British troops in their positions; he also conferred with the Commander-in-Chief, Lord Gort, and met French leaders, including President Lebrun, Daladier, and General Gamelin. It is interesting, in view of his chronic seasickness when serving as a junior officer in the Royal Navy during the First World War, that the King suffered no ill-effects while crossing the Channel during the worst weather conditions for several weeks:

Throughout the one and a half hour trip he stood at the bridge of the warship that brought him over. The deck below was frequently awash as the man-of-war buried her nose in the swirling waves.

The King, who had walked to the bridge as soon as the warship nosed out of harbour to face the gale, stood serene and calm, revelling in the battle against the elements.[7]

It was pointed out in the British press that the King "stepped ashore twenty-five years to within two days after his father King George V paid his first visit to the Front in 1914". The King's programme was also similarly outlined: "he will tramp through the mud just like [the troops] do. He will see their trenches, their forts, their guns. And, equally important, how they live." The *Daily Mirror* understood "that this is to be the most democratic royal visit ever made". Sir Piers Legh wrote to Queen Elizabeth, "the really salient feature to my mind was that the King showed a vital interest & understanding of the difficulties and problems which confront the highest and the lowest of all ranks of the BEF, and this fact was mentioned to me again & again during the visit."

The King also visited civilian workers during the Phoney War period. At the end of October 1939 he inspected a munitions factory "somewhere in the Midlands", where one of the female workers sorting out live bullets said to him, "If I had my way, each one of these would have Hitler's name on it." Standing by her side, George VI tried to sort out, as she had to do, the live bullets from the dud ones. After a while, "he laughed and said: 'I'm no good at it.'"[8]

In March 1940, he spent several hours inspecting the Dover Patrol and, for a while, acted as the ticket-collector for troops from the BEF entraining at a port to begin a spell of leave. This piece of light-hearted fun was reported in the press:

A sergeant of the BEF, coming ashore at a south-east coast port yesterday on leave, hurried to the barrier to reach the waiting train. He thrust his papers into the hands of a man in naval uniform standing by the ticket collectors.

Suddenly he gave a gasp of surprise, straightened to attention, and saluted. The ticket collector was the King.

The King tore the sergeant's ticket from his book of passes and handed the book back with a smile, and the sergeant hurried on.

The King was on the quayside to watch nearly a thousand men come ashore and few, in their eagerness to continue their journey, recognized him.[9]

Still the war in the West seemed curiously muted, although there had been one or two British successes at sea. In December 1939, a British cruiser squadron had eliminated the "pocket battleship" *Graf Spee* in the Battle of the River Plate, and in the middle of February 1940 a Royal Navy destroyer had rescued three hundred British merchant seamen from the German prison-ship *Altmark*.

Neville Chamberlain's government remained in power during this time, but was embarrassed, in January 1940, by the resignation of Leslie Hore-Belisha, the controversial and energetic Secretary of State for War. In March 1940 George VI declared himself "very worried over the general situation", and his anxieties were not lessened by the clear indication that President Roosevelt could not give aid to Britain on the scale suggested during his conversations with the King at Hyde Park during the royal tour of 1939. "The fact is," the King recorded rather despondently in his diary, "the U.S. is not coming in to help us, & nothing yet will make them, but they are pro-British in the main."

In April the war entered a new and more threatening phase. On 4 April, Neville Chamberlain announced over-optimistically, "Hitler has missed the bus." On 9 April Germany attacked Denmark and Norway. Although initially there were high hopes that the Royal Navy would come into its own in helping Norway resist a German attack, this was not realistic. By 4 May, except for a pocket of Allied resistance at Narvik, Norway was in Nazi hands. The Allies' foothold at Narvik could not be sustained for long, and Britain and France had quite clearly suffered a serious defeat.

The humiliating failure of the Norwegian campaign precipitated a crisis in the House of Commons. On 7 May, on the first day of the Commons debate on Norway, speaker after speaker turned upon Neville Chamberlain and his administration. Lloyd George, "the man who had won the war" of 1914–18, appealed to the Prime Minister to "give an example of sacrifice, because there is nothing that can contribute more to victory than that he should sacrifice the seals of office." Leopold Amery, a distinguished Conservative minister between the wars, quoted the words of Cromwell as he dismissed the Long Parliament in a passionate denunciation of Neville Chamberlain: "You have sat here too long for any good you have been doing. Depart, I say, and let us have done with you. In the name of God, go!"

George VI's first reaction to the opening of the Norwegian debate was to rally to his Prime Minister's support. He told Chamberlain that he would speak to Attlee, the Labour Party leader, to try and persuade Labour to join a national government. Still unwaveringly loyal to Neville Chamberlain, and perhaps disconcerted by the breaking of ranks in the Conservative party, George VI said of his Prime Minister, "I did not like the way in which, with all the worries and responsibilities he had to bear in the conduct of the war, he was always subject to a stab in the back from both the H of C and the Press."[10]

The next day in the House of Commons, Chamberlain accepted the challenge of the Labour opposition to press for a vote on a motion of adjournment – in effect, a vote of confidence. The vote on the motion showed a dramatic collapse of support for the Government: the normal majority of over two hundred had been reduced to eighty-one. When the figures were announced there was: "A gasp, and shouts of 'resign, resign,' . . . Chamberlain stood up, erect, unyielding, sardonic, and walked out past the Speaker's Chair and over the feet of his colleagues, who then followed. The Government benches cheered, while the Socialists shouted: 'Go, in God's name, go!'"[11]

Two days of feverish political intrigue followed this vote on 8 May 1940. At first, Chamberlain attempted to form a National Coalition Government with the support of the Labour Party. If his own resignation should prove the necessary price to pay for forming a national administration, Chamberlain indicated that his preferred successor would be Lord Halifax. 9 May closed with the Prime Minister awaiting the response of the Labour Party's Executive to the proposition that they should enter a National Government either under the present Prime Minister or under another.

On 10 May, Britain's political crisis was put into even sharper and more urgent perspective by the news that Germany had at last mounted a full-scale assault on the Low Countries and upon France. Chamberlain came under renewed and persistent pressure to resign, and at the same time the Labour Party Executive announced that they would only enter a National Government under another Prime Minister.

In the early evening of 10 May, Chamberlain went to Buckingham Palace and offered the King his resignation. George VI's response to these dramatic events was predictably loyal, but perhaps lacked a real understanding of the situation. The day before he had declared, "It is most unfair on Chamberlain to be treated like this after all his good work. The Conservative rebels like Duff Cooper ought to be ashamed of themselves for deserting him at this moment." When the Prime

Minister tendered his resignation, the King, ". . . told him how grossly unfairly I thought he had been treated, and I was terribly sorry that all this controversy had happened." The King suggested Halifax as Chamberlain's successor, but the Prime Minister indicated that Halifax was not enthusiastic. George VI "was disappointed over this statement, as I thought H. was the obvious man".[12]

The King "knew that there was only one person that I could send for to form a Government, who had the confidence of the country, & that was Winston." Churchill accepted the King's invitation to form a government, and on the next day, 11 May, completed the composition of his wartime coalition administration. Neville Chamberlain stayed on as Lord President of the Council, and the Cabinet now consisted of ministers from all three parties.

Although he carried out his constitutional duty and sent for Winston Churchill to form an administration, George VI seems at first to have regretted it. On 11 May he wrote, "I cannot yet think of Winston as PM . . . I met Halifax in the garden & I told him I was sorry not to have him as PM." The King's misgivings over Churchill were partly due to the regret he felt at losing Neville Chamberlain as his Prime Minister, and partly reflected the anxieties over Churchill's past conduct. After all, Churchill had been a leading supporter of Edward VIII during the abdication crisis, had resigned the Conservative whip, and had bitterly denounced the policy of appeasement with which the King had become identified. Churchill's career had been too erratic, and his capacity to break the rules too marked, for the King to feel comfortable with him at first. The King, moreover, was shy and modest, whereas Churchill was ebullient and convinced of his own superior abilities.

Fortunately, Churchill also had an abundance of charm and tact, and the King, with practical good sense, wanted the arrangement to work:

It was not long before the King was regarding the Prime Minister's audiences with pleasurable anticipation. He had fruitful opportunities for a common unburdening of mind, and by September [1940] the formal audiences had been replaced by regular Tuesday luncheons, at which the King and his Prime Minister, serving themselves from a side-table, would transact State business undisturbed save by an occasional air-raid."[13]

For his part, Churchill "valued as a signal honour the gracious intimacy with which I, as First Minister, was treated, for which I suppose there has been no precedent since the days of Queen Anne and Marlborough during his years of power". By February 1941, George VI had set aside any of his initial doubts, writing in his diary, "I could not have a better Prime Minister." As it happened, the King and Winston Churchill provided a well-suited and in many ways complementary dual leadership of the British Empire during the Second World War. Churchill became a figure of world repute: dramatic, eloquent, passionate and indomitable; George VI provided an inspiration which was simple, straightforward, and heartfelt. Oddly, it was perhaps easier for ordinary men and women to identify with George VI's low-key, earnest and self-effacing style of leadership than with Churchill's more grandiose and grandiloquent deportment.

On Empire Day, 24 May 1940, George VI, despite his continuing dislike of the microphone, broadcast a message to all his people. This speech, confidently delivered, was a plainer counterpart of the inspiring and moving speeches with which Winston Churchill was to uplift the spirits of all those who fought against the fascist powers:

> The decisive struggle is now upon us. I am going to speak plainly to you, for in this hour of trial I know that you would not have me do otherwise. Let no one be mistaken; it is no mere territorial conquest that our enemies are seeking. It is the overthrow, complete and final, of this Empire and of everything for which it stands, and after that the conquest of the world. And if their will prevails they will bring to its accomplishment all the hatred and cruelty which they have already displayed. . . .
>
> Against our honesty is set dishonour, against our faithfulness is set treachery, against our justice, brute force. There, in clear and unmistakable opposition, lie the forces which now confront one another. The great uprising of the peoples throughout the Empire shows without doubt which will prevail . . . In perfect unity of purpose they will defend their lives and all that makes life worth living.[14]

The German attack upon the Low Countries and France in May 1940 changed the map of Western Europe and faced Britain with the very real prospect of invasion and defeat. Not merely were the Netherlands and Belgium overrun, but within a few weeks the French Army was utterly broken and demoralized, and the French government on the point of surrender. The fall of France, which had been preceded by Italy's attack upon that stricken country, left Britain alone to face the *Luftwaffe*'s attempt to break the Royal Air Force and to destroy the morale of the civilian population by the mass bombing of her cities.

George VI was touched at a personal level by the German conquest of the Low Countries, when in the middle of May he gave hospitality to the Dutch royal family, headed by the redoubtable Queen Wilhelmina, who had escaped from the Nazi forces. King Haakon of Norway also found refuge in Great Britain, but King Leopold III of Belgium chose to make a premature surrender of his forces to the Germans on 27 May, and then proceeded to stay in his occupied country. Belgium's surrender exposed the flank of the British Expeditionary Force in France, and was bitterly attacked in the United Kingdom. George VI tried to persuade Leopold to escape to Britain, there to rally resistance to the German occupation of his country, but his personal intervention failed to move King Leopold. Although sympathizing with his fellow-monarch's dilemma, the King was disappointed by his inaction, and with German armoured columns driving towards the Channel ports, there was no alternative but to evacuate as much of the British Expeditionary Force as possible. During the last days of May and the early days of June, the Dunkirk evacuation took place. By 6 June the bulk of the BEF had been brought home, together with over 111,000 French troops.

Even while the Dunkirk operation was taking place, the French government was slipping towards surrender. Both the King and Winston Churchill tried to sustain the French leaders by messages of encouragement and exhortation, but by 16 June it was all over – Reynaud, the French Prime Minister, resigned, and Marshal Pétain, the hero of Verdun, formed a government and immediately sued for armistice terms. The Vichy régime and collaboration speedily followed. Britain and her Empire now faced Germany and Italy alone. Although head of an Empire which comprised approximately one-fifth of the human race, Britain could draw upon few of these Imperial resources in the perilous months which lay ahead. When, at the end of July, Hitler gave his final orders to the *Luftwaffe* to prepare the way for the invasion of Britain, it was the British people alone, with such Allied forces that were sheltering within their frontiers, who had to defend the British Isles.

*　　*　　*

As the Battle of Britain opened, and the RAF and the *Luftwaffe* fought for control of the skies, and as the German bombers began to pound Britain's cities and military installations, King George VI's leadership was at its most effective. After the fall of France, he had expressed feelings which were shared by the great majority of his subjects, "Personally I feel happier now that we have no Allies to be polite to and to pamper." Although there were plans to remove the Court and the administration to the country, King George VI refused to leave his capital, but travelled to Windsor each evening. Quite a considerable number of those who could afford it sent their wives and children overseas to escape from the blitz, but the King merely sent his two daughters to Windsor, just as children from London's East End were evacuated to the countryside. It had been suggested that the two Princesses should go to America, to which Queen Elizabeth replied, "The Princesses could not go without me; I could not leave the King; and of course the King will never leave."

By insisting on remaining in London, and thus claiming no special privileges or protection from the air-raids, the King and Queen established themselves and the monarchy still more firmly in the affections of the British people. This bond was strengthened on 9 September 1940, when a bomb fell on the north side of Buckingham Palace and exploded early the next morning. Although no damage was done to the main structure of the Palace, and there were no casualties, all the windows, including those of the royal apartments, were shattered by the explosion. Fortunately the King and Queen had been at Windsor, where they now slept each night.

Three days later, however, they faced a far greater hazard. As the King recorded in his diary, while he and the Queen were talking upstairs in his little sitting-room with Alex Hardinge, "All of a sudden we heard an aircraft making a zooming noise above us, saw 2 bombs falling past the opposite side of the Palace, & then heard 2 resounding crashes as the bombs fell in the quadrangle about 30 yds. away. We looked at each other & then we were out into the passage as fast as we could get there. The whole thing happened in a matter of seconds. We all wondered why we weren't dead."

Although it was not immediately known by the public that the King and Queen had been so close to death, the fact that the Palace had been bombed for a second time was, in a curious way, a boost for the nation's morale. The sense of shared danger and common cause, were

[183]

enhanced still further and the royal couple felt more at ease when making their tours of the bombed areas of London. The King wrote in his diary, "I feel that our tours of bombed areas in London are helping the people who have lost their relations & homes, & we have both found a new bond with them, as Buckingham Palace has been bombed as well as their homes, & nobody is immune from it." Queen Elizabeth said with more feeling, "I'm glad we have been bombed. It makes me feel we can look the East End in the face." The Palace was hit by bombs nine times in all.

Contemporary accounts of the King and Queen's visits to the bombed areas of British cities illustrate beyond any doubt the warm emotions which were generated on both sides. On 10 September 1940, the day the first bomb exploded at Buckingham Palace, the King visited East London, where he was given a tremendous reception:

> "It is wonderful – really wonderful – to know how brave everyone has been," he said. . . .
>
> Mrs Margaret Price was busy scrubbing her floor clear of falling debris caused by a bomb which had dropped 90 yards from her house when the King walked by. "Lor'" said Mrs Price. "If it's not the King – and me so untidy." She jumped up and waved to him excitedly. The King smiled back.
>
> His Majesty had to climb over a heap of debris to inspect some wrecked houses. "Nice work, mate!" a workman called out to him. . . .
>
> A woman broke through the crowds in one street to grasp the King's hand and say: "God bless and save you Sir, and the Queen and the Princesses." The King, obviously touched, shook the woman's hand and thanked her.[16]

In April 1941, the *Daily Mirror* printed a photograph of the King and Queen smiling at a crowd of East Enders who were smiling almost joyfully back at them. The *Mirror* caption read: "Look at this photograph – the King and Queen, the cop, the kids, the crowd – and not a gloomy face among them. The picture was taken yesterday when the King and Queen were in the bombed areas of London's East End; everyone in it has known the horror of Nazi hate raids, but knows, too, that though the War news is grave, IT'S NOT ALL BLACK."[17]

George VI found a sense of personal fulfilment that many of his subjects felt amid the perils and trials of the Second World War. In a way, wartime conditions suited him admirably. No great lover of luxury, the privations of total war made it easier for him to live simply. Food rationing was strictly enforced in the royal palaces, though perhaps an exception was made when Winston Churchill came to lunch. Once the King offered a sandwich to a visitor, exclaiming "I don't know what's in these, sawdust, I expect." He drank draught beer from preference, although in 1943 at one of his weekly luncheon meetings with Winston Churchill he produced a rare bottle of French wine, refusing to say, much to the annoyance of the Prime Minister, how he had got hold of it. (In fact, the bottle had been brought back to England by Group Captain "Mouse" Fielden, a member of the King's Flight, who ferried secret agents across the Channel in small aeroplanes.)[18]

Neither did the King require sumptuous entertainment in the evening. He detested opera, had no great love for serious theatre, and preferred musical plays and the music hall. He would infinitely rather listen to *Annie Get Your Gun* than to *Fidelio*. In any case, he liked best of all in the evenings to be at home with his family, listening to the radio – his favourite radio entertainer during the war was Tommy Handley of the ITMA shows. He also enjoyed projecting films in his small private cinema, showing a marked taste for instructive documentaries as well as the Marx Brothers. In all these ways, George VI was able to identify with the vast majority of his subjects.

He also set great store by hard work, and the Second World War gave him ample opportunity to work more zealously than any British sovereign, before or since. He was tireless in his round of duties, and insisted on decorating all ranks himself with service medals, which no king had done before. He made many visits to the fighting forces in Britain and overseas, and visited factories even more enthusiastically than before. He was still able to astonish industrialists and government officials by his detailed technical knowledge. He tried, too, to be of some practical use: when he learnt that there was a shortage of parts for anti-tank guns, he had a lathe installed at Windsor Castle, and worked on it at weekends.

A.J.P. Taylor has remarked, "The King loved working to rule. The War brought plenty of rules to which he could work." Certainly he took his duties as head of his household as seriously as any suburban father. During the blackout, he often stepped out into the courtyard to check whether any light was escaping from the Palace windows, and when it became necessary to conserve fuel, he insisted that the rooms of Windsor Castle and Buckingham Palace were kept in an appropriately chilly state. He even went round the family's bathrooms and marked the hot-water limit, five inches from the bottom, in each bath (he painted the mark himself, having measured the distance with a foot ruler). Although he always appeared in public in uniform, he made do with his pre-war stock of clothes, of which he admittedly had a plentiful supply. When his collars and cuffs wore out, he had new ones made from his shirt-tails.

Although King George VI and the Royal Family shared the wartime dangers of ordinary people, the King was especially at risk – there was the very real possibility that the Germans might somehow attempt to kidnap him. Aware of this eventuality, the King spent half an hour each morning at revolver practice in the grounds of Buckingham Palace. When he drove out in his car he always had a sten gun at his side, and the chauffeur had strict instructions to drive on in case of attack while the King shot it out with his assailants. He made it clear that, in the event of an enemy invasion, he was determined to die fighting for his life in the grounds of Buckingham Palace.

At the height of the blitz, the King devised a special decoration to reward the gallantry daily being demonstrated by the civilian population. This was the George Cross and Medal. Suspended from a dark blue ribbon, the decoration consisted of a plain silver cross with the royal cipher G.VI on the angle of each limb; in the centre was a representation of St George and the Dragon, surrounded by an inscription "For Gallantry". Although members of the military services could also win the George Cross, they could only do so in actions for which purely military honours would not normally have been granted. The King announced the creation of the George Cross, which he had himself designed with meticulous care, in a broadcast to Britain and the Empire, on 23 September 1940. For the work he did for his country during the worst years of the war, the King might well have merited the award of the George Cross himself.

The King's devotion to duty during the war years was matched by that of the Queen. Queen Elizabeth was endlessly busy: leading a working party which met twice weekly to make surgical dressings and comforters for the troops; sending thousands of letters of thanks to those who had received evacuees from the cities; travelling – sometimes with the King and sometimes not – to visit areas devastated by German bombing. The Queen gave considerable thought as to what clothes to wear when she toured the bomb sites. Deciding that uniforms did not suit her, she tended to wear clothes in a series of dusty shades, especially blue, lilacs and dirty pinks. The restrained colour of the Queen's clothes was both practical, in that they did not show dust from the ruined buildings, and sensitive, since they would not appear too light-hearted a choice to the victims of the blitz. The Queen always made an effort to wear her best clothes, saying, "If the poor people came to see me, they would put on their best clothes." Like her husband, she was determined to offer real resistance to any German invasion, and also practised firing a revolver in the grounds of Buckingham Palace. When Harold Nicolson, the National Labour MP and diarist, expressed his surprise, she said to him, "Yes, I shall not go down like the others." In fact the Queen did suffer an attack, of a sort:

> One day a half-crazed deserter whose family had all been killed in a raid found his way into the Queen's bedroom, threw himself at her feet and seized her by the ankles. It was like something from the Middle Ages. "For a moment, my heart stood absolutely still," remembered the Queen. Then, "Tell me about it," she said quietly, realizing that if she screamed he might attack her. He poured out his tale as she moved step by step towards the bell. "Poor man, I was so sorry for him," she said afterwards.[19]

The two Princesses also did their share of visiting, and towards the end of the war, on her own insistence, Princess Elizabeth was allowed to become a junior transport officer with the Auxiliary Territorial Service, the ATS. Like others, the Royal Family suffered bereavement during the war: in August 1942 the King's youngest brother, George, Duke of Kent, was killed when his RAF plane crashed in Scotland en route for Iceland. The King was naturally shocked at the death of his handsome and charming brother, but recorded proudly in his diary, "He was killed on Active Service."

While the RAF was winning the Battle of Britain and Hitler's bombers were pounding Britain's cities and towns, the King did his best to promote the country's war effort overseas, exerting whatever diplomatic pressure he could. He telegraphed an exhortation to Marshal Pétain in October 1940, urging the Vichy government not to collaborate with the Germans; he sent a strongly worded letter to King Farouk of Egypt to ensure that his government would fully support the

British in North Africa; and he tried to strengthen the spirit of resistance to Axis aggression among his Balkan cousins. Among these, George VI interceded personally with King Boris of Bulgaria, Prince Paul of Yugoslavia and King George of Greece. However, George VI's personal pressure did not alter the policies of the Balkan governments overnight – indeed, Prince Paul of Yugoslavia's vacillation led to a military revolution which proclaimed the end of his regency and put King Peter in power in his place. But in any case, the Axis invasion and conquest of the Balkans had the desired effect of bringing these states fully into the war.

By 1941, if Britain had successfully avoided a German invasion, and if the Empire's armies were at the very least holding their own in North Africa, victory still seemed very far away. The two great powers who could help turn the tide still held back from the conflict. In June 1941, however, Hitler launched his long-awaited attack upon the Soviet Union, giving the British Empire a potentially mighty ally in the East. Tactfully setting aside any ideological differences with Communist Russia, the British Government and people were relieved to find themselves allied with a nation which gave early proof that it was prepared to fight back with terrible determination against the advancing German armies. If Winston Churchill – who had earlier wanted to strangle Bolshevism in its cradle – could become the enthusiastic supporter of Soviet Russia's war effort, King George VI could equally try to forget the murder of his Romanov relatives after the Russian revolution. There is no doubt that the King admired the heroic resistance of the Soviet people in the face of the Nazi invasion, and in 1943 he warmly supported the sending of the specially made Stalingrad sword to Marshal Stalin. The two-edged blade was made of the hardest steel, and bore the inscription, "To the steel-hearted citizens of Stalingrad, the gift of King George VI, in token of the homage of the British People." When Winston Churchill presented the sword to Stalin at the Teheran Conference at the end of November 1943, the Soviet leader raised the weapon to his lips and kissed it. He was, according to eye witnesses, "deeply affected" – he had difficulty in replying, and when he did speak his voice was so low that he could scarcely be heard.

Although the Soviet Union was actively engaged in the war against the fascist powers by the middle of 1941, the United States still held aloof. Although three-quarters of American public opinion favoured the Allied cause at the outbreak of war, more than ninety-five per cent of the population were opposed to their country becoming involved in a war which seemed conveniently far away. For over two years, therefore, the best that Britain could hope for from her friendship with the United States was aid. George VI played a central and constructive part in the often difficult negotiations over the extent and nature of this American aid, and the warmth of the relationship which the King and Queen had established with President and Mrs Roosevelt during their American visit in 1939 stood Britain in good stead during these discussions. The King and the President exchanged a large number of letters during this period, the correspondence undoubtedly helping to oil the wheels of Anglo-American diplomacy.

At the same time, there was much hard bargaining between the two powers. Although in 1939 Roosevelt had proposed to the King a Western Atlantic Patrol operating from British bases, there were long delays before this was implemented. While the United States was prepared to send millions of dollars worth of arms in return for cash payments, there was initially resistance in Congress to the proposal to transfer fifty reconditioned United States destroyers of First World War vintage to the Royal Navy. These warships were desperately needed to provide escorts for the Atlantic convoys until British shipyards were able to produce vessels for the Royal Navy in sufficient numbers. In exchange for the outdated destroyers, the United States wanted the establishment of air and sea bases on ninety-nine-year leases in a variety of British possessions from Newfoundland down to British Guiana. Although the King had intervened personally with Roosevelt to bring about this agreement, he was also sympathetic to the anxieties of West Indian colonists who feared that the American leases were merely the thin end of the wedge of American economic penetration. He felt he had not become King-Emperor to preside over the dissolution of the British Empire, and was responsive to West Indian anxieties, minuting to his private secretary, Alexander Hardinge, on 30 December 1940: "The Americans have got to understand that in leasing the bases the question of Sovereignty does not come in. These islands are part of the British Colonial Empire, & I am not going to see my West Indies subjects handed over to the US Authorities." By the time the final agreement over the bases was signed in March 1941, most of the difficulties over the deal had been overcome.

On 12 December 1940, the British Ambassador to Washington, Lord Lothian, died suddenly of food poisoning. The question of his successor was vitally important to Britain's policy of maintaining the closest possible links with the United States, and although the name of the veteran Liberal statesman Lloyd George was touted as a possible replacement, the choice eventually fell upon Lord Halifax, still Foreign Secretary. The King played an important part in beating down Halifax's objections to taking up the embassy, and recorded the conversation in his diary:

> He was very unhappy at the thought of leaving here now, & was perplexed at what might happen if anything happened to Winston. The team was not a strong one without a leader, & there were always some hot heads among it. I told him he could always be recalled. By way of helping him, I suggested that the post of my Ambassador in the USA was more important at this moment than the post of Foreign Secy. here.[20]

When Lord Halifax reached the United States on 4 January 1941, he was honoured by being welcomed by the President in person. The King wrote a grateful letter of thanks to Roosevelt for this supportive gesture, and a fortnight later was able to offer repayment in kind when he met J. G. Winant, the new American Ambassador, personally at Windsor Station. Winant was fully aware of the significance of the meeting, writing later, "It was the first time in the history of Great Britain that a King had gone to meet an Ambassador."

Winant replaced Joseph Kennedy as American Ambassador. Kennedy departed largely unlamented, since, for all his undoubted abilities, he had not shown himself to be a true friend of Britain. With Roosevelt re-elected for an unprecedented third term, Halifax in Washington, and Winant in London, Anglo-American relations were now notably improved. In March 1941, despite opposition in Congress, cash payments for materials of war were replaced by the Lend-Lease agreement. The American Navy also began to give information to the Royal Navy as to the movements of German surface raiders and U-Boats in the Atlantic. The United States was now very close indeed to actively participating in the hostilities themselves.

Anglo-American accord was given further symbolic strength when Winston Churchill and President Roosevelt signed the Atlantic Charter in August 1941. George VI had urged the necessity for such a meeting upon the American government six months previously, and was now delighted at the meeting between the two "former naval persons" aboard the USS *Augusta* anchored in Placentia Bay, New-foundland. The eight points of the joint declaration by the President and the Prime Minister of 12 August 1941 involved sweeping wartime and post-war undertakings on the part of both powers. The King's first reaction to the charter centred very practically upon the fear that America would not fulfil her part of the declaration. He also believed that the provisions would be very difficult to carry out, ". . . as we should have to do it ourselves. The USA had deserted us after the Great War in Europe, & might easily do so again if she does not come in and feel the effects." The King's misgivings were substantially dispelled when Churchill, on 19 August, reported personally on the conference with Roosevelt. Among the reassurances that the Prime Minister could offer to the King was the news that "FDR has got £3,000,000,000 to spend on us here."

During the autumn of 1941, public opinion in the United States became more favourably disposed towards Great Britain and the prospect of eventual American involvement in the fighting. In November, the House of Representatives passed by eighteen votes a bill to amend the Neutrality Act, thus allowing American merchantmen to sail into war zones. The King noted in his diary, "This is a very great help to us, though it appears the President had to send a special message to Congress to have it passed. America is not nearly ready for War. But she will wake up when the enemy sink armed US merchantmen."[21]

Within a month, however, the United States was in the war. On 7 December, the Imperial Japanese Air Force, flying from carriers, bombed the American naval base at Pearl Harbor in Honolulu. Although unexpected, the Japanese attack was not without some provocation. For some time, the United States government had been perturbed by the rate and extent of Japanese expansion in East Asia and the south-west Pacific. Indeed, shortly after the signing of the Atlantic Charter, President Roosevelt had issued a serious warning to the Japanese government against any further encroachment in this part of the Pacific.

With the American Pacific fleet crippled, the Japanese now turned their attention to the Royal Navy, sinking the battleship *Prince of Wales* and the battle-cruiser *Repulse* off the coast of Malaya on 10 December. The King, with his close identification with the Royal Navy, was shocked and depressed by the virtual elimination of the British naval presence in Far Eastern waters, and within days, the

Japanese attacks upon Hong Kong and Malaya threatened to tear apart the British Empire in the Far East.

But at least, as 1941 drew to a close, Britain had two powerful allies on her side. The conflict had truly become a world war, but at the same time there was now a clear prospect of victory.

14

THE GRAND ALLIANCE

1941–1945

Says a Cockney, also gawking [at Buckingham Palace]: "He's a decent bloke, you know. Works hard. I wouldn't have his job." Says G.I. Joe: "Yeah, not much chance for promotion."
Time magazine, 6 March 1944

It was most encouraging to know that it was possible for me to land on the Normandy beaches only 10 days after D-Day.
George VI, 16 June 1944

ALTHOUGH BRITAIN BEGAN THE YEAR of 1942 with two great allies at her side, the next seven months were marked more by military catastrophe than by victory. Indeed, the turning of the tide seemed as far away as ever. On the night of 11 February, three German warships, the *Scharnhorst*, the *Gneisenau* and the *Prinz Eugen*, slipped out of the blockaded port of Brest and passed into the North Sea. Within four days of this naval humiliation, a far greater disaster occurred when the Imperial island fortress of Singapore, complete with garrison of nearly seventy thousand men, surrendered to the Japanese. The surrender of Singapore has been called "the greatest capitulation in British history". Certainly it dealt a massive, and perhaps fatal, blow to British prestige in the Far East, and allowed the Japanese navy to penetrate deep into the Indian Ocean. Meanwhile, there had been further disasters in North Africa. The German army there was now commanded by Rommel, and at the end of January the British, equipped with inferior tanks, had been driven out of Cyrenaica and pushed back to Tobruk.

George VI was deeply disturbed by these setbacks, writing to his mother, "I am very depressed over the loss of Singapore and the fact that we were not able to prevent the 3 German ships from getting through the Channel. We are going through a bad phase at the moment, and it will take all our energies to stop adverse comment and criticism from the Press and others." Also for the first time since becoming Prime Minister, Winston Churchill found himself the object of criticism, something he compared to "hunting the tiger with angry wasps about". The King defended Churchill as loyally as he had earlier defended Neville Chamberlain – rebellion and acts of opposition were disturbing to him, and he remarked in a letter to his uncle, the Earl of Athlone, then Governor-General of Canada, "I do wish people would get on with the job, and not criticize all the time". However, he had enough sense of perspective to add, ". . . but in a free country this has to be put up with."

Churchill weathered the criticisms, reshuffled the War Cabinet (to which was now added Sir Stafford Cripps), and although refusing to give up the post of Minister of Defence, won an overwhelming vote of confidence from the House of Commons on 25 February. The King expressed relief at Churchill's triumph, but commented shrewdly, "The House of Commons wants Winston to lead them; but they don't like the way he treats them. He likes getting his own way with no interference from anybody and nobody will stand for that sort of treatment in this country."[1]

At the end of February 1942, a mood of pessimism enveloped both the King and the Prime Minister, and Churchill, usually so ebullient and optimistic, confided to the King at one of their weekly luncheons, "Burma, Ceylon, Calcutta & Madras in India & part of Australia may fall into enemy hands." For his part, the King wrote in his diary on 28 February, "I cannot help feeling depressed at the future outlook. Anything can happen, & it will be wonderful if we can be lucky anywhere."

On the home front, a good deal was done to promote the cause of Anglo-Soviet friendship: Mrs Churchill raised a fund for Russian aid, Red Army Day was celebrated by leading figures of the establishment who generally hated communism, and the BBC added the *Internationale* to its roll-call of Allied anthems. There was some agitation, particularly from those on the political left, for the opening of a second front in Europe – something which did not happen for over two years. George VI received the Soviet Foreign Minister, Molotov, on 22 May, recording, "he looks a small quiet man with a feeble voice, but is really a tyrant. He was quite polite." Molotov's visit eventually produced an Anglo-Soviet Treaty of Alliance.

The spring of 1942 brought no relief to the Allies, and in Britain, the *Luftwaffe* began a series of "Baedeker" raids, bombing attacks upon historic cities like Exeter, Bath, Norwich and York. The King reacted angrily, "It is outrageous that the Germans should come and bomb our Cathedral cities and towns like Bath, which they know are undefended

& contain no war industries, as 'Reprisal' raids for what we are doing to their war industries."

Overseas, worse things than Baedeker raids were going on: the Japanese were pressing on the frontiers of the Indian Empire, the Americans had been driven out of the Philippines, the British and Dutch colonies in the East Indies had been conquered, and Japan was now completely dominant in the South Pacific. Elsewhere, the Russian armies had been beaten back across the Don river to Rostov, and in North Africa the German counter-offensive under Rommel was to result in the fall of Tobruk and the penetration of the *Wehrmacht* to El Alamein, sixty miles west of Alexandria, on 1 July. Early that month, the Prime Minister faced another vote of censure in the House of Commons, though surviving it by 475 votes to 25, with about 30 abstentions.

The vote of censure against Winston Churchill, however, immediately preceded a dramatic shift in the fortunes of the Allied Powers. On 2 July, Rommel's army was halted at El Alamein, and although not defeated, was never again to mount a major offensive in North Africa. In Russia, the Red Army began a summer campaign, which marked the beginning of the ultimately devastating counter-attack against the German forces. In Asia and the Pacific, where the Japanese advance had at last ground to a halt, there had been earlier encouraging signs in the defeat of the Japanese navy by the United States navy at the battles of the Coral Sea on 4 May and of Midway Island a month later. On 7 August, American troops landed on the Solomon Islands, thus taking the first step in a campaign of reconquest that was to end with the ultimate surrender of Japan.

At the end of October 1942, Anglo-American accord was further strengthened by the visit of Mrs Roosevelt to the King and Queen. Before his wife's arrival, President Roosevelt had written to the King, saying, "I want you and the Queen to tell Eleanor everything in regard to the problems of our troops in England which she might not get from the Government or military authorities. You and I know that it is the little things which count but which are not always set forth in official reports."[2]

Mrs Roosevelt's stay at Buckingham Palace brought home to her with full force the very real privations that were being endured in Britain. She arrived at a battle-scarred palace, and was lodged in the Queen's own bedroom which, because of the effect of bombing, had no glass in its windows, which were filled instead by small wooden frames glazed with mica. In keeping with the need to preserve fuel, Buckingham Palace was decidedly chilly, causing Mrs Roosevelt to write wonderingly in her diary, "I do not see how they keep the dampness out. The rooms were cold except for the smaller sitting-room with an open fire. In every room there was a little electric heater." She also noted that both the King and Queen were suffering from colds. The Palace's food was equally austere, including delicacies like dehydrated, reconstituted eggs, and pies, puddings and jams made out of root vegetables – this wartime fare was incongruously served to the President's wife on gold and silver plates. She was, at the same time, no doubt impressed by the comment of Lord Woolton, the Minister of Food, that the meals "might have been served in any home in England and . . . would have shocked the King's grandfather".

Having been personally conducted by the King and Queen on a tour of the bombed areas of London, Mrs Roosevelt left on 25 October, far better informed of the difficulties facing the British people. She later wrote of her visit:

The King and Queen treated me with the greatest kindness. The feeling I had had about them on their visit to the United States – that they were simply a young and charming couple, who would have to undergo some very difficult experiences – began to come back to me, intensified by the realisation that they now had been through their experiences and were anxious to tell me about them. In all my contacts with them I have gained the greatest respect for both the King and Queen.[3]

During Mrs Roosevelt's stay at Buckingham Palace, it was noticed one evening at dinner that Churchill, who was among the guests, was showing signs of suspense and anxiety. Eventually, he made his apologies and went to telephone Downing Street for news of the battle that was developing at El Alamein. Things were evidently going well for when he returned he was singing "Roll out the Barrel" with great enthusiasm.

After twelve days of heavy fighting, the Eighth Army, now led by General Bernard Montgomery, achieved the long-awaited defeat of the German Afrika Corps and their Italian allies at El Alamein. The news was telephoned through to the King on 4 November while he was rehearsing with Lionel Logue the speech from the throne which he had to make at the opening of Parliament on 11 November. Lógue recorded, "He said excitedly: 'Well, read it out, read it out', and I could hear coming across the wire the glorious news of the Libyan battle & Rommel's defeat: 'The enemy is in full retreat.' The King said: 'good news, thanks,' and turned to me smiling."⁴ The King wrote in his diary, with evident relief, "A victory at last, how good it is for the nerves."

Not merely were the Germans and Italians in full retreat before Montgomery's victorious army, but on 8 November, an Anglo-American force landed in French North Africa. The success of "Operation Torch", following so soon after the victory of El Alamein, was an enormous boost to Allied morale. It was the first tangible proof that the Anglo-American alliance was capable of mounting an operation of considerable weight with secrecy and efficiency, and on 13 May 1943 the Axis forces in North Africa surrendered to the Allies.

Between the launching of Operation Torch and the final surrender, events did not run altogether smoothly for the Allies. One of the main difficulties was in dealing with the French, in whose North African colonies the action was now taking place. The problem centred on who to recognize as the true representatives of free France. Three groups competed for Allied recognition: the French of North Africa, who had originally acknowledged the Vichy regime, but had dropped their allegiance after the Allied landings in North Africa; the followers of General Giraud, who was officially recognized by the Allies and had been appointed commander-in-chief of the French forces; and finally there were the followers of General de Gaulle who, proud, obstinate and brilliant, considered himself to be the true leader of free France, but whose bearing antagonized both Winston Churchill and, later, President Roosevelt, with the result that he was excluded from authority.

George VI picked his way deftly through the problems created by these internecine conflicts. Shortly after the successful Allied landings in French North Africa, the King expressed his misgivings over the tendency of General Mark Clark, the American Commander, to deal with Admiral Darlan and other French officers who had collaborated under the Vichy regime. At least, on 27 November 1942, Darlan fulfilled an earlier promise to Britain, when he ordered the scuttling of the French fleet at Toulon. George VI confided to his diary, "I wish I could understand this Darlan business. We must use him now, but for how long?" The Darlan problem was, in fact, solved on Christmas Eve

1942, when he was assassinated at the door of his office in Algiers.

However, this did not solve the problem of the conflicts between Generals Giraud and de Gaulle. The King tended to be sympathetic to de Gaulle, admiring him as a symbol of the stubborn and independent spirit of a France that had somehow managed to survive the humiliating collapse of 1940 and the subsequent collaborations of the Vichy government. George VI tried to moderate Churchill's dislike of de Gaulle's tactics, warning the Prime Minister after his return from the Casablanca conference in North Africa in January 1943 not to be too hasty with their awkward ally.

Although both Generals Giraud and de Gaulle were invested with joint authority in North Africa, this did not remove the friction between them, and the political situation there continued to be chaotic. These problems were compounded on 12 February 1943, when Rommel struck westward and attacked the United States forces on the Tunisian front, driving them back in confusion through the Kasserene Pass. The King reacted firmly and with good sense to this accumulation of difficulties in North Africa, writing to Churchill, who was in bed with influenza, urging him to strengthen the hand of Harold Macmillan, then British Minister at Allied Headquarters in North Africa, and General Alexander, Commander-in-Chief of British Forces in the Middle East. Thus strengthened, he hoped that Macmillan and Alexander could "make the two French sides come together". George VI was also thinking ahead to the projected invasion of Sicily, "Operation Husky", as he wanted the British commanders to work out a firm programme for this with the American generals. As a result of the King's suggestions, and flowing from the conclusions of the Casablanca conference of January, the Allied High Command in the Mediterranean area was reorganized: General Eisenhower became Allied Commander-in-Chief of that area (with General Alexander as his deputy), with control over all British, American and French forces in North Africa; Admiral Sir Andrew Cunningham became Commander-in-Chief of all naval forces, and Air Chief Marshal Sir Arthur Tedder was appointed Commander-in-Chief of all air forces. Harold Macmillan, as the King had proposed took up the important co-ordinating position of Minister-President at Allied Headquarters in North Africa.

By the spring of 1943, with the Allies on the offensive and confidence in their ultimate victory growing, George VI occupied an important central role in the prosecution of the war. Although he could not over-rule his War Cabinet or control the decisions of his ministers, the King showed sound judgement in areas of politics and strategy, and his advice was always well considered and generally highly valued. Churchill, in particular, set great store by the King's views, sometimes using his sovereign's backing to force a decision through the Cabinet. Perhaps the Prime Minister romanticized the relationship between himself and his monarch, and his letters to the King contain humble and rather misleading sentences like, "The orders you gave me on August 15, 1942 have been fulfilled." Or, "I now await your further instructions." Nonetheless, the relationship between the two men was close, cordial, and founded on mutual respect. The King was particularly worried that Churchill would be killed on one of the often lengthy journeys he undertook to promote the war effort, and was particularly anxious over Churchill's long journey to Casablanca in January 1943, confiding in a letter to Queen Mary, "Ever since he became my Prime Minister, I have studied the way in which his brain works. He tells me, more than people imagine, of his future plans & ideas & only airs them when the time is ripe to his colleagues & Chiefs of Staff. But I do hope & trust he will return home at once."[5]

As Churchill's trips to meet with Allied leaders became more frequent, George VI sought his advice as to who should replace him if he were killed during one of these missions. Churchill's formal advice was that in this case he should send for Anthony Eden, the Foreign Secretary. Later, when both Eden and Churchill attended the Yalta Conference, the Prime Minister nominated, though with some reservations, the Chancellor of the Exchequer, Sir John Anderson.

The King invested an inordinate amount of confidence in Churchill, and although his relations with other ministers were cordial, they were far less intimate. Although George VI had come to admire Anthony Eden, he found that the Foreign Secretary nearly always kept strictly to his brief, and it was impossible to discuss foreign affairs in the wide-ranging way he often did with the Prime Minister. Clement Attlee was shy, formal and correct, like the King himself, and not given to lengthy expositions. Nor did the King have much opportunity to speak to Ernest Bevin or Herbert Morrison. Early in 1941, George VI expressed his regrets to Anthony Eden that, ". . . it was not made easy for him to meet the Labour Party leaders. At about the same time, in a conversation with R. A. Butler, the King showed his concern that the junior Labour and Conservative ministers should work well together, and he asked pertinent questions about their accommodation in the House of Lords and Church House, after the Commons chamber had been hit by bombs."[6]

George VI's close relationship with Churchill was rewarded by his being made privy to the most innermost secrets of the war – on no substantive issue could the King complain that he had not been kept fully informed. In turn, he was himself fully aware of the wartime stricture that "careless talk costs lives". George VI was one of only four senior people, the others being Churchill, Sir John Anderson, and the scientist Lord Cherwell, who knew the full story of the development of the atomic bomb. The King showed his appreciation of the vital need to keep the bomb as secret as possible, and when in August 1945 the American Secretary of State, James Byrnes, began to talk at lunch with the King about the imminent use of the bomb against Japan, he swiftly and tactfully said, "I think we should discuss this interesting subject over our coffee." Both Byrnes and Admiral Leahy, Chief of Staff to President Truman, were astonished at the King's informality and wide-ranging knowledge.

The demands of the home front were also well known to the King. Through his own example and that of his family, he did his best to impress upon the public the necessity of accepting wartime rationing regulations and other restrictions, and when he visited the Ministry of Food he emphasized how vital to the war effort the work of its civil servants was. He warmly and consistently supported what Lord Woolton, the Minister of Food, called the "kitchen front", and he was careful to praise all those who worked in demanding and not particularly glamorous jobs like the Women's Land Army, who the Queen and he thought "were not well treated". He was particularly anxious to prove that as a landowner himself he could "dig for victory" as well as anybody, and in August 1942 *Picture Post* featured an article headed THE KING SHOWS THE WAY: WINDSOR PARK UNDER THE PLOUGH. The article began:

The Royal Farm (the King's private farm) at Windsor provides an outstanding example of British Agriculture at war; the scale of food production here is symbolic of the industry's finest achievements. Milk production is maintained at the pre-war level on wartime stock rations, and a large area of grassland has been ploughed to grow food for human consumption.

Of the total of 541 acres, 300 are now arable – three times the area ploughed in 1938. There are 109 acres of wheat, 70 acres of barley and 35 acres of oats, the remainder having been planted with potatoes and roots for stock feeding.[7]

Photographs of the King inspecting the new arable land at Windsor, looking at his Jersey cows and engaged in an apparently intimate conversation with a large white pig that lived on kitchen waste from Windsor Castle, could only promote national solidarity and good sense. The two Princesses were also photographed on bicycles accompanying their father, during one of his forays as "Farmer George".

In May 1943 the King's very real contribution to the war effort as counsellor and overseer was put before the public in a somewhat fulsome editorial in The Times. Seizing on a telegram sent from the Prime Minister to the King which said, "No Minister of the Crown has ever received more kindness and confidence from his Sovereign than I have done during the three fateful years which have passed since I received your Majesty's commission to form a National Administration," The Times said:

> Mr Churchill's telegram ... revealing the help that one of the strongest Prime Ministers has received from his Sovereign, is a powerful reminder that King George VI is doing a work as indispensable for English governance as any of his predecessors, just as he has set his people from the first day of the war an unfailing public example of courage, confidence, and devoted energy; and it conveys a hint of how much His Majesty's advisers continue to owe to His Majesty's advice.[8]

More significant was the King's visit to Allied forces in North Africa in June 1943. The idea had been broached as early as March by Churchill, and the King had responded enthusiastically to it. The greatest secrecy surrounded the preparations and since the long journey had to be made by air, the King, who disliked flying, summoned a solicitor the day before his departure and placed his affairs in order, writing in his diary, "I think it better on this occasion to leave nothing to chance." Before leaving, the King also appointed five Councillors of State: Queen Elizabeth, the Duke of Gloucester, his sister – the Princess Royal, Princess Arthur of Connaught, and the Countess of Southesk.

The flight to Algiers was not without its adventures, for although the aeroplane was scheduled to stop at Gibraltar for refuelling, such a dense fog surrounded the Rock that it was decided to fly straight on to

Algiers and land there. In London, the Queen, who knew the difficulties of landing at Gibraltar, had several anxious hours. "I imagined every sort of horror, & walked up & down my rooms staring at the telephone." When eventually the King landed in Algiers, shortly after noon on 12 June, despite his having made the journey under the alias "General Lyon", his arrival was soon known all over the city. He was lodged in the Villa Germain, and noted in his diary, "like all French houses, the plumbing was defective, and erratic."

For the next two weeks George VI undertook a gruelling programme. He visited units of the Allied forces, met Generals Alexander, Montgomery and Eisenhower, sat between the rival Generals de Gaulle and Giraud one day at lunch, and perhaps contributed to both withdrawing the resignations they had submitted the same morning. He also visited General Mark Clark's United States Fifth Army at Oran, and the Fourth Indian Division in Libya. Although travelling long distances by air, suffering digestive disorders from "desert tummy", and journeying in all some 6700 miles, often under a scorching sun, the King was a sharp-eyed and insatiable observer. Having inspected the troops of the British First Army at Bone, he commented, "The men looked very fit & well, and the smiles on their faces showed that they were pleased with what they had done." After visiting Clark's US Fifth Army at Oran, he observed frankly, "They have at last realized that their troops are not fit & hard, so they are copying our battle schools & PT."

On Sunday 13 June, the King received a moving and dramatic welcome from some three thousand British troops who were on the beach. A contemporary newspaper account recorded the incident:

> As he walked out on the verandah of his villa, first one man, then another, recognized him.
>
> And as if called by one voice, the thousands of men, most of them semi-nude, many of them still dripping with water, raced up the beach like a human wave.
>
> Then, as if the wave had suddenly frozen, they stood silently below the verandah, a solid mass of tanned and dripping men.
>
> There was one of those strange silences one sometimes gets among a huge crowd.
>
> A voice started "God Save the King". In a moment the National Anthem was taken up everywhere. It swelled deep-throatedly from a mass of soldiers.

[202]

In a campaign that has been drama without end it was one of the most dramatic scenes of all.

As the last notes of the Anthem died out, the King suddenly turned, stepped down from the verandah. He stood there, surrounded by hundreds of men, talking to them, asking them about their experiences.

Then the men broke into song again, this time with "For he's a jolly good fellow".[9]

On 20 June, the King also paid a visit to the battered, but still unconquered, island of Malta. The heroic resistance of the island to air attacks had already resulted in the King's awarding it the George Cross, and so he was determined, while on his visit to North Africa, to pay special tribute to the Maltese people and to the British garrison there for their tremendous contribution to the maintenance of British naval power in the Mediterranean. George VI made a dramatic entry into the Grand Harbour of Valletta, standing upon the bridge of the cruiser *Aurora* in bright morning sunlight, a slim figure in dazzling white naval uniform, his hand held at the salute. His reception in Malta provided the King with great emotional satisfaction, and he later recounted his experiences in a letter to Queen Mary:

> The real gem of my tour was my visit to Malta. I had set my heart on that, and it was not difficult to persuade the Naval & Air C in Cs of its importance, or of the effect on the Island itself. The question was which was the safest route, by sea or by air. I knew there was a risk in any case, but it was worth taking. I went by sea & by night. I shall never forget the sight of entering the Grand Harbour at 8.30 am on a lovely sunny day, & seeing the people cheering from every vantage viewpoint, while we were still some way off. Then later, when we anchored inside, hearing the cheers of the people which brought a lump into my throat, knowing what they have suffered from, 6 months constant bombing. . . .[10]

Shortly after the King's return to Britain from North Africa and Malta, his Private Secretary, Sir Alexander Hardinge, resigned through ill-health. He was succeeded by Sir Alan Lascelles, who remained the King's Private Secretary for the rest of his reign.

The summer of 1943 abounded in Allied victories. Sicily was invaded on the night of 9 July by Anglo-American forces, and six weeks later was in Allied hands. On 3 September, exactly four years after the outbreak of war, British troops landed on the mainland of Italy, north of Reggio, and almost a week after that an Anglo-American force under General Mark Clark went ashore in the Gulf of Salerno to the south of Naples. Mussolini had been deposed at the end of July, and although the advance on the Italian front was soon slowed down by the resistance of several German divisions, the Allied campaign to rid Europe of fascist rule had begun at last. On the Eastern front, five months before the Anglo-American invasion of Sicily, the Red Army had received the surrender of Field-Marshal von Paulus and nearly one hundred thousand German troops at Stalingrad. Russia now began her massive counter-offensive against the Axis powers, which was to bring the Red Army to Berlin and beyond. At sea, off the coast of Norway, *Tirpitz* was crippled, and *Scharnhorst* was sunk.

As the Allies began the process of dismantling Hitler's New Order in Europe, the leaders of the "Big Three" powers prepared to meet in conference at Teheran in Persia at the end of November 1943. At Teheran, although Churchill, Roosevelt and Stalin saw eye to eye on most issues, and indeed agreed upon the necessity of an Allied invasion of the north coast of France in the comparatively near future, the divergent, long-term interests of the three great powers were soon to assert themselves.

For the moment, however, these problems belonged to the future, and it was possible to feel a guarded optimism as the year drew to its close. In his Christmas Day broadcast for 1943, George VI hit exactly the right note when he said, "Since I last spoke to you, many things have changed. But the spirit of our people has not changed. As we were not downcast by defeat, we are not unduly exalted by victory. While we have bright visions of the future, we have no easy dreams of the days that lie close at hand. We know that much hard working and hard fighting, and perhaps harder working and harder fighting than ever before, are necessary for victory."[11] In his diary that same evening the King allowed his optimism full rein when he wrote, "Let us hope next Christmas will see the end of the War."

In the early part of 1944, the King gave thoughtful consideration to the future status of his elder daughter, Princess Elizabeth, who would reach her eighteenth birthday on 21 April 1944. In September 1943, a new Regency Bill had provided for the heir apparent to become a Councillor of State at the age of eighteen, rather than twenty-one, as before, and there arose in some circles the suggestion that, to mark the occasion of the Princess's birthday, she should be created Princess of Wales. This romantic proposal somewhat offended the King's sense of convention, and on 12 February 1944 it was announced in the press that there would be no change in the style and title of Princess Elizabeth when she attained her eighteenth birthday. In private, the King put his objections more bluntly in a letter to Queen Mary, "How could I create Lilibet Princess of Wales when it is the recognized title of the wife of the Prince of Wales? Her own name is so nice and what name could she be called by when she marries, I want to know." So Princess Elizabeth's birthday was simply celebrated in homely fashion at a family lunch given at Windsor.

The early months of 1944 were taken up with the preparations for the Allied landings on the north coast of France. In the autumn of 1943 the King had expressed his misgivings over these plans and, prompted by General Smuts, the South African Prime Minister, who arrived in London in October 1943 for a meeting of Commonwealth Prime Ministers, the King tried to convince Churchill that the Prime Minister's original plan to open up an Allied Mediterranean front on "the soft underbelly of the Axis" should be revived. George VI accepted Smuts' analysis that the Allies' commitment to launching "Overlord", planned for May 1944, might ". . . mean a stalemate in France. . . . If you have a good thing, stick to it. Why start another front across the Channel. . . . The Russians do not want us in the Balkans. They would like to see us fighting in France, so as to have a free hand in the east of Europe."[12] In pursuit of this argument, the King invited Churchill and Smuts to dine with him alone, and it was at this private dinner that Churchill succeeded in convincing both Smuts and the King of the impossibility of changing the plans for "Overlord". As a sop to George VI's feelings, however, Churchill revealed that he had already sent the King's letter advocating the conquest of Italy before "Operation Overlord" began to the Chiefs of Staff. This advice was ignored, and the conquest of Italy was far from complete when the D-Day landings were eventually made on 6 June 1944.

With General Eisenhower appointed as Supreme Commander of the Allied Expeditionary Force on Christmas Eve 1943, the King now embarked on an intense programme of inspecting and encouraging the troops that were to make the eventual assault on the north coast of France. On 15 May 1944 in a classroom at St Paul's School in London, the details of "Overlord" were explained to the King, the War Cabinet and the Chiefs of Staff. After General Eisenhower, General Montgomery, Admiral Ramsay, and others had spoken, the King rose from his chair and, quite unexpectedly, stepped on to the platform and spoke to the Allied Commanders. He was brief and to the point:

> I have known of the existence of this Operation ever since it was first mooted, and I have followed all its preparations very carefully . . . This is the biggest Combined Operation ever thought out in the world. But it is much more than this. It is a Combined Opn. of two countries, the United States & the British Empire. As I look around this audience of British & Americans I can see that you have equally taken a part in its preparation. I wish you all success, & with God's help you will succeed.[13]

Two months earlier, in March 1944, *Time* magazine had described the prelude to D-Day:

> British and U.S. Troops practised all-out landings along England's coast, splashing ashore under live gunfire. Brick courtyards of country houses echoed to the boots of Texas, Devonshire, Yorkshire, Boston.
>
> Thousands of other small, sharp vignettes of approaching action constituted the English scene. All through that scene threaded the sometimes tactless-tongued, sometimes careless, always curious U.S. soldier. The hedged lanes, the pleasant parks, the thatched pubs teemed with G.I. Joes.
>
> For the American soldier, England is a stopping-place on the long road home through Fortress Europe . . . when he can, he makes for London. There he and his buddies fill the subways, the buses, the cabs, the theaters, the pubs and hotel bars. In astonishing numbers they go to gawk through the iron fence at Buckingham Palace in the hope of seeing the King.[14]

While the Allied forces prepared themselves for the great invasion, the King was obliged to fight an unexpected private action of his own. At lunch on 30 May, Churchill told the King that he planned to watch the D-Day landings personally from one of "the bombarding ships". The King promptly suggested that he should go too, and Churchill reacted favourably to this idea. On hearing of this conversation, the King's

48

WARTIME RELAXATIONS

48 The King and his stamps, 1944. On the left is Sir John Wilson, royal philatelist, and on the right Sir Alan Lascelles, the King's Private Secretary. 49 Shaking hands with England's soccer team before the 1944 international with Scotland at Wembley. England's captain, Stan Cullis, is on the right.

49

With comedian Tommy Trin- (right) during a Christmas cert in a village hall

POST-WAR
RELAXATION

51 South Africa bound. The King and Queen aboard HMS *Vanguard* in early 1947.

51

52

52–54 The Royal Family, July 1946, the Royal Lodge, Windsor. The photographs clearly show the strength of the bonds, especially between the King and his elder daughter.

53   54

55 The Queen's wedding group: amongst the many guests are (centre row), above the royal couple, Queen Mary, the bride's grandmother; (front row, 2nd from left), Princess Alice, Prince Philip's mother; HRH Princess Margaret; pageboy, HRH Prince William of Gloucester; 3rd Marquess of Milford Haven (best man); HRH Princess Elizabeth; HRH Prince Philip; pageboy, HRH Prince Michael of Kent; HRH Princess Alexandra of Kent; a pensive King George VI; Queen Elizabeth; the Duke of Gloucester, with his hands on shoulders of his younger son; standing slightly behind him, the Duchess of Gloucester; (3rd row from front, 2nd from left), a contented Louis Mountbatten

56 Losing a daughter . . . The King and Queen in Westminster Abbey during Princess Elizabeth's wedding. Behind Queen Elizabeth is a beaming Queen Mary, and behind the King is Princess Alice of Battenburg, the Duke of Edinburgh's mother and sister of Lord Louis Mountbatten.

57 Gaining a son-in-law . . . Prince Philip and Princess Elizabeth, December 1948

58 Festival of Britain. The King and Queen arrive a
South Bank site in May 1951.

THE KING UNDERWENT AN OPERATION
FOR LUNG RESECTION THIS MORNING.
WHILST ANXIETY MUST REMAIN
FOR SOME DAYS HIS MAJESTY'S
IMMEDIATE POST-OPERATIVE CONDITION
IS SATISFACTORY.

DANIEL DAVIES   GEOFFREY MARSHALL
THOMAS DUNHILL   C. PRICE THOMAS
HORACE EVANS   JOHN WEIR.
R. MACHRAY   ROBERT H. YOUNG.

23rd SEPTEMBER, 1951

59 The bulletin on the railings of Buckingham Pa
giving brief details of the operation for the remov
the King's cancerous lung

Proud grandparents with Prince Charles
and Princess Anne, 14 November 1951

A picture taken for Prince Charles' third
birthday party and the first of the King after
lung resection

61

62 The King, looking tired and il
bids his daughter farewell on
February 1952 as she flies off wit
Prince Philip from London Airport fo
her Commonwealth Tour

62

THE KING IS DEAD

63 Shocked Birmingham schoolgir
read the news on 6 February 1952

Four Royal Dukes walk behind George VI's
ffin in the grounds of Windsor Castle, 15
bruary 1952. From left, the Duke of
linburgh, the Duke of Gloucester, the Duke of
indsor and the Duke of Kent.

OURNING

The widowed Queen and the Dean of
indsor at the funeral   (66) miners observe
wo-minute silence underground

Private Secretary, Sir Alan Lascelles, expressed horror at the idea, and argued that neither the King nor the Prime Minister should put themselves at risk in this way. The King, sensibly, straight away wrote to Churchill, saying, "My dear Winston ... I don't think I need emphasise what it would mean to me personally, and to the whole Allied cause, if at this juncture, a chance bomb, torpedo, or even a mine should remove you from the scene; equally a change of Sovereign at this moment would be a serious matter for the country and Empire.. We should both, I know, love to be there, but in all seriousness I would ask you to reconsider your plan." A battle of wills now ensued. Churchill counter-attacked the King's anxieties by declaring that he would feel obliged to seek Cabinet approval for the monarch's parti-cipation in the expedition, and that he would not feel able to re-commend them to give it. The King maturely accepted this point of view, but continued to press Churchill not to go himself. On 2 June, with the invasion imminent, the King made one more appeal to Churchill, saying, "Please consider my own position. I am a younger man than you, and a sailor, & as King I am the head of all three Services. There is nothing I would like better than to go to sea, but I have agreed to stop at home; is it fair that you should then do exactly what I should have liked to do myself?"

Despite these entreaties, the Prime Minister remained obdurate – indeed, he set off in his special train for General Eisenhower's head-quarters near Portsmouth, and by 11 pm on 2 June, he had sent no reply to the King's letter. George VI now played his last card: he threatened to set off from Windsor by car at dawn the next morning to personally prevent the Prime Minister from embarking with the invasion force. Sir Alan Lascelles telephoned Churchill's train with the King's threat, and received his somewhat grudging assurance that he would abandon his plan of going to sea.

On 6 June, "Operation Overlord" at last swung into action. That night, at 9.00 pm, the King broadcast a simple and moving appeal to his people, "calling them to prayer and dedication for this great enterprise, the liberation of Europe". It was a message delivered in the style that was now familiar to his listeners – restrained, sensible, and lacking any ostentation; the exhortation of a practical man to a practical people.

Only ten days after the D-Day landings, the King did cross a choppy Channel to spend the day on a Normandy beach-head, meeting

[207]

General Montgomery, decorating some of the troops, and seeing, as he arrived, the cruiser *Hawkins* firing its guns in support of the landward attack.

In July, he visited the Allied armies in Italy. During a hectic eleven days he travelled eight thousand miles by air and a thousand miles by road, anxious to restore morale in forces which had begun to believe that the world had all but forgotten them. The King recorded in his diary what his host, General Alexander, had told him: "He was particularly glad I had come out just at this moment, as the troops rather feared that their campaign had been put in the shade by the Press ever since the landing in Normandy." George VI's visit to the Italian front coincided with substantial Allied advances in Northern Europe, and on 15 August 1944 an Allied landing was made on the south coast of France. Paris was liberated by the end of August, and on 3 September British troops entered Brussels. By October the German forces had been almost completely driven from France, Belgium and the southern part of the Netherlands. Between 11 and 16 October the King visited his 21st Army group, led by General Montgomery, campaigning in the Low Countries. As a result of these successful visits, the King toyed with the idea of going to India early in 1945 to visit his troops fighting on the South-East Asian front, but despite the warm support of Lord Louis Mountbatten, Supreme Allied Commander in South-East Asia, it did not prove possible to arrange the trip.

While the Allies were driving the enemy back in Europe and beyond, the Germans launched their V1 and later their V2 attacks upon Britain. The V1 was a pilotless plane, the V2 a rocket; both exploded on impact. Queen Elizabeth thought that there was "something very inhuman about death-dealing missiles being launched in such an indiscriminate manner", and the King later took some pleasure in visiting an anti-aircraft battery in Sussex and watching the gunners trying to shoot down the V1s as they passed overhead. In the spring of 1971, an ex-Nazi air chief claimed in Madrid that an attempt had actually been made to kill the King with a flying bomb during the latter part of 1944. According to the newspaper article, a German agent in London sent daily radio messages suggesting fresh targets for the flying bombs to aim at, and on one occasion reported that the King was to take part in "... a morale march down one of London's main streets. The German High Command authorized the attempt on his life with a flying bomb." In the story, published in a popular Madrid daily newspaper, the man, then in his seventies and living in retirement in Spain, added, "We planned to hit the demonstration, but the bomb struck 500 yards from where the King was standing." A Buckingham Palace spokesman reacted to the article by saying, "We have not heard this story before."[16] If the King escaped injury as a result of V1 and V2 attacks, several thousands of his citizens in the area of London and the south-east were not so fortunate, and in the first two weeks after the flying bombs were launched 1600 people were killed, over ten thousand injured, and more than two hundred thousand houses damaged in the London area alone.

As the German forces fell back on both the western and the eastern front, towards the frontiers of the Reich, the Allies held a series of summit meetings to plan for peace as well as for victory. These meetings culminated in the Yalta Conference of February 1945. Although George VI welcomed the decision taken at Yalta to call a conference of the United Nations in San Francisco in April to prepare a charter for a permanent international organization to succeed the League of Nations, he expressed disquiet at the concessions made to Stalin. In essence, Roosevelt, with Churchill unable to restrain him, conceded a vast sphere of influence in Eastern Europe to Russia. The King, who had always viewed Russia as a long-term threat to the West, saw the abandonment of Britain's obligations to Poland and the other Allies of 1939 as a retrograde step, and he doubted whether Stalin would "play fair".

In April 1945, the King was deeply affected by the sudden death of President Roosevelt in Georgia, and wrote in his diary, "He was a very great man, & his loss will be felt the world over. He was a staunch friend of this country, & Winston will feel his loss most of all in his dealings with Stalin."[17] Roosevelt's successor was the then comparatively unknown Vice-President Harry S. Truman. Though completely different from his predecessor in his social origins, personality and methods, Truman was to provide the United States with firm and courageous leadership as the war drew to its close.

Although the British and American advance westwards was delayed by stubborn German resistance in the Low Countries and on the Rhine, by the end of April the Third Reich, destined to last "for a thousand years", had been totally destroyed. American and Russian armies met on the Elbe on 25 April 1945. Three days later Mussolini was executed by Italian partisans. On 2 May the German armies in Italy surrendered unconditionally, and on the same day Berlin capitulated to the Russians. Hitler had committed suicide on 30 April, so it was left to Admiral Doenitz to open negotiations for the surrender of Germany. The instrument of unconditional surrender was signed on the morning of 7 May, and the war finally came to its official conclusion at a little before midnight on 8 May.

Winston Churchill lunched with the King and his family that day. The two men congratulated each other quietly, but with great feeling. Vast crowds gathered round Buckingham Palace, and the Royal Family, with the Prime Minister standing in the middle of them, appeared on the balcony to acknowledge the applause. The King wrote in his diary, "we went out 8 times altogether during the afternoon and evening. We were given a great reception." Afterwards, the King let his two daughters go out, escorted by some young officers, to take part in the celebrations below. He wrote in his diary, "Poor darlings, they have never had any fun yet."

For the next two weeks, the King and his family shared their nation's heartfelt rejoicings. The King wrote in his diary, while enjoying a short rest at Windsor Castle, "We have spent a very busy fortnight since VE Day, & feel rather jaded from it all. We have been overwhelmed by the kind things people have said over our part in the War. We have only tried to do our duty during these 5½ years. I have found it difficult to rejoice or relax as there is still so much hard work ahead to deal with."[18]

Among the hard work ahead was the successful prosecution of the war against Japan. This war was by no means over when the Prime Minister, having come to the conclusion that a period of caretaker government before the overdue general election would not serve Britain's best interests, asked for a dissolution of Parliament. Polling day was set for 5 July 1945. From Balmoral, the King believed, "The outcome of it is uncertain, as no Party may secure a clear working majority, which will make things difficult for any Govt. to try & deal with USA, Russia and France, let alone setting up a Govt. in Germany, and with all the problems of demobilisation and housing at home. Then there is the war with Japan to deal with as well. The outlook as far as I am concerned does not look very peaceful or restful."[19]

The General Election campaign of 1945 was the first to be held for ten years, and although Churchill campaigned on the basis of his war record, as the man who had saved the nation, the electorate, though applauding him for his wartime efforts, declined to send him back to finish the job. Perhaps Churchill's notorious blunder when he claimed in an election speech that socialism could only be established in Britain by the use of Gestapo-like methods lost him the goodwill of many moderate men and women. The Labour leaders, though not confident of victory, had mostly established themselves as national figures during the wartime coalition government, and their party seemed to offer a more positive and constructive approach to the post-war problems that the nation must face.

When the result of the election was announced on 26 July, three weeks having been necessary to collect all the votes of the troops overseas, the result was a sensational landslide for Labour: the Conservatives lost 160 seats while Labour gained 230. The combined number of Liberal and Independent MPs was cut by 55, nearly all of which were Liberal losses. The Labour Party ended up with 393 seats and an overall majority of 180.

When Churchill came to the King on 26 July to tender his resignation it was, in George VI's words, ". . . a very sad meeting. I told him I thought the people were very ungrateful after the way they had been led in the War. He was very calm. . . . I asked him if I should send for Mr Attlee to form a Government and he agreed. We said goodbye & I thanked him for all his help to me during the 5 War years."[20]

That evening, Clement Attlee went to Buckingham Palace and agreed to form a government. Many felt it was fitting that, with the urgent need to create a new democratic order out of the confusion of post-war Europe, the administration of the United Kingdom should be in the hands of a government committed to a programme of social and economic reforms.

15

THE KING AND
THE LABOUR GOVERNMENT
1945–1951

". . . he was essentially broad-minded and was ready to accept changes that seemed necessary."

Clement Attlee

"My new Government is not too easy & the people are rather difficult to talk to."

George VI, 1945

GEORGE VI APPEARED AN UNLIKELY monarch to oversee a period of dramatic and far-reaching, albeit peaceful, social change. When he had ascended the throne in 1936, one of his wishes was to preserve the traditions of a highly traditional monarchy. He was deeply conservative, apt to worry over change, and positively obsessional over the formalities of ceremonial and dress – during the war he had rebuked his godson, King Peter of Yugoslavia, for wearing a gold watch-chain with the uniform of the Yugoslav Royal Air Force, with the words, "Take it off. It looks damned silly and damned sloppy." Nor was the King, by inheritance or conviction, in any way a socialist. He disliked political extremism and perhaps feared that some of the more radical proposals in the Labour Party's election manifesto, notably the huge programme of nationalization, had a revolutionary flavour about them. The fact that Labour had never before formed a majority government also aroused the King's doubts as to whether they would be fit to carry through their huge legislative programme at the same time as they grappled with the enormous and complicated problems of post-war reconstruction.

For some time, also, George VI was in a state of depression at losing Winston Churchill as his Prime Minister. He wrote to General Smuts of South Africa after the results of the election became known: "It was a great shock to me to have to lose Churchill as my chief adviser, and I am sure the People did not want to lose him as their leader, after all the years of stupendous work he did on their behalf in the War."[1] Since the King had expected that Churchill would win the election, Labour's surprisingly large majority came as an even greater surprise to him. Given a choice, he would undoubtedly have preferred the wartime coalition to have continued in office as the symbol of a united national desire to cope with the problems of the changed world together.

Despite these personal misgivings, however, it is inaccurate to caricature the King as being simply pro-Conservative or even reactionary. His work in the inter-war period with the Industrial Welfare Society, and the principle of social mixing that had been so central to the concept of his Boys' Camps, were all indications of a sympathy with the idea of greater equality of opportunity and with the need for more understanding between the classes. His official biographer perhaps exaggerates when he calls the King "a progressive in political thought and a reformer in social conscience", but it seems clear that he was prepared to welcome liberal methods of reconstruction and reform rather like those envisaged by the Beveridge Report. That he understood some of the details of the poverty and disadvantage of so many of his subjects, is illustrated by a story recounted by Lord Woolton. In 1943, Woolton's wife was explaining to the King the difficulties of extending a proper water supply to remote country cottages and the poorer parts of towns where for generations there had been resort to a common pump. The King replied, "It isn't enough. What you want is a plug in every house," and waved his arm to express his point.[1]

Looking back on his premiership, Clement Attlee recalled that, having been the King's Prime Minister for six and a half years, "there had never been any difficulty between us." Attlee also said in his speech to the House of Commons in February 1952 after the King's death, "The longer I served him, the greater was my respect and admiration. . . . It was his fate to reign in times of great tension. He could never look round and see a clear sky. . . . He was a very hard worker. Few people realised how much time and care he gave to public affairs, and visitors from overseas were often astonished at his close familiarity with all kinds of questions. With this close study went a good judgement, and a sure instinct for what was really vital."[2]

Although Attlee probably exaggerated the extent of the harmony which existed between him and the King on all issues, his impressions of George VI certainly do not indicate a reactionary ogre, desperate to frustrate the reforms of the Labour Government. Interestingly, Attlee also wrote of the possibility that Queen Mary, brought up in the traditions of Victorian England, ". . . might have resented the coming

[213]

into power of a Labour Government, but it was not so. She had a forward-looking mind."[3] Queen Mary had a special regard for two of Attlee's ministers: George Tomlinson, who served as Minister of Education, and whom the Queen called "My Minister", and Ernest Bevin, the Foreign Secretary, who, since he lived in Carlton House Terrace near to Marlborough House, Queen Mary insisted on calling "My neighbour". Still the influential matriarch of the House of Windsor, Queen Mary was prepared to be an open-minded observer of the Labour government's activities.

Whilst George VI welcomed government measures which clearly helped to relieve poverty and suffering, he was sometimes irritated and surprised by more trifling egalitarian and progressive attitudes. When the servants at Buckingham Palace, for example, organized a union and demanded higher wages, he was both shocked and puzzled, although he readily acceded to the demands. He also disliked strikes, especially unofficial ones, and commented when the gas workers struck unofficially during the winter of 1945 that "the liberty of the subject was at stake if a strike interfered with home life." "He was puzzled, too, when a Cabinet Minister, Aneurin Bevan, declined to wear evening dress on the ground that it was an upper-class uniform".[4]

Not that the King viewed all the leading members of the Labour Party with an impartial and friendly eye. The left wing of the party had, in the inter-war period, advocated policies which some contemporaries considered to be extremist. For example, Harold Laski in his *Democracy in Crisis* had argued that a future Labour government would have to govern by decree, and Sir Stafford Cripps, in his somewhat wayward period as a founder member of the Socialist League, had even advocated that emergency powers should be used to prevent a "capitalist dictatorship". When Labour came to power in 1945, however, Cripps had for some time been a respectable member of the War Cabinet, Laski had become Chairman of the Labour Party, and the Cabinet, which had an average age of over sixty, was by no means top heavy with Bolshevik revolutionaries. Generally, George VI could feel safe with a government dominated by such figures as Attlee, Herbert Morrison, Ernest Bevin, Arthur Greenwood, J. Chuter Ede, and Arthur Creech Jones. Even Hugh Dalton and Aneurin Bevan proved amenable.

*   *   *

The crucial relationship, of course, was with the Prime Minister, Clement Attlee. Despite Attlee's warm words upon looking back on his time of close contact with George VI, their personal relationship was not at first easy. Although Attlee was a moderate, a product of Haileybury and University College, Oxford, had served with distinction in the First World War, and had undertaken social work in the East End of London, he was also a shy man. He was not a great conversationalist, expansive, self-confident, sparkling with quips and asides, in the fashion of Winston Churchill. The King, with his own history of conversational awkwardness, found his early meetings with Attlee hard-going, and "At the outset the Prime Minister's audiences were not infrequently marked by long silences. This, however, quickly wore off. Both persevered – and with success. The King writes in his diary later of 'long talks' with Mr Attlee."[5]

When Attlee had first come to the Palace for the King's permission to form a government, the King had thought that he "looked very surprised", and Attlee later admitted, "indeed I certainly was at the extent of our success."[6] The victorious leader of the Labour Party was perhaps even more surprised when he began to discuss with the King the composition of his Cabinet. Taking advantage of his constitutional right to advise his Prime Minister, George VI, as he wrote in his diary, ". . . asked him who he would make Foreign Secy. & he suggested Dr Hugh Dalton. I disagreed with him & said that foreign affairs were the most important subject at the moment & I hoped he would make Mr Bevin take it. He said he would. . . ."[7] Although Attlee later insisted that it was by his own choice that Bevin went to the Foreign Office, this is not how it appears from the King's diary. Later, when the Foreign Secretary came for an audience with the King, he was told that it was at the King's suggestion that he was going to the Foreign Office – something that Bevin confessed "was news to him".

George VI had greatly admired Bevin's work as Minister of Labour during the war, and believed that he was a solid and reliable man to have in control of foreign affairs. He may also have been guided by his dislike of what seemed to him the looming danger of Russian territorial expansion, and he doubtless knew that Dalton tended to be sympathetic to the Soviet Union whereas Bevin had an abiding dislike of Communism. Perhaps the King also knew of the animosity, amounting sometimes to hatred, that existed between Bevin and Herbert Morrison, and reckoned that, with Bevin in charge of foreign policy and Morrison established as Lord President of the Council, the two men would have less opportunity to quarrel. It has also been argued that, "perhaps there was a deeper factor. George VI took easily to the Socialists from the working class. He was more doubtful about Old Etonians, particularly about one [Dr Dalton] whose father had been a close friend of the Royal Family."[8]

Whatever the reasons, the decision to substitute Bevin for Dalton was one of great weight and significance. Bevin knew little of foreign affairs. On the other hand, he might have made a solid and effective Chancellor of the Exchequer, and could perhaps have prevented that combination of economic austerity and financial inflation which later undermined the popularity of the Labour government. Hugh Dalton, though not particularly good at figures, was far better qualified to become Foreign Secretary than Bevin. Certainly the two men had very different views on foreign policy: to cite just two examples, Dalton was far more sympathetic than Bevin to opening the British Mandate of Palestine to full-scale Jewish immigration; Bevin was also less hostile to Germany than was Dalton.

Despite the extraordinary way in which Bevin's appointment as Foreign Secretary was made, it had been vital to make an immediate decision, as the Potsdam Conference was meeting in Berlin and was waiting for the British delegation's return in order to proceed with the settlement of German and European affairs. Within twenty-four hours of receiving the King's permission to form an administration, Attlee was back in Berlin with Ernest Bevin at his side as Foreign Secretary. The Conference was therefore resumed, with the continuity of British representation hardly ruffled by the results of a general election which had so drastically altered the composition and personnel of the British Government.

Quite apart from the settlement in Europe, there was still the war against Japan to be won. The King had very much wanted to arrange a meeting with President Truman of the United States at this time. The Russian government, however, objected to the proposal that Truman should meet with the King before the opening of the Potsdam Conference, and when the King went on to suggest that he should visit Germany to review his troops and there meet Stalin and Truman together, this proposal, too, was vetoed because Field-Marshal Montgomery declared that he could not answer for his sovereign's safety in devastated Berlin. Eventually, Truman did manage to meet the King on his way home from the Potsdam Conference aboard HMS *Renown* at Plymouth. The two men got on well. Truman declared himself "impressed with the King as a good man", and, before they parted company, George VI asked Truman if he would give him his autograph "for my wife and daughters".

Amid these homely exchanges, the dropping of the atomic bomb on Japan was also discussed, and the King demonstrated his considerable knowledge of the development of the weapon, going on to talk about the possible uses of atomic energy after the war. Admiral Leahy, the President's Chief of Staff, was sceptical, saying, "It sounds like a professor's dream to me." To which the King quickly responded, "Would you like to lay a little bet on that, Admiral?"[9] On 6 August 1945, the first atomic bomb was dropped on Hiroshima. Three days later the city of Nagasaki was similarly devastated, and the Japanese government now hastily accepted the Allies' terms of unconditional surrender. Britain celebrated victory over Japan, vj Day, on 15 August. That afternoon and evening, as the crowds once more gathered around Buckingham Palace, the King and Queen and their daughters appeared half a dozen times on the balcony. Clement Attlee, however, was not with them. Where the King's true feelings of gratitude lay was demonstrated when he received Winston Churchill that evening, and noted in his diary, "I wish he could have been given a proper reception by the people." That night, at nine o'clock, the King broadcast his victory message to his subjects:

The war is over. You know, I think that those four words have for the Queen and myself the same significance, simple yet immense, that they have for you. Our hearts are full to overflowing as are your own. Yet there is not one of us who has experienced this terrible war who does not realize that we shall feel its inevitable consequences long after we have all forgotten our rejoicings of today. But that relief from past dangers must not blind us to the demands of the future.[10]

Appropriately, the end of the war against Japan coincided with the King's speech from the throne at the opening of Parliament outlining the Government's enormous legislative programme. Among the major items to which it was committed were the nationalization of the mines, the railways, the Bank of England, the gas and electricity systems, and the creation of a national health service. The Government also announced its intention to retain controls over economic development in order to prevent what has been described as "the relapse into a private enterprise free-for-all which had marred recovery after 1918". The King's speech also emphasized the Government's steadfast commitment to social revolution by improving educational opportunity and by accomplishing the transfer of wealth from the richer to the poorer classes.

Despite the King's basic acceptance of the mandate to attempt what amounted to a peaceful economic and social revolution, he proceeded to express his misgivings whenever he thought it necessary. It is clear that he found it hard to move in the same direction as the Labour government with great enthusiasm. In November 1945, while Attlee was in the United States and Herbert Morrison was acting Prime Minister, the King objected to the pace of the Labour legislative programme: "We discussed the whole of the Labour programme. I thought he was going too fast in the new nationalizing legislation." The King's explanation of his objections – that, "Bill drafting takes time, especially with reduced staff," seems a little lame in retrospect. As it happened, the Government was proved right in its determination to press ahead as quickly as possible with its restructuring of British society since after 1947 conditions in general, and perhaps the national mood, were not so favourable.

Apart from deploring the rate at which the Labour government began its legislative initiative, George VI kept a careful eye on the constitutional forms within which that change was brought about. In 1947, for example, he objected to the introduction of the Supplies and Services Bill, which was meant to enable the Government to increase its range of controls and restrictions during that year of economic crisis. Perhaps the King accepted too readily the assertion of Churchill and the Conservative opposition that the Bill was "a blank cheque for totalitarian government". Attlee tried to present the Bill as a minor piece of legislation, but the King was not convinced, and sent his Prime Minister a letter requiring a full explanation of the Government's intentions. Attlee's response was to point out the exaggerated nature of the Tory accusations against his Government, and the Bill was passed through Parliament. In the event, Labour did not need to rule by decree as the King had feared.

George VI showed his anxieties at the effects of Labour policies in other ways. Privately he deplored the effects of estate duties and heavy taxation upon the wealthy classes, and when the novelist Vita Sackville-West told him that her family's house, Knole, had been given to the National Trust, he raised his hands in despair, and said,

"Everything is going nowadays. Before long, I shall also have to go." The monarchy's future, however, was perfectly safe under a Labour government – the King's obvious integrity and wartime contribution were powerful factors in ensuring that. Nor need he have feared that there would be an abrupt and irreversible shift in the balance of wealth and power. Although there was some debate over the value of the House of Lords, the monarchy was too popular, and perhaps too evidently useful, to be threatened by extinction.

Though the King continued to give Attlee various pieces of advice, there is no evidence that the Prime Minister acted upon any of them. For instance, the King told Attlee that "he must give the people here some confidence that the government was not going to stifle all private enterprise"; and when the two discussed housing and clothing, the King expressed his worry over the delay in getting the house-building programme started; as for clothing, the King struck a personal note when he said, "we must all have new clothes & my family are down to the lowest ebb."[11]

The King was convinced that he knew the mood of the country as well as his government. Despite his generally cordial relations with Attlee, he sometimes felt that he was not confided in, as had been the case when Churchill was Prime Minister. Also, Attlee, placid and in command of himself, was a far less obvious worrier than the King, and in 1947, when the Government faced a host of crises, George VI complained, "I have asked Mr Attlee three times now if he is not worried by the domestic situation in this country, but he won't tell me he is, when I feel he is. I know I am worried." Perhaps one of the problems was that the King's first three Prime Ministers – Baldwin, Chamberlain and Churchill – had demonstrated a very gratifying friendliness towards him, and had thus perhaps exaggerated the Crown's influence upon matters of state. Attlee continued to be more detached, and, in a sense, asserted a more honest relationship between a constitutional sovereign and the Prime Minister of a majority government.

With some of his ministers, George VI established really good working relationships. Apart from his good opinion of Ernest Bevin during the War, he also took, perhaps surprisingly, to Aneurin Bevan, the Minister of Health, and a member of the Labour left. Perhaps Bevan's proletariat origins endeared him to the King, certainly the two men had a common bond as former stammerers. Bevan, with typical charm, told the King at his first audience with him of his long-felt

[219]

admiration for the way in which he had overcome his speech defect, ". . . adding that, as one who had himself stammered very badly as a boy, he appreciated his achievement in full measure."

The King's hard work on state papers impressed all of his departmental ministers, even though some disapproved of the attitudes he expressed in private. Herbert Morrison remembered from his days as Home Secretary in the wartime coalition that whenever he discussed the possibility of a reprieve for a convicted murderer with the King, the latter had always carefully gone through the report of the trial before they met. (When the *Sunday Times* serialized six extracts from his autobiography in the spring of 1960, a reference to the two occasions on which Morrison had differed from the King on the question of a reprieve were eliminated from the final text, presumably so as not to embarrass the Home Secretary of the day.)[12] Morrison, at any rate, certainly continued to go to audiences with the King well primed, knowing George VI's disconcerting habit of firing penetrating and detailed questions at him.

To add to Britain's economic and financial difficulties, the abrupt ending by President Truman of the Lend-Lease arrangements on 17 August 1945 meant that she had to cope with the implications of an enormous uncovered external debt of £3,355,000. As well as this, Britain's "invisible" income had been cut by more than fifty per cent because of the sale of over four thousand million pounds worth of overseas assets and investments, there was a huge internal debt, a deficit on the balance of payments of three hundred million pounds for 1946, and an export trade that had shrunk to forty per cent of its 1938 total. Although four thousand million dollars were eventually raised in the United States at two per cent interest, the Americans insisted that sterling must be made freely convertible into dollars after twelve months.

The winter of 1946–47 (the worst on record for sixty-six years), the coal and fuel shortages, the rationing of bread, and the raising of income tax and indirect tax, all conspired to constrict the Government's freedom of action. These were the years of austerity and utility, and many began to question whether living conditions in peacetime were in reality any better than those of war. The King shared the pessimism of many of his subjects, writing from Balmoral in September 1947, "I do wish one could see a glimmer of a bright spot anywhere in world affairs. Never in the whole history of mankind have things looked gloomier than they do now, and one feels so powerless to do anything to help." Two years later, the devaluation of the pound from its old exchange rate of \$4.03 to \$2.80, which was accompanied by yet more demands for national sacrifices and greater austerity, seemed to symbolize the Government's failures.

In February 1950 a General Election was held at Attlee's choice, and although the Government had not lost a single by-election in its period of office, its huge majority vanished. Labour now had 315 seats, the Conservatives, 298, and the Liberals, 9. Attlee could thus form another administration, but with such a small overall majority that the normal toll of death and illness could, within a short time, make the Government's position untenable. Given the terribly difficult circumstances of the post-war period, the result was not a bad one for Labour. Clearly the electorate had not rejected socialism utterly. They had, however, refused to give it a further extensive mandate. In the event, the Government was only destined to remain in office for another twenty months.

In matters of foreign policy, the Government's task was no easier than at home. Britain's relative impoverishment, and her reduction to client status with the United States, were not the foundations upon which a vigorous and constructive foreign policy could be based. The expansion of Russian influence in Eastern Europe, moreover, continued steadily after the peace of 1945. With America holding back until 1947 from a full-blooded commitment to uphold western influence, Britain, in her reduced circumstances, had to do the best that she could. The King, with his lengthy experience of world affairs, now saw himself as something of an elder statesman in the formulation of foreign policy.

George VI became a dedicated opponent of Soviet expansion and approved enthusiastically of Winston Churchill's speech at Fulton, Missouri, in March 1946, where the ex-Prime Minister warned against "the indefinite expansion" of Soviet power and doctrine. Stalin reacted angrily to Churchill's speech, denouncing it as warmongering. The King, however, told Churchill "how much good it had done in the world, and that Stalin's tirade against him personally showed he had a guilty conscience". George VI also was much preoccupied with the defence of Europe, and frequently criticized France for evading what he considered to be her true responsibilities. As the Cold War developed, he was gratified that more people came to share his views as to the dangers of Soviet foreign policy. When, in June 1950, there was a Commons debate on the Communist attack upon South Korea, the King gave whole-hearted backing to Attlee in his support of the United Nations' intervention, saying, "It is naked aggression and it must be checked." The King was anxious throughout that Britain should maintain her great power status, and to this end was an enthusiastic supporter of conscription, despite its electoral unpopularity.

If, in the field of foreign affairs, the United Kingdom was slowly being reduced to second-class power status, her Empire, in the period 1945–51, had undergone even more radical changes. The granting of independence to India, Pakistan, Burma and Ceylon in rapid sequence between 1947 and 1948 signalled the real beginning of the end for the old Imperial system. In 1942 the King had expressed amazement that Churchill was apparently, ". . . quite prepared to give up India to the Indians after the War . . . I disagree & have always said India has got to be governed & this will have to be our policy."[13]

Despite these convictions, and although very anxious over the prospect of communal conflict between his Indian subjects, George VI played an important part in facilitating the partition of the Indian Empire. He did this by the appointment of Lord Louis Mountbatten as the last Viceroy of India. Towards the end of 1946, Attlee had decided to recall the Viceroy, Lord Wavell, whose plan for a gradual with-drawal of British power seemed to resemble a not particularly glorious military retreat. Mountbatten was not, at first, anxious to undertake the enormously complex task of ending British rule in India, but the King, his cousin and a close friend, played a substantial part in persuading him to accept, and insisted that Mountbatten had approp-riately clear instructions: "Lord Mountbatten must have concrete orders as to what he is to do. Is he to lead the retreat out of India or is he to work for the reconciliation of Hindus and Moslems?"

As it happened, Mountbatten was committed to the principle of granting independence to the Indian Empire. Upon his arrival in March 1947, he swiftly decided that the tension and deadlock between various Indian factions necessitated an earlier withdrawal than planned, and during the summer of 1947 some abrupt boundary surgery partitioned India. On 15 August 1947, the new Dominions of India and Pakistan were established. Burma seceded from the Empire shortly afterwards.

In the aftermath of the British withdrawal from India, the King spent some time considering how best to amend his title. Since he could no longer sign himself Georgius Rex Imperator, the King worried for some time as to when to drop the "I" of G.R.I. Eventually, Attlee decided for him, and after 15 August 1947, with the exception of the final India Honours List issued on 1 January 1948, the King signed himself "George R". It was symptomatic of a sentimental regard for his Indian Empire that he asked that the last of the Union Jacks to be flown above the besieged residency at Lucknow during the Indian Mutiny of 1857 should be given to him so that he might hang it at Windsor.

There were soon other problems of style and title to perplex the King. In 1949 Southern Ireland, which had been a reluctant Dominion ever since 1922, was formally declared the Republic of Ireland. Citizens of the Republic, however, were not to be considered as foreigners in the United Kingdom, thus prompting the King, a few weeks after the declaration of the Republic, to ask the Eire Minister for External Affairs, "What does this new legislation of yours make *me* in Ireland, an undesirable alien?" The King was also much exercised over India's request, soon after Independence, to become a republic itself. How was this compatible with continuing membership of the Commonwealth? The King was sovereign of his Dominions within the Commonwealth, but how could he be head of a republic? In October 1948, he spent some time discussing this problem with India's Prime Minister, Jarwarhalal Nehru, during the latter's visit to London. After talking with Nehru at dinner, the King found that he "liked him very much". He also believed that Nehru wished devoutedly to keep India within the Commonwealth. Under these pressures, a compromise was found: a constitutional formula was devised whereby the King became Head of the Commonwealth, not of India, and in that capacity Indians could still owe him allegiance. George VI was declared Head of the Commonwealth at the Conference of Commonwealth Prime Ministers held in April 1949.

Although the King was to die regretting that he had never visited India, in 1947, he at last took up Smuts' frequent invitations to visit South Africa. There was political expediency behind the invitation, as Smuts, facing a General Election in the fairly near future, wished to consolidate support, particularly amongst English-speaking South Africans, for his United Party. The King, too, was anxious to defuse the secessionist agitation of the Afrikaner South African Nationalist Party, led by Dr Malan. It is indicative of his strong desire to help Smuts keep South Africa within the Commonwealth that he was prepared to make this visit during 1947, a most critical year in the fortunes of Great Britain, even though he was risking unfriendly suggestions that he and his family were basking under the South African sun merely to avoid austerity and restrictions at home.

Sailing to South Africa in the newly commissioned but soon out-dated battleship *Vanguard*, the Royal Family landed at Cape Town towards the end of February 1947. The King was conscience-stricken over leaving his people, and wrote to his mother back in snow-bound Britain, "I am very worried over the extra privations which all of you at home are having to put up with in that ghastly cold weather with no light or fuel. In many ways I wish I was with you, having borne so many trials with them."[14] Queen Elizabeth was well aware of her husband's anxieties, writing to Queen Mary, "This tour is being very strenuous as I feared it would be & doubly hard for Bertie who feels he should be at home." The King, in fact, suggested to Attlee that he should return home from South Africa early, but the Prime Minister advised against it.

By the time the royal tour of South Africa ended, on 24 April, the party had travelled thousands of miles by car, train and air, visiting all the provinces of the Union and also including Southern Rhodesia in their travels. Princess Elizabeth celebrated her twenty-first birthday during the tour, and on 21 April had broadcast to the peoples of the Empire, saying, "I declare before you all that my whole life, whether it be long or short, shall be devoted to your service, and the service of our great Imperial Commonwealth, to which we all belong." Although the royal party were greeted by large crowds throughout their travels in South Africa, it was noticeable that the Nationalists boycotted official gatherings, and the Afrikaner people in general were unenthusiastic. Although the King, on his own initiative, paid a private visit to the aged widow of Martinus Steyn, last president of the independent Orange Free State at the time of the Boer War, the Afrikaner oppo-nents of the Imperial connection were not impressed. When, in 1948, South Africa went to the polls, the result was a convincing victory for the Nationalist Party, and a defeat for Smuts. Although the royal visit did not win Smuts the election, it may have reduced the size of the swing to the Nationalists. That the King was personally respected by many Nationalist leaders was to be demonstrated during his last illness, when Dr Malan, then Prime Minister, invited him to come to South Africa to recuperate. A visit was arranged for March 1952, which, though it never took place, provoked some criticism in Britain and the Commonwealth, and led the *New Statesman* to publish in

January 1952 a cautionary article headed 'The King Must Condone No Wrong' which hoped that the proposed visit would not associate the monarchy with apartheid.

The enormous strain of the war and the difficulties and anxieties of the post-war years all put a great strain upon the King's health. In July 1946, the London correspondent of *Time* magazine, Alfred Wright, saw the Royal Family in the flesh, and commented, "The King looked considerably older than I had expected. His sandy-coloured hair is well streaked with grey, and his face is prominently lined. . . . The King appeared to lack the composure of the Queen. He continually works the muscles of his jawbone, a reflex common among nervous people."[15] The correspondent also noticed that the King seemed to find his tour of the Tate Gallery, ". . . more of a duty than a pleasure. Several times I noticed he ducked away from the lecture to pass a pleasantry with some member of the party."

The King had, in fact, come back from the South African tour greatly fatigued and having lost seventeen pounds in weight. From January 1947 he had also been suffering from cramp in both legs: the first symptom of arteriosclerosis which by the end of the year threatened him with the danger of gangrene and the very real possibility that his right leg might have to be amputated. Although his condition improved, his doctors decided in March 1949 that an operation was necessary to relieve the thrombosis which threatened him. This was carried out at Buckingham Palace, and the King seemed to make a good recovery. He had not, however, seen the last of illness.

Despite these difficulties, the King's family life continued to be a source of great happiness to him. The royal tour of South Africa had provided the Royal Family with one of their last experiences of being a close-knit unit of four people – shortly after the royal party returned to the United Kingdom, King George agreed that Princess Elizabeth could marry Philip Mountbatten. The wedding took place in November 1947. In April 1948, the King and Queen celebrated their Silver Wedding.

The King's health continued to give cause for concern during the last years of the Labour government. Indeed, in a way, his illnesses brought about the fall of the Government in 1951. On 23 September of that year, the whole of the King's left lung was removed after his doctors had discovered that part of it was cancerous. This was his second operation in two years, and the King made another good recovery, beginning to think seriously again about the plans for his tour of Australia and New

Zealand, which had been postponed once already due to his illness. However, he was now beset by doubts of a constitutional nature.

The Labour government's overall majority was down to six, and MPs were sometimes brought from hospital, at the risk of their lives, to vote in the House of Commons, and so prevent a defeat. Therefore, the King felt uncertain about touring Australia and New Zealand if the Government might be defeated by a snap vote in the House of Commons while he was away. On 24 June 1951, he put these anxieties to the Prime Minister who, with some relief, said that he would ask for a dissolution of Parliament in the autumn. In his memoirs, Attlee confirms that it would have been "a constant anxiety to the King if there were a possibility of a fall of the Government or a General Election during his absence from the country".[16]

Polling day in the General Election was on 25 October 1951, and although the Labour Party received nearly fourteen million votes, 231,000 more than their Conservative opponents, they lost the election. The Conservatives were returned to power with 321 seats against Labour's 295 and the Liberals' 6. The new government had a not uncomfortable majority of 17.

In the early evening of 26 October 1951, Winston Churchill drove to Buckingham Palace to receive, for the third time, the King's commission to form a government. Thus the wartime partnership which had given the King so much satisfaction was restored. Attlee was received by the King on 5 November and awarded the Order of Merit. Over six years of Labour rule were at an end.

16

A SUITABLE ADDITION:
THE ROYAL FAMILY
AND PHILIP MOUNTBATTEN

[Prince Philip] was the man with whom Princess Elizabeth had been in love from their first meeting.

Sir John Wheeler-Bennett

I suppose one thing led to another. I suppose I began to think about it seriously, oh, let me think now, when I got back in forty-six and went to Balmoral.

Prince Philip

IF THE YEAR 1947 BEGAN with blizzard conditions, fuel shortages, economic gloom and personal privation, July brought what Winston Churchill, then Leader of the Opposition, called a "flash of colour on the hard road we have to travel" – the announcement of the engagement of Princess Elizabeth to Lieutenant Philip Mountbatten, RN. The Princess had first noticed Prince Philip of Greece eight years before, when she and her sister had accompanied their parents on a visit to Dartmouth Naval College at the end of July 1939. The college, however, was stricken with a double epidemic of chicken-pox and mumps, and it was thought necessary to keep the Princesses away from possible infection. They were taken to the house of the officer in charge of the college, while their parents, accompanied by the King's personal aide-de-camp, Lord Louis Mountbatten, inspected the college. How, in the meantime, were the two Princesses to be entertained? At this point, Prince Philip of Greece, "a fair-haired boy, rather like a Viking, with a sharp face and piercing blue eyes", according to Marion Crawford who was with the Princesses, made his entrance. It was an entirely understandable choice of companion – he was a distant cousin and he was on the spot.

A member of the Greek Royal House, Prince Philip's ancestry was a mixture of Danish, Russian, German and English, and, like Princess Elizabeth, he was a great-great-grandchild of Queen Victoria. In contrast to Elizabeth, however, his upbringing had not been marked by great security nor designed to produce a passive, uncontentious personality. Indeed, chance and misfortune had paid a substantial part in his early development. Although his father was Prince Andrew of Greece, son of George I, King of the Hellenes, and his mother Alice of Battenberg, sister of Lord Louis Mountbatten, in December 1922 the eighteen-month old Prince Philip had been carried into exile with his family aboard HMS *Calypso* where he was given a cot hastily constructed from an orange box.

From December 1922, until his marriage to Princess Elizabeth twenty-five years later, Prince Philip was effectively stateless, and lacking a permanent home. In exile he lived first in France, then at various times in England, Germany and Scotland. His father had little money, and was partly dependent upon financial help from the more fortunate members of his family. After periods of education in France, England, and Germany, Prince Philip underwent the most formative of his educational experiences at Gordonstoun School, founded in Scotland by Dr Kurt Hahn. Hahn, who had been hounded out of Germany by the Nazis in 1933, was a charismatic, quirky and unconventional educationalist who believed in offering his pupils rigorous intellectual and physical challenges, thus helping them to stave off the alleged decays of contemporary society. Prince Philip flourished at Gordonstoun, and Hahn said of him, "He has the greatest sense of service of all the boys in the school . . . [he] is a born leader."

By the time he had reached the age of eight, Prince Philip had had to face the dispersal of his family, as his three much older sisters gradually moved to Germany and their future husbands, and his parents' marriage broke down. Although nothing as vulgar as divorce was suggested, Prince and Princess Andrew drifted apart, and for some years Philip was shuttled between one set of aristocratic and royal relatives to another, from the homes of his elder sisters to those of his mother's brothers – particularly her oldest brother George, Marquis of Milford Haven.

When Philip's uncle, George of Milford Haven, died in 1938, it was the younger brother, Lord Louis Mountbatten, who stood *in loco parentis*. Partly in the martial tradition of his father, and partly due to the influence of his sailor Mountbatten uncles, Prince Philip had entered the Naval College at Dartmouth early in 1939.

What did cadet Prince Philip of Greece make of his cousin Elizabeth, and she of him, at their famous meeting at Dartmouth in July 1939? Certainly they could not have provided greater contrasts in terms of experience and personality: Prince Philip was a tall, confident, ebullient eighteen-year-old; Princess Elizabeth was a shy and rather sheltered thirteen-year-old. Marion Crawford remembers that, "He said 'How do you do?' to Lilibet, and for a while they knelt side by side playing with the trains." Apparently at first Philip found it easier to relate to Margaret, who was rather plump and far less shy than her sister, teasing her a lot and provoking her to ask, with royal disdain, "Who is that boy?"

For a good deal of the time, Prince Philip seems to have spent a lot of energy in showing off. When they went outside, he played croquet with his visitors, and proceeded to jump over the net on the tennis court. Princess Elizabeth seems to have been impressed by this athletic prowess. According to Miss Crawford, "Lilibet said 'How good he is, Crawfie! How high he can jump!' He was quite polite to her."[1] To say wonderingly "How good he is" seems to have been Elizabeth's main contribution to the conversation. Years later, Prince Philip, remembering, said to his wife, "You were so shy. I couldn't get a word out of you."[2]

The next day, contact was renewed, as Lord Louis Mountbatten, Philip's Uncle Dickie, had ". . . steadfastly procured his nephew an invitation to lunch on the royal yacht. Philip contributed to the conversation mainly by teasing Margaret, and laughing a good deal." When eventually the *Victoria and Albert* sailed from Dartmouth, a flotilla of small craft manned by cadets followed in her wake. Aboard, George VI grew apprehensive, telling his captain, "This is ridiculous and quite unsafe. You must signal them to go back!" All but one of the cadets obeyed the signal. Prince Philip of Greece rowed on, causing George VI to exclaim angrily, "The young fool!" Or, in another version, "damned young fool!" Eventually the solitary oarsman turned back, but at least had bade his cousin Elizabeth farewell with a flourish.

Sir John Wheeler-Bennett's official biography of George VI, approved and closely scrutinized by Queen Elizabeth II, says plainly of Prince Philip, "This was the man with whom Princess Elizabeth had been in love from their first meeting." Prince Philip has subsequently been studiously vague about the first flowering of his romance with Princess Elizabeth, though admitting that, in the early years of the war, he was on the list of eligibles, "I mean, after all, if you spend ten minutes thinking about it – and a lot of these people spent a good deal more time thinking about it – how many obviously eligible young men . . . were available? Inevitably, I must have been on the list, so to speak."[3]

What is clear is that during the war, in which Prince Philip served in the Royal Navy with great distinction, an understanding developed between Princess Elizabeth and her Greek cousin. Prince Philip had several match-makers busy on his behalf. First of all, there was his uncle, Lord Louis Mountbatten, who had arranged the introduction at Dartmouth in July 1939, and a powerful figure who skilfully and persistently advocated Philip's case afterwards. There were also various Greek relatives closely connected with the British Royal Family: his uncle, King George II of Greece, exiled in Britain after the Nazi invasion of his country, certainly put in a warm word for Philip to King George VI in 1944; also, there was already a Greek member of the Royal Family – Princess Marina, Duchess of Kent – to advance his cause.

From the early years of the war, Prince Philip and Princess Elizabeth kept up a correspondence. On 21 January 1941, "Chips" Channon recorded his attendance at a Greek cocktail party in Athens: "Prince Philip of Greece was there. . . . He is to be our Prince Consort, and that is why he is serving in our Navy." Channon apparently based his information on a conversation with Princess Nicholas of Greece, mother of the Duchess of Kent. In the summer of 1941, Prince Philip's cousin, Princess Alexandra of Greece, was with him in Cape Town. Observing him writing a letter, she enquired who it was to:

"Lilibet", he answered.
"Who?" I asked, still rather mystified.
"Princess Elizabeth, in England."
"But she's only a baby," I said, still rather puzzled, as he sealed the letter. Aha, I thought with family candour, he knows he's going to England, and he is angling for invitations.[4]

At the end of 1941, after some pressure, Princess Elizabeth got Philip's name added to her father's family Christmas mailing list. By Christmas 1943, Philip had indeed got the invitation for which his cousin Alexandra had suspected him of angling and, having in his own words "nowhere particular to go", was invited to spend the festivities with the Royal Family at Windsor Castle. At dinner with the King and Queen, Princesses Elizabeth and Margaret, and four others, the young naval officer entertained the company with a humorous account of German dive-bombers attacking his ship, HMS *Wallace* off the coast of Sicily; the King, with his taste for naval heroics, was doubtless as impressed as his daughter.[5]

All the same, King George VI did not take kindly to the prospect of his elder daughter's marriage, partly on the quite justifiable grounds that she was too young and inexperienced. The King, moreover, had difficulty in believing that Princess Elizabeth had fallen deeply in love with the first eligible male she had met. Yet as the correspondence between Elizabeth and Philip grew more intense, as the young naval officer made more visits to Windsor and Buckingham Palace, all the signs of an increasingly serious attachment were there. In March 1944, George VI had delivered an interim and authoritative pronouncement, telling Queen Mary that he was not prepared to give King George II of Greece any encouragement on Philip's behalf, "We both think she is too young for that now, as she has never met any young men of her own age. . . . I like Philip. He is intelligent, has a good sense of humour & thinks about things in the right way. . . . We are going to tell George that P had better not think any more about it for the present."

The King's belief that Princess Elizabeth was too young to contemplate an engagement was shared by his wife, and there was something more to the King's attitude than mere paternal common sense. George VI was, in a way, extremely possessive. His strong attachment to his immediate family was easy enough to understand: having missed the pleasures of a warm and close childhood himself, the family love and loyalty which he had experienced after his marriage brought him such intense pleasure that he found it difficult to contemplate the break-up of the royal family of four. Within a decade of his marriage his family had become, ". . . a perfect quartet. To remove one member of this team would inevitably spoil it; not only for himself, but for his younger daughter also, who might be left lonely and exposed."[7] The idea that the King felt possessive about his daughters is substantially reinforced by his failure during and after the war to provide them with sufficient social contact with young men of their own ages. Although some belated efforts were made by the King to introduce his elder daughter to suitable young men, especially from 1945 onwards, it was too late to deflect her affections from Philip of Greece. Packs of suitably blue-blooded young Guards officers were encouraged to cluster around Elizabeth at rather self-consciously jolly parties at Windsor and elsewhere, with the King himself leading congas round the ballroom.

Queen Mary supported her grand-daughter's preference for Prince Philip, and rather disapproved of the clumps of young men organized by the King, referring to them scathingly as the "Body Guard". Queen Mary's own marriage to George V had hardly resulted from a chance meeting: she had originally been engaged to his elder brother, the Duke of Clarence, but on the latter's death had been prudently handed on to the second son. Perhaps because of these experiences, Queen Mary in her old age seems strongly to have approved of Princess Elizabeth's "unarranged" choice of a future husband. Certainly she once told Lady Airlie, "Elizabeth seems that kind of a girl. She would always know her own mind. There is something very steadfast and determined about her." For her part, Lady Airlie speculated, during 1946, on the King's feelings about his daughter's desire for marriage: "His affection for her was touching. I wondered sometimes whether he was secretly dreading the prospect of an early marriage for her – by then her name had been linked for some time with that of Prince Philip of Greece."[8]

If by the end of the war Princess Elizabeth was quite sure that she wanted to marry Prince Philip, and if he was equally sure, as seems to be the case, what ensued was a long rearguard action fought with great persistence by George VI against the inevitable outcome. There are a good many indications that this was so. Towards the end of the war, Princess Alexandra of Greece, now Queen Alexandra of Yugoslavia, spoke to Princess Marina about Philip and Elizabeth. "Well let's touch wood they don't have to wait so long for their engagement and wedding as we did." To which Marina replied, "They will probably have to wait much longer than you did. I won't be able to influence Uncle Bertie for Lilibet nearly as easily as I did for you."[9] By the middle of 1946 things were no more settled, although Prince Philip was invited to spend part of the summer holiday at Balmoral Castle with the Royal Family. This was undoubtedly part of the vetting process that was going on, but did not result in the announcement of the couple's engagement. The impending royal tour of South Africa was another reason why no engagement could be announced: although Princess Elizabeth would be twenty-one while in South Africa during the early part of 1947, the King wished her to set aside her personal wishes until the tour was completed. Later, the King recognized her forbearance in this matter, writing to her perhaps a little guiltily, "I was rather anxious that you had thought I was being very hard-hearted about it. I was so anxious for you to come to South Africa as you knew. Our family, us four, the 'Royal Family', must remain together with additions of course, at suitable moments!"[10]

As it happened, Prince Philip proposed to Princess Elizabeth during his stay at Balmoral in the summer of 1946. The proposal had been accepted, and a discreet, unofficial engagement party had been held. Even so, things were not easy. Philip outstayed his welcome, and George VI finally grew impatient, saying, "The boy must go south!" Early in September 1946, rumours of a royal engagement led to an official statement being issued from Buckingham Palace firmly denying the story.

Although Princess Elizabeth dutifully accompanied her family on the tour of South Africa in the early part of 1947, her return did not result in a prompt announcement of her engagement. This was surprising, since several difficulties in Prince Philip's background had already been cleared up: the Greek royal family were back on the throne and apparently winning the battle against the Communist-led insurrection, and early in 1947 Prince Philip had been naturalized, and had thus become a British subject. Even this development led George VI to worry over further insubstantial obstacles – for example, what should the newly-anglicized young man's surname be? Various proposals, including Oldcastle, were suggested and rejected, and finally the obvious surname of Mountbatten was adopted. As to his religion, Prince Philip, who had been baptized into the Greek Orthdox Church, indicated that he would be willing to become a member of the Church of England.

By the summer of 1947, no substantive reason existed to prevent the official announcement of the engagement, and, on 10 July, Prince Philip at last produced an engagement ring that incorporated some stones from a ring of his mother's, and the announcement was made from Buckingham Palace. The wedding day was fixed for 20 November, despite a last-ditch effort by George VI to delay the ceremony until June 1948 when, he argued, the weather would be kinder. His daughter, however, had waited long enough, and her wedding ceremony was to enliven with warmth and light a dull November day.

It was a grey, gloomy, typical November morning – but fine. Enormous crowds lined the ceremonial route, many having camped overnight in inclement weather.

The bride and her father alighted from the Irish State Coach. Richard Dimbleby described the scene for radio audiences:

The doors of the coach are open. The crowds shout with excitement and love. The King, in the uniform of Admiral of the Fleet, comes forward to help his daughter alight carefully. Now she steps down. A great cheer arises to sustain her.

[233]

She pauses for a moment and looks at the Abbey. And perhaps – perhaps she is a little nervous in her heart as she passes from the grey of the morning outside into the warmth and colour of the Abbey.

As the King escorted his daughter down the aisle, he experienced that mixture of pride and loss that is commonplace in fathers about to give away their daughters, but which in his case was particularly deeply felt. He later told his daughter of his feelings, writing to her during her honeymoon:

> I was so proud of you & thrilled at having you so close to me on our long walk in Westminster Abbey, but when I handed your hand to the Archbishop I felt that I had lost something very precious. You were so calm & composed during the Service & said your words with such conviction that I knew everything was all right.
>
> I am so glad you wrote & told Mummy that you think the long wait before your engagement & the long time before the wedding was for the best.[11]

Princess Elizabeth was certainly outwardly calm, triumphant even. She looked particularly pretty – "like an English rose" observers were to say predictably – yet, at the same time, unassuming, ordinary in demeanour. There was nothing ordinary, though, about her wedding dress which shimmered as she moved; it was embroidered with the white roses of York, with orange blossom, and with ears of corn and wheat, emblems of harvest and fertility.

After the wedding service in the Abbey and the triumphant procession back to Buckingham Palace through the cheering crowds, the reception for the married couple saw the King like a man liberated from both doubt and grief, moving among his guests, joking and chaffing. However, when the bridal pair had driven off to embark on their honeymoon, the King, according to his niece, Alexandra of Yugoslavia, looked depressed. "I tried to cheer up Uncle Bertie, who was looking quite miserable, 'Now Philip's got you and Aunt Elizabeth, as well as Lilibet,' I said. 'He *belongs* now.' 'That's right, Sandra,' said Uncle Bertie, suddenly smiling. 'He does belong. *You're so right!* Come and have a drink!'"[12]

The King's sense of loss jostled with his better feelings in a letter he wrote soon afterwards to his daughter. "Your leaving us has left a great blank in our lives. Do remember that your old home is still yours,

& do come back to it as much & as often as possible. I can see that you are sublimely happy with Philip, which is right, but don't forget us is the wish of Your ever loving & devoted Papa."[13]

No doubt the King hoped that many years of life lay ahead of him, during which he could, little by little, acquaint his daughter with the realities of the responsibilities and obligations that would one day be hers. This was not to be – the last years of his life were marred by ill-health and doubt.

Before he died, his daughter produced two grandchildren; Prince Charles on 14 November 1948, and on 15 August 1950 a daughter, Princess Anne. There is little evidence to indicate the quality of the relationship between the King and his two grandchildren, only that he had a "growing interest" in them. Perhaps something of the affection that existed between them can be gauged more accurately by some of the photographs that exist picturing them together. There is a particularly touching set taken on Prince Charles' third birthday in November 1951, which shows the smiling Queen Elizabeth holding a bouncing Princess Anne, and the King engaged in affectionate conversation with his grandson; all four are sitting on a sofa.

The King, of course, had another daughter, and although he was not to see her married, she had already fallen in love. When she was fourteen years old, her father had appointed a new equerry, Group Captain Peter Townsend, a thirty-year-old war veteran who had flown with "the Few" during the Battle of Britain. Townsend was an attractive man with blue eyes, fine features, wavy hair and a slim, graceful build. He was also married, to Rosemary Pawle, by whom he had two sons. By the time of her father's death, Princess Margaret was in love with Peter Townsend.

Princess Margaret had been quite closely involved with her sister's courtship with Prince Philip. On the surface, she seems to have been a caring and supportive younger sister, sympathizing with Elizabeth in the face of the King's reluctance to treat her attachment to Philip as seriously as it deserved. She also seems to have been something of a nuisance, frequently joining the couple when they would have preferred to have been alone. Marion Crawford noticed, "The constant presence of the little sister, who was far from understanding, and liked a good deal of attention herself, was not helping the romance." However, there seems to have been no resentment felt on this score by either Philip or Elizabeth.

Almost certainly, though, Princess Margaret's involvement with her sister's courtship, her "constant presence", was partly a displacement of her own feelings for Peter Townsend. Her infatuation with him was hardly respectable; he was, after all, already married, her father and mother would not have approved of such feelings. Even if, in Princess Margaret's fantasies, Townsend might one day get divorced, the Royal Family and divorce evidently did not mix – as the self-imposed exile of the Duke and Duchess of Windsor clearly indicated. Margaret's affection for Townsend may have been strengthened by her father's evident respect and liking for his equerry. Some have even argued that Townsend, in some ways, became to the King the son he had never had. Her father's liking for and dependence upon Townsend thus rendered Princess Margaret's admiration for him, in a sense, more respectable.

In 1951 Peter Townsend separated from his wife, and in December 1952 he was granted a divorce decree *nisi* on account of his wife's adultery. What would have happened if the King had lived several years longer than he did is impossible to say. No doubt, with Townsend finally divorced, Margaret's affection for him, and his for her, would in some way have been brought to the King's notice. Although it seems extremely unlikely that George VI would have sanctioned the marriage of his daughter to a divorced man, Princess Margaret herself apparently believed that, had he lived, "Papa would have found a way." The King's premature death, however, removed even this remote possibility, but he at least died knowing that his elder daughter's marriage was a success. Not merely did she seem happy with her husband, but she had provided the House of Windsor, with commendable efficiency, with a male heir. Moreover, although the King may not have appreciated it at the time, Prince Philip's marriage to the Royal Family was to provide it with a capable and stimulating recruit.

Princess Elizabeth had been brought up in such a way as to render Lord Altrincham's criticisms of her, published in the *National and English Review* in August 1957, tellingly accurate. Altrincham wrote, "The personality conveyed by the utterances that are put into her mouth is that of the priggish schoolgirl, captain of the hockey team, a prefect, and a recent candidate for confirmation." All this was hardly her fault, and simply reflected the sheltered, rather restricted quality of her upbringing. George VI and Queen Elizabeth's social circle and intellectual capacities had been limited, and her own were similarly narrow. Prince Philip, however, could in no way be described as the male equivalent of a "priggish schoolgirl". His obvious intelligence, his capacity to think about the problems of the modern world, his ability to write and make speeches which could cause people to sit up and take notice, his physical drive and the spontaneity which characterized his public appearances, were qualities that could only enhance the standing of the House of Windsor.

Despite the essential simplicity of his manner and of his tastes, King George VI was too respectful of archaic tradition. While preserving enough mystique to mystify, a constitutional monarchy must also be prepared to move with the times, and there is little evidence to suggest that, if he had lived longer, George VI would willingly have undertaken its modernization and refurbishment. In his daughter's husband, however, there existed a modernizing influence within the family that could bring about relevant change and at the same time preserve the dignity and prestige of the institution of monarchy. Although he might not have approved of the methods employed, George VI would undoubtedly have welcomed the net result: the monarchy's increased relevance, its enhanced standing, and the continued widespread affection felt for it by the public in Britain and overseas.

17

LAST YEARS
1951–1952

The King is not likely to live more than 18 months. The end will probably come suddenly. The operation was six months too late.
Sir Harold Graham Hodgson, royal radiologist, September 1951

This was by any standards, anywhere, a good man.
The Daily Mirror

ALTHOUGH THE LAST FEW YEARS of George VI's life were enriched by the arrival of his two grandchildren, they were also plagued by anxiety and illness. One observer had written, "Racked with ill health, puzzled where his duty lay, George VI withdrew increasingly to the country life at Sandringham, which he had always preferred."[1] Although few of his subjects could have known it, the King was fighting a losing battle from 1949 to regain his health, and had never fully recovered from the enormous strain imposed upon him during the Second World War. During the royal tour of South Africa in 1947, a snapshot taken of him towards the end of the tour by a student showed a tense and drawn profile: "The King's features are clear-cut and taut – almost too taut for comfort – and his eyes have a faraway look. It is a profile to love, admire – and fear for."[2] Within two months of his return from South Africa, he began to feel cramps in his legs – the first symptoms of the illness which was soon to overtake him.

By October 1948 the King's cramps were painful and permanent, and on 20 October he summoned Sir Morton Smart to Buckingham Palace for a medical consultation. Sir Morton was alarmed at the condition in which he found the King's right foot, and insisted upon seeking further medical advice. On 30 October George VI was examined by Sir Maurice Cassidy, Sir Morton Smart, Sir John Weir and Sir Thomas Dunhill. All four specialists agreed that the King's condition was serious, and they decided to call in Professor James Learmonth, Regius Professor of Clinical Surgery at Edinburgh University, and one of the greatest authorities on vascular complaints in the country.

Professor Learmonth arranged to examine the King on 12 November, when the results of blood tests and X-ray photographs would be known. In the interim, George VI, with his characteristic devotion to duty, insisted upon carrying out a number of tiring official engagements, including a review of the Territorial Army in Hyde Park on 31 October, and the Remembrance Day Service at the Cenotaph on Sunday 7 November. He attended this service against medical advice, and also insisted that Princess Elizabeth, who was very soon due to give birth to her first child, should not be told of the serious nature of his condition.

After examining the King on 12 November, Professor Learmonth diagnosed that he was suffering from a case of early arteriosclerosis. The other consultants present agreed with the diagnosis, and it seemed to the King's medical advisers that there was a danger of gangrene developing, and that his right leg might have to be amputated.

Fortunately, amputation was avoided. The King accepted, although with some reluctance, that a period of rest and inactivity, coupled with treatment to improve the circulation of blood through the arteries in his legs, was unavoidable. By the beginning of December 1948, his health had improved so rapidly that all danger of amputation had disappeared. He wrote to his mother, "I think even Learmonth is surprised & pleased with the fortnight's treatment, so I am feeling happier today. But I am getting tired & bored with bed as I am feeling so much more rested which is a good thing." Although the proposed royal tour of Australia and New Zealand had to be postponed, he went to Sandringham for Christmas and the new year, was able to enjoy some limited shooting there after 18 January, and returned to London at the end of February 1949. There he resumed a limited programme of audiences and held an investiture. It seemed to the King and his family that he was already well on the road to a complete recovery.

A full consultation with his doctors on 3 March 1949, however, brought bitter disappointment. Although satisfied with the progress he had made, the King's consultants believed that the improved state of his health could only be maintained if he continued to lead the life of an invalid. Given the King's impatience with inactivity, his capacity to fret, and his high sense of his public duty and obligations, it was unthinkable that he should live out the rest of his life in so restricted a fashion. To avoid this, his doctors proposed that he should undergo an operation to relieve the obstruction to the blood supply in his right leg.

George VI was not pleased at this suggestion, exclaiming wrathfully, "So all our treatment has been a waste of time!" His good sense prevailed, however, when it was pointed out to him that as a result of his recent forbearance and co-operation he would be much better able to stand the strain of the proposed operation. Where should the surgery be performed? One proposal was the Royal Masonic Hospital, to which the King, albeit a devoted Freemason, replied, "I have never heard of a King going to a hospital before."

In the event, the operation was carried out in rooms in Buckingham Palace, in a temporary but fully equipped surgical theatre. It was performed by Professor Learmonth, assisted by Professor Paterson Ross. The operation, a right lumbar sympathectomy, was not a particularly dangerous piece of surgery: a small incision was made in the skin at the side of the body, then the nerve controlling the blood supply to the foot was cut in order to give a freer circulation of blood to the right limb. Once the nerves were cut, the muscles in the walls of the leg artery relaxed, thus allowing much more blood to get down to the tissues of the foot. The operation lasted for about half an hour.

The King had sufficiently recovered from this operation to hold a Privy Council on 29 March 1949, but despite his rapid progress he was under no illusions that he would be completely restored in health. A change in the tempo of his life was necessary, and Professor Learmonth warned him that a second attack of thrombosis would be much more difficult to survive. The King promised not to overtire himself, but went to some lengths to ensure that he could still pursue his passion for shooting as fully as possible. Nonetheless, he started to live a quieter life.

If the King, his family, and the British public felt relief at his apparently successful recovery from the operation in March 1949, the underlying cause of the King's ailment, though not a subject for official speculation, was far more worrying. What had brought about the inflammation in the arteries which had slowed down the circulation of the blood in the King's feet and legs? The American press, with its traditional lack of inhibition, had speculated on the nature of the King's illness at the end of 1948. *Time* magazine had reported that George VI was suffering from a variation of Buerger's Disease, and it commented, "The cause of Buerger's Disease is unknown. Many, but not all, patients are cigarette smokers (smoking constricts the small arteries). The King's doctors are reported to have ordered him to stop his heavy smoking."[3]

Here, in all probability, was the underlying cause of the King's ill health – his heavy smoking. Back in July 1941, *Time* magazine had reported that, in order to share the hardships of his people, the King had cut down his consumption of cigarettes from twenty or twenty-five a day to a mere fifteen.[4] After the war, however, the King's rate of smoking again increased.

It is odd that so little attention was paid to the King's smoking habits amid the immense publicity that was given to every aspect of his ill health from 1948 onwards. In 1957, a book published by Dr Lennox Johnston, *The Disease of Tobacco Smoking and Its Cure*, asserted that far too much secrecy had surrounded George VI's smoking habits. Dr Johnston claimed that heavy smoking was one of the causes of Buerger's Disease, and wrote, "Not until after the King's death from coronary thrombosis, following an operation for lung cancer, was it revealed by one of the surgeons, himself a heavy smoker, that the King had been a consistently heavy smoker."[5] Dr Johnston criticized the BBC, the *British Medical Journal*, the *Lancet*, and the Medical Research Council for their obstructive attitudes to anti-smoking propaganda. (His wife Frieda said, on the publication of his book, "It has taken my husband thirty years to complete his research into the evils of smoking – and to find a publisher for his book."[6])

Despite the ominous implications of his taste for tobacco, there seemed no reason why, if he was sufficiently prudent, the King should not look forward to a reasonable span of life. As he recovered from the operation, his sense of optimism and well-being returned, and until the end of 1949 he had frequent consultations with Professor Learmonth, whose care and advice helped the King to adjust to the necessary change in the tempo of his life. On the occasion of his final consultation with Learmonth, the King showed that his sense of humour was as lively as ever. When the examination was over, he picked up a sword which had been discreetly concealed and said, "You used the knife on me, now I am going to use one on you," and, bidding the professor kneel before him on a stool, bestowed a knighthood upon him.

For all his sense of regained health, developments both at home and internationally gave the King ample cause for anxiety. In Britain the post-war reconstructions and reforms of the Labour government were clouded by the nation's deteriorating economic position, culminating in the devaluation of the pound in 1949. Nor did the narrow Labour majority in the General Election of February 1950 promise a lengthy period of stable domestic government. Abroad, the opening of the Korean War in June 1950 and the continuing menace of the Cold War were clear indications that harmony and tranquillity would be even more difficult to achieve internationally than at home.

1951, however, saw Britain attempt to prove its regeneration and continuing vitality through the Festival of Britain. This enormous enterprise, which had been planned four years previously, was intended not only to mark the hundredth anniversary of the Great Exhibition of 1851, but also to provide an advertisement for Britain's industrial and technological strength. Although interest was centred on the exhibition on the South Bank and the funfair in Battersea Park, the spirit of the festival was expressed in various events and celebrations throughout the nation during that year. George VI opened the Festival of Britain from the steps of St Paul's Cathedral on 3 May 1951.

On 24 May 1951 the King installed his brother, the Duke of Gloucester, as Great Master of the Order of the Bath at a special service in the King Henry VII Chapel at Westminster Abbey. Many who saw him during the service remarked on the fact that he looked ill. He was indeed running a high temperature, and that evening he took to his bed with influenza.

The King was slow to recover from this attack and was also troubled by a persistent cough. A distinguished team of doctors, Sir Horace Evans, Sir Daniel Davies, Sir John Weir and Dr Geoffrey Marshall made a thorough examination of the King's condition, and as a result discovered a small area of what was called catarrhal inflammation in the left lung. George VI was relieved that his doctors had found an explanation for his continued high temperature, and he told Queen Mary:

> I have a condition on the left lung known as pneumonitis. It is not pneumonia though if I left it it might become it. I was X-rayed, & the photograph showed a shadow. So I am having daily injections of penicillin for about a week. This condition has only been on the lung for a few days at the most so it should resolve itself with treatment . . . The doctors think the cause of the cough was below the larynx, & has now moved into the lung . . . Everyone is very relieved at this revelation & the doctors are happier about me tonight than they have been for a week.[7]

There was little cause for this optimism – the King could not shake off his ill health, and complained at "not being able to chuck out the bug". His doctors ordered him to rest and convalesce during June and July, and on 3 August he moved to Balmoral for two months' recuperative holiday.

Meanwhile, speculation grew as to the nature of his illness, and the prospects for his full recovery. Early in June 1951 the *Sunday Pictorial* published an article under the headline, WILL THE KING RETIRE? The article, by a Special Correspondent, began, "The King has been seriously ill – how seriously the general public does not fully appreciate. His convalescence is going slowly." The paper pointed out, "The precise nature of his leg trouble has never been publicly diagnosed. But informed medical opinion is that he had Buerger's disease. . . . This disease is recurrent. An operation such as the King underwent two years ago could afford only temporary relief. Most men would be lucky to survive another five years without amputation."[8] Suggesting that the proposed tour of Australia and New Zealand in 1952 would have to be cancelled, and pointing out that Lloyds of London were already refusing to underwrite the risk of cancellation of the tour, the *Sunday Pictorial* continued, "The King's health has now prompted the question: Will he now retire into private life and pass the reigns of sovereignty to his daughter, Princess Elizabeth. . . . It would be a saddening thing to see a much-loved King step down from his throne. But it would be callous, indeed, to demand that he should sacrifice himself on the altar of duty."[9]

Of course there was no question of the King abdicating. For one thing, he still retained the hope that he would sufficiently recover his health; for another, the true nature of the illness that was affecting him was as yet unknown. By the end of August 1951, however, the benefits that the King had earlier felt from his holiday at Balmoral had all but vanished. He developed a chill and a sore throat. Two of his doctors flew to examine him at Balmoral on 1 September. They strongly advised him to return to London for further examination and X-rays.

On 8 September the King came down to London by train for consultation with his team of doctors, which now included Clement Price Thomas, a surgeon specializing in malignant diseases of the chest. The *Sunday Pictorial* of 9 September published on its front page, under the heading, A PICTURE WE ARE PROUD TO PRINT!, a photograph of the King leaving the front door of his Wimpole Street radiologist, Dr George Cordiner. The King is carrying his hat in his right hand, and is looking drawn and ill as he steps onto the pavement towards his car. In the comment under the photograph, the *Sunday Pictorial* says, somewhat ingenuously, "Why are we proud to print this picture? Because it is news, because it is human, because it is symbolic. It is a happy and reassuring picture of a monarch about whom his people have been anxious for a long time. . . . Now he makes the arduous double journey in twenty-four hours so that no groundless rumours about his health would develop. It is a picture of a King who is secure in his people's affections. Of a King who always puts his country before himself."[10]

Ironically, the photograph is anything but reassuring: it shows a sick, anxious and prematurely aged man. The King's doctors now feared that he was suffering from cancer of the lung and they unanimously advised him to undergo a bronchoscopy, so that a small piece of the tissue from his left lung could be removed and analyzed. The King returned to London on 15 September, where, on the next day, Mr Price Thomas carried out the examination. The bronchoscopy revealed that the King was indeed suffering from a malignant growth. On 18 September, Price Thomas informed the King that his doctors considered it necessary to remove his left lung as soon as possible.

George VI did not know that he was suffering from cancer. The reason given for the proposed operation was that his illness was caused by a blockage of one of the bronchial tubes in his chest. He dreaded the prospect of a second operation, telling a friend, "If it's going to help me get well again I don't mind, but the very idea of the surgeon's knife again is hell."

The operation was carried out by Price Thomas on the morning of Sunday 23 September. The removal of the King's diseased left lung went smoothly, but there was throughout the operation, and after it, the serious possibility that the King might suffer a thrombosis which could cause his death. During the operation it had also been found necessary to sacrifice certain nerves of the larynx, which meant that the King might never be able to speak again above a whisper. The medical bulletin issued after the operation said, "The King underwent an operation for lung resection this morning. Whilst anxiety must remain for some days, His Majesty's immediate post-operative condition is satisfactory."

The nation reacted to the news of the King's operation with anxiety and concern. The day before the operation, the *Daily Express* had carried a front page banner headline, THE KING: AN OPERATION. "Lung condition causes concern."[11] On the Monday after the operation, the *Daily Herald* proclaimed on its front page, THE KING: 'SATISFACTORY'. But anxious days follow operation." Crowds gathered outside Buckingham Palace to wait for further news and on 13 October, *Picture*

Post published a series of photographs showing the daily and nightly vigils of the King's subjects, headlining the article, TEN DAYS OF ANXIETY. Princess Elizabeth and Prince Philip postponed the departure date of their projected visit to Canada, which had been set for 1 October; they eventually left by air on 7 October. Two days later it was announced that the King would not, after all, be able to undertake his own tour of Australia and New Zealand in the coming year.

By mid-October the King had made satisfactory progress in his convalescence. He wrote, in reasonably good spirits, to his mother, "At last I am feeling a bit better after all I have been through in the last 3 weeks. I do seem to go through the most serious operations anybody can do, but thank goodness there were no complications & everything has gone according to plan."[13]

In fact, the King was less than four months away from death. Although the British public were reassured that he was making a slow but satisfactory recovery from his operation, within a small and well-informed circle there were real anxieties about the state of the King's health, and, apparently, some controversy among the royal doctors over whether the cancer could have been diagnosed earlier. Looking back on the death of George VI twenty years after the event, John Gordon, writing in the *Sunday Express*, said:

> Was his death a surprise? Not to me. On the day that the decisive operation was performed in September, the lung tissues were sent for clinical examination. I asked my friend, Sir Harold Graham Hodgson, the royal radiologist for many years and one of the shrewdest diagnostic experts I ever knew, what he thought. After consulting other experts, in whose judgement he had infallible faith, he replied: "The King is not likely to live more than 18 months. The end will probably come suddenly. The operation was six months too late."[14]

Could the King's cancer have been discovered earlier? In an article published in the *St Mary's Hospital Gazette* in the middle of 1967, the distinguished surgeon Arthur Dickson Wright alleged that one of the doctors who had attended the King had recognized a tumour early, but "was ignored, and brooded over it so much that he committed suicide".[15] Sir Geoffrey Marshall, who had been the physician in the team of doctors and surgeons that had attended the King, took issue with Dickson Wright, claiming that the doctor in question, in reports

[245]

dated 31 May, 6 June, 12 June and 10 July 1951, had merely described an inflamed area in the left lung, and had not suggested that there was a tumour present, either cancerous or otherwise. Marshall went on:

> The clinicians still suspected a growth in the lung, and at their request the doctors took a series of chest films by a different technique, known as tomography.
>
> These again failed to establish the diagnosis so, again at their request, a second doctor was invited to co-operate with the first one, and take a further series of tomographs with a modified apparatus.
>
> These films for the first time showed the presence of a tumour at the root of the lung, and on the same day a chest surgeon was called in.[16]

Sir Geoffrey Marshall also denied that the doctor referred to had committed suicide in 1957. He said, "He died suddenly; but the verdict of suicide is that of the writer of the article, and is not in accordance with the findings of the inquest." In reply to this point, Mr Dickson Wright stuck to his views, and wrote, "From my own personal knowledge, I believe that this sincere and dedicated doctor did brood, because his early diagnosis was ignored." *The Times* report of the inquest of the dead doctor on 12 April 1957 was headlined "Doctor died from overdose", but went on to state that, "Although Dr —— died from an overdose of barbiturates, there was no evidence pointing to suicide."[17]

Altogether, a good deal of secrecy surrounded the real reasons for the King's second operation. In the medical bulletin issued on 18 September, which prepared the public for the surgery that was now deemed essential to save the King's life, the reference to the "structural changes . . . in the lung" was unspecific.

One of the results of the King being kept in ignorance as to the real reason for the removal of his lung was that his family – who did know – and indeed the Government, were obliged to act as if the future was relatively secure. Thus Princess Elizabeth and the Duke of Edinburgh had been obliged to set off for their tour of Canada, which included a brief visit to the United States, and on 31 January 1952 the couple embarked on their lengthy and ambitious tour of East Africa, Australia and New Zealand, on the King's behalf.

Meanwhile, George VI appeared to be in better health, and on 14 November 1951 had been photographed for the first time since his operation at Prince Charles' third birthday party. A day of national thanksgiving for the King's recovery was celebrated on 2 December 1951. The King continued to gain strength, and indeed felt fitter than he had done for a long time – he was even able to give much thought to the problem of Winston Churchill's failing health. Churchill had already had one stroke, and he was demonstrably slowing down. George VI felt that it was time for Churchill to make way for Anthony Eden, who was the obvious heir to the premiership. Since none of Churchill's cabinet colleagues stood a chance of persuading him to stand down for Eden, only the King had the necessary prestige to undertake the delicate task of suggesting that the time had arrived for Churchill's retirement. He decided that he would broach the subject in the new year.

On 21 December, George VI, having celebrated his fifty-sixth birthday quietly, travelled with his family to Sandringham. For the first time for many years, he was relieved of the worry of delivering his Christmas broadcast live, for the frequent examinations of his chest and throat had left him hoarse, and it was decided that he should pre-record his address, sentence by sentence, as his strength allowed. About a month later, on 29 January 1952, the King's doctors examined him and declared themselves well satisfied with his progress. The next evening, the Royal Family went to the theatre together for the first time since the King's illness – they saw *South Pacific* at Drury Lane. The outing was in the nature of a celebration for the King's recovery, and a final gathering of the family before Princess Elizabeth and the Duke of Edinburgh embarked on their Commonwealth tour.

The next morning, 31 January 1952, King George VI waved goodbye to his daughter and son-in-law, standing on the tarmac of London Airport. The newsreel film shows him bare-headed, his hair ruffled by the keen, cold wind, and his face, as he at last turned away, seemed drawn with anxiety, and perhaps a premonition of death.

The King returned to Sandringham where a small party of friends awaited him. He had told the surgeons that now they had had their fun with him, he was going to have some fun himself – shooting. Although the King used special shells in his gun to reduce recoil, he shot game with his usual dexterity, and on 5 February, a clear, crisp and sunny day, he excelled himself at shooting hare. He was apparently "as carefree and happy as those about him had ever known him to be". At the end of the outing, which had bagged 280 hares, the King planned the next day's sport, and after dinner retired to his room at 10.30 pm. He finally went to sleep at about midnight.

When the King's valet went to wake him early on the morning of 6 February he found him already dead. Not long after he had finally gone to sleep at midnight, he had suffered the coronary thrombosis which had for some time threatened his life. There had not been enough pain to wake him.

The tributes to George VI, both national and international, reflected both the affection and the respect that was felt for him. The *Evening Standard* of 6 February wrote, "Modest and gentle, he gave a moral lead to all his people." The *Evening News* called him "A good and great King". The *Daily Mirror* wrote of him, "Not at all palace-minded, but with the right dignity of kings, and an upholder of the decencies. This was by any standards, anywhere, a good man." The Prime Minister of Canada, Louis St Laurent, said, "For Canadians, the death of the Sovereign comes as a personal sorrow. The King was a great King and a good man." An Australian MP was reported as saying, "We have lost a great bloke," and in Pakistan a salute of fifty-six guns, one for each year of the King's life, was fired. In Egypt, King Farouk ordered his Court in mourning for two weeks, and the Prime Minister of Italy, de Gasperi, said in Parliament, "King George represented the civic virtues of the British people, and exercised them with simplicity and a high sense of duty." In the West German parliament the speaker, Dr Dehlers, announced the news "with deep sorrow" while members stood silently. The Prime Minister of Belgium, van Houte, said in a broadcast, "Never have we felt the loss of a foreign monarch so deeply." In India, the parliament adjourned for two days, and the French Prime Minister, Faure, calling at the British Embassy, said "King George carried out noble traditions with dignity and greatness, and devotion." On the edge of no-man's land in Korea, British troops fired a salute of 101 guns.

George VI was the man *not* born to be king who nonetheless rescued the British monarchy during the confusion of the abdication crisis and its aftermath. He was no Renaissance prince, the fountainhead of a cultured and sophisticated Court, but the times he lived in were not those of the Renaissance: his kingship coincided with a global struggle to the death between the forces of democracy and enlightenment and those of tyranny and evil. Throughout this conflict the King, by his example, symbolized those qualities of unassuming decent and modest self-sacrifice that made it possible for his subjects to identify closely with him. Although sometimes intolerant and obsessional in small matters like correct dress and styling, he was maturely tolerant in the face of great issues and choices.

The King did not possess a fully rounded and tranquil personality: he could be bad-tempered, irritable and querulous, prone to self-doubt, and, for much of his life, easily discouraged. But he also had the courage and will to overcome or contain his inadequacies and disabilities and to find, in the process, much personal happiness. Amid shifting times and new moral standards, George VI stood for the old-fashioned virtues of monogamy, domesticity, hearth and home. He was a faithful and loving husband, and an adoring and reliable father. Although he lived his life in palaces, indulging aristocratic sporting tastes, he would have been perfectly content in a mock-Tudor semi-detached house with his family, his stamp collection and the radio.

The widespread and genuine grief that greeted his death was not merely a ritual reaction to the passing of a king. It also reflected his people's perception of him as a monarch who cared, and who had apparently worked himself sacrificially to death on the nation's behalf. The King was a great worrier: sometimes he worried about himself, far more often he worried about others – about his subjects in Britain and the Empire, about the people of Europe, and the international community at large. This did not make for an easy life, but at least he had a comfortable death. After fifty-six years of endeavour, duty and anxiety, it was wholly fitting that King George VI should die peacefully in his sleep.

On 15 February King George VI was buried with the solemn pomp and ceremony of state. Among the millions who mourned his passing was Queen Mary, alone in her sitting-room at Marlborough House with Lady Airlie, looking out into the mist and gloom: "As the cortège wound slowly along the Queen whispered in a broken voice, 'Here *he* is,' and I knew that her dry eyes were seeing beyond the coffin a little boy in a sailor suit. She was past weeping, wrapped in the ineffable solitude of grief. I could not speak to comfort her. My tears choked me. The words I wanted to say, would not come. We held each other's hand in silence."[18]

Among the wreaths in tribute to the dead King was one bearing the signature "Winston S. Churchill' and inscribed, "In loyal and affectionate memory of their august Sovereign King George VI, the royal

[249]

founder of the George Cross, with humble duty from Her Majesty's Government." The wreath was in the shape of the George Cross, made out of white lilac and white carnations, and bearing in purple lettering at its centre the words "For Gallantry".

BIBLIOGRAPHY

BOOKS

Airlie, Lady, *Thatched With Gold*, 1962
Alexandra, ex-Queen Consort of Yugoslavia, *Prince Philip; A Family Portrait*, 1959
American Resident, An, *The Twilight of the British Monarchy*, 1937
Amery, L. S., *My Political Life*, Vol. 3, 1955
Asquith, Lady Cynthia, *The King's Daughters*, 1937
Attlee, Clement R., *As It Happened*, 1956
Bagehot, Walter, *The English Constitution*, 1949 edition
Baxter, Beverley, *Destiny Called Them*, 1939
Beal, Erica, *King-Emperor; The Life of King George VI*, 1941
Bolitho, Hector, *George VI*, 1937
Bolitho, Hector, *Their Majesties*, 1951
Boorman, Henry R. P., *Merry America: Their Majesties' Tour of Canada, the United States of America and Newfoundland, 1939*, 1939
Boothroyd, Basil, *Philip: an informal biography*, 1971
Bowen, Marjorie, *Royal Pageantry*, 1937
Broad, Lewis, *Crowning the King*, 1937
Buchan, John, *The King's Grace*, 1935
Buxton, Aubrey, *The King in His Country: an Account of King George VI's Game Shooting Activities*, 1955
Carnegie, Robert K., *And the People Cheered: an Account of the Visit of the King and Queen to Canada, 1939*, 1940
Channon, Henry, *Chips: the Diaries of Sir Henry Channon* (Ed. R. Rhodes James), 1967
Churchill, Winston, *The Second World War*, 6 vols., 1948–54, 1960
Cook, Elsie T., *Royal Cavalcade; the Coronation Book of King George VI and Queen Elizabeth*, 1937
Crawford, Marion, *The Little Princesses*, 1950
Dalton, E. H. J. N., *The Fateful Years*, 1957

Darbyshire, Taylor, *The Royal Tour of the Duke and Duchess of York*, 1927

Darbyshire, Taylor, *The Duke of York*, 1929

Darbyshire, Taylor, (Ed.), *In the Words of the King: selected speeches of George VI*, 1938

Donaghue, Bernard, and Jones, G. W., *Herbert Morrison*, 1973

Donaldson, Frances, *Edward VIII*, 1974

Donaldson, Frances, *King George and Queen Elizabeth*, 1977

Feiling, Keith, *The Life of Neville Chamberlain*, 1946

Fife, Charles W. D., *King George VI and His Empire*, 1937

Fife, Charles W. D., *King George VI and Queen Elizabeth*, 1937

Frischauer, Willi, *Margaret, Princess Without a Cause*, 1977

Gordon, Keith V., *The King in Peace and War*, 1940

Gorman, J. T., *King George VI: King and Emperor*, 1937

Harewood, Earl of, *The Tongs and the Bones*, 1981

Hibbert, Christopher, *The Court at Windsor*, 1964

Holden, Anthony, *Charles, Prince of Wales*, 1979

Hough, Richard, *Mountbatten: Hero of our Times*, 1980

Hyde, Robert R., *The Camp Book*, 1930

Industrial Welfare Society, *King George VI and Industry: a Tribute*, 1952

Jacob, Alaric, *Scenes from a Bourgeois Life*, 1949

Johnston, Lennox, *The Disease of Tobacco Smoking and its Cure*, 1957

Judd, Denis, *The Life and Times of George V*, 1973

Judd, Denis, *The House of Windsor*, 1973

Judd, Denis, *Prince Philip; A Biography*, 1980

King George VI to His Peoples, 1936–1951: selected speeches, 1952

Lacey, Robert, *Majesty: Elizabeth II and the House of Windsor*, 1977

Lascelles, Gertrude, *Our Duke and Duchess*, 1932

Longford, Elizabeth, Countess of, *The Queen Mother*, 1981

Longford, Elizabeth, Countess of, *The Royal House of Windsor*, 1974

Lucas, Ian F. M., *The Royal Embassy: the Duke and Duchess's Tour of Australasia*, 1927

Magnus, Philip, *Edward VII*, 1964

Mee, Arthur, *Salute the King*, 1937

Middlemas, Keith, *The Life and Times of George VI*, 1974

Middlemas, Keith, and Barnes, John, *Baldwin*, 1969

Moffatt, James, *King George Was My Shipmate*, 1940

Morrah, Dermot, *Princess Elizabeth, Duchess of Edinburgh*, 1950

Morrah, Dermot, *The Work of the Queen*, 1958

Nicolson, Sir Harold, *King George V: His Life and Reign*, 1952

Nicolson, Sir Harold, *Diaries and Letters*, 1930–39 (Ed. Nigel Nicolson), 1966

Nicolson, Sir Harold, *Diaries and Letters*, 1939–45 (Ed. Nigel Nicolson), 1967

Nicolson, Sir Harold, *Diaries and Letters*, 1945–52 (Ed. Nigel Nicolson), 1968

Oman, C., (preface) *The Reign of George VI, 1900–25*: a forecast written in the year 1763, republished 1899

Paneth, P., *King George VI and His People*, 1944

Petrie, Sir Charles, *The Modern British Monarchy*, 1961

Pope-Hennessy, James, *Queen Mary, 1867–1953*, 1959

Pudney, John, *His Majesty King George VI*, 1952

Roosevelt, Eleanor, *This I Remember*, 1949

Shewell-Cooper, W. E., *The Royal Gardeners*, 1952

Sitwell, Osbert, *Queen Mary and Others*, 1974

Stuart, Dorothy M., *King George the Sixth*, 1937

Taylor, A. J. P., *English History 1914–45*, 1963

Townsend, Peter, *The Last Emperor*, 1975

Townsend, Peter, *Time and Chance: an autobiography*, 1978

Wheeler-Bennett, Sir John, *George VI: His Life and Reign*, 1958

Windsor, Duchess of, *The Heart Has Its Reasons*, 1956

Windsor, HRH, Duke of, *A King's Story*, 1960

Windsor, HRH, Duke of, *A Family Album*, 1960

Wilson, Sir John, *The Royal Philatelic Collection*, 1952

Wulff, Louis L. V., *Silver Wedding: of George VI and Queen Elizabeth*, 1948

NEWSPAPERS AND JOURNALS

Globe
Daily Mail
Daily Mirror
Daily Express
Daily Worker
Evening News
Evening Standard
Illustrated
Illustrated London News
Listener
Manchester Guardian
New Statesman
News of the World
News Review

The Observer
The People
Picture Post
Punch
Saturday Evening Post
The Sphere
Star
Sunday Chronicle
Sunday Express
Sunday Graphic
Sunday Pictorial
Sunday Telegraph
Time
The Times

ENDNOTES

Chapter 1
1. Sir John Wheeler-Bennett, *King George VI: His Life and Reign* (1965), p. 5
2. *The Globe*, 14 December 1895
3. *The Standard*, 16 December 1895
4. Wheeler-Bennett, p. 6
5. *Ibid.*, p. 8
6. Frances Donaldson, *Edward VIII* (1976 edition), p. 8
7. Wheeler-Bennett, p. 16
8. HRH THe Duke of Windsor, *A King's Story* (1960), p. 26
9. Harold Nicolson, *Diaries and Letters, 1945–62* (1966), p. 137
10. Earl of Harewood, *The Tongs and the Bones* (1981), p. 14
11. *Ibid.*, p. 15
12. Marion Crawford, *The Little Princesses* (1950), p. 16
13. Lady Airlie, *Thatched with Gold* (1962), p. 112
14. *Ibid.*
15. *Ibid.*, p. 113
16. Donaldson, p. 13
17. Sir Harold Nicolson, *King George V: his Life and Reign* (1952), p. 51
18. Airlie, p. 112
19. *Ibid.*
20. Osbert Sitwell, *Queen Mary and Others* (1974), pp. 23–4
21. Airlie, p. 113
22. Nicolson, 366
23. Wheeler-Bennett, p. 17
24. *Ibid.*, p. 18
25. Airlie, pp. 113–114
26. Erica Beal, *King-Emperor; the Life of King George VI* (1941), p. 114
27. Wheeler-Bennett, p. 27.
28. Robert Lacey, *Majesty: Elizabeth II and the House of Windsor* (Revised ed. 1978) p. 59

29. Wheeler-Bennett, p. 29
30. *Ibid.*, p. 28
31. *Ibid.*, p. 25
32. *Ibid.*, p. 121
33. Nicolson, p. 328
34. James Pope-Hennessy, *Queen Mary* (1959), p. 390
35. Lacey, p. 71
36. Pope-Hennessy, p. 511
37. *Ibid.*
38. Wheeler-Bennett, p. 22
39. *Ibid.*, p. 28

Chapter 2
1. Nicolson, p. 15.
2. Hector Bolitho, *George VI* (1937), pp. 32–5
3. Wheeler-Bennett, pp. 45–6
4. *Ibid.*, p. 52

Chapter 3
1. Wheeler-Bennett, p. 70
2. *Ibid.*, p. 73
3. *Ibid.*, p. 84
4. *Ibid.*, p. 86
5. *Ibid.*, p. 87
6. *Ibid.*, p. 93
7. *Ibid.*, pp. 95–6

Chapter 4
1. Wheeler-Bennett, p. 108
2. *Ibid.*, p. 109
3. *Ibid.*, p. 113
4. *Ibid.*, p. 126
5. Walter Bagehot, *The English Constitution* (1949 edition), pp. 35–37, p. 53
6. Beverley Baxter, *Destiny Called Them* (1939), p. 12
7. Wheeler-Bennett, p. 140

Chapter 5
1. Baxter, p. 10
2. *Ibid.*
3. Wheeler-Bennett, p. 142
4. *Ibid.*, p. 146
5. Elizabeth Longford, *The Queen Mother; a Biography* (1981), p. 18
6. Lacey, p. 53
7. *Ibid.*, pp. 53–4
8. Airlie, pp. 166–7
9. *Ibid.*, p. 166
10. *Ibid.*, p. 167
11. Wheeler-Bennett, p. 150
12. Longford, p. 23
13. Quoted in Lacey, p. 56
14. Airlie, pp. 167–8
15. *Ibid.*, p. 168

Chapter 6
1. Graham Brooks, *The Dukes of York*, p. 11
2. *The Times*, 26 April 1923
3. Longford, p. 26
4. Wheeler-Bennett, p. 153
5. *Ibid.*
6. Longford, p. 28
7. Wheeler-Bennett, p. 154
8. *Ibid.*, pp. 154–5
9. Longford, p. 29
10. Wheeler-Bennett, pp. 155–6

Chapter 7
1. Wheeler-Bennett, p. 160
2. *Ibid.*, p. 163
3. *Ibid.*, p. 166
4. *Ibid.*, p. 167
5. *Ibid.*, p. 171
6. Baxter, p. 30
7. *Daily Mirror*, 27 November 1940

Chapter 8
1. Wheeler-Bennett, p. 176
2. Robert R. Hyde, *The Camp Book* (1930), p. 11
3. Article in the *Bedfordshire Times and Independent*, 26 August 1926
4. Wheeler-Bennett, p. 180
5. *Ibid.*, pp. 184–5
6. *News Review*, 5 August 1937
7. Hyde, pp. 38–9
8. *Ibid.*, p. 38
9. *Ibid.*, p. 39

10. *Ibid.*, pp. 39–40
11. Colonel Paterson's memorandum, quoted in Wheeler-Bennett, p. 398
12. *Ibid.*, p. 399

Chapter 9
1. Wheeler-Bennett, p. 198
2. *Ibid.*, p. 199
3. *Ibid.*, p. 201
4. *Ibid.*, p. 205
5. Lacey, p. 38
6. Wheeler-Bennett, p. 209
7. *Ibid.*, p. 210
8. *Ibid.*, p. 212
9. Hannen Swaffer, *The People*, 31 December 1950
10. Reginald Pound, *Harley Street* (1967), extract in *Sunday Express*, 29 October 1967
11. *Ibid.*
12. *Ibid.*
13. Wheeler-Bennett, p. 214
14. Pound, *Harley Street*, extract in *Sunday Express*
15. Wheeler-Bennett, p. 214
16. Pound, *Harley Street*
17. *Ibid.*
18. *Ibid.*
19. *Ibid.*
20. *Ibid.*
21. *Ibid.*
22. Wheeler-Bennett, p. 216
23. *Ibid.*, p. 220
24. *Ibid.*, p. 228
25. *Ibid.*, p. 230
26. *Ibid.*, p. 232
27. HRH The Duke of Windsor, p. 224

Chapter 10
1. Wheeler-Bennett, p. 254
2. *Ibid.*, p. 253
3. *Ibid.*, p. 257
4. Robert Lacey, *Majesty*, pp. 75–6
5. Wheeler-Bennett, p. 259
6. Lacey, pp. 51–2, also Dorothy Laird, *Queen Elizabeth the Queen Mother* (1966), p. 94
7. Lacey, p. 57
8. *Ibid.*, p. 52
9. *Ibid.*, pp. 61–2
10. *Ibid.*, p. 66
11. Beal, p. 241

12. Lacey, p. 69
13. HRH The Duke of Windsor, p. 62
14. Lacey, p. 72
15. *Ibid.*, pp. 69–70
16. Lady Cynthia Asquith, in *Illustrated*, 4 April 1953
17. Lacey, p. 74
18. Crawford, p. 9
19. *Ibid.*
20. *Ibid.*, p. 19
21. Frances Donaldson, *King George VI and Queen Elizabeth* (1977), extract in *Evening News* 4 May 1977
22. Lacey, p. 79
23. Crawford, p. 25
24. Crawford, p. 48
25. Airlie, p. 225
26. Crawford, p. 33
27. *Ibid.*, p. 48
28. Airlie, p. 225
29. Wheeler-Bennett, pp. 259–60
30. W. E. Sheweil-Cooper, *The Royal Gardeners* (1952), p. 5
31. *Ibid.*, p. 6

Chapter 11
1. Wheeler-Bennett, p. 266
2. HRH The Duke of Windsor, p. 278
3. Interview in U. S. magazine, *Parade*, 16 June 1957
4. The Duchess of Windsor, *The Heart has its Reasons* (1956), p. 224
5. Lady Hardinge, *Loyal to Three Kings* (1967), p. 61
6. Airlie, p. 202
7. Lacey, p. 94
8. Duchess of Windsor, pp. 224–5
9. Lacey, p. 94
10. *Ibid.*, p. 105
11. *Ibid.*
12. *Ibid.*, p. 115
13. Donaldson, *Edward VIII*, pp. 169–70
14. Wheeler-Bennett, p. 280
15. Lacey, p. 120
16. Wheeler-Bennett, p. 285
17. Donaldson, *King George VI and Queen Elizabeth*, p. 50
18. K. Middlemas and J. Barnes, *Baldwin* (1969) pp. 1009–10
19. Wheeler-Bennett, pp. 308–9
20. Lacey, p. 129

21. Dermot Morrah, *Princess Elizabeth, Duchess of Edinburgh* (1950), p. 62
22. Wheeler-Bennett, p. 286
23. *Ibid.*
24. *Ibid.*, pp. 286–7
25. Frances Donaldson, *Edward VIII*, p. 197 (See Chapter 15, 'The King and Nazi Germany').
26. Lacey, pp. 108–9
27. *Chips; The Diaries of Sir Henry Channon* (ed. Robert Rhodes James) (1967), p. 84
28. Lacey, p. 109

Chapter 12
1. Wheeler-Bennett, p. 293
2. *Ibid.*, p. 294
3. Baxter, p. 8
4. Airlie, p. 202
5. Quoted in Lacey, p. 135
6. Airlie, pp. 202–3
7. Wheeler-Bennett, p. 296
8. Airlie, p. 203
9. *Ibid.*
10. Lady Cynthia Asquith, *The King's Daughter* (1937), p. 96
11. Crawford, p. 39
12. Wheeler-Bennett, p. 288
13. *Sunday Telegraph*, 9 December 1979
14. Wheeler-Bennett, pp. 294–5
15. Donaldson, *Edward VIII*, p. 292
16. Longford, p. 68
17. *Ibid.*
18. *Ibid.*
19. A. J. P. Taylor, 'The Improbable King', *Sunday Express*, 22 September 1957
20. Quoted in Donaldson, *Edward VIII*, pp. 310–11
21. Duchess of Windsor, *The Heart has its Reasons*, p. 295
22. Donaldson, *Edward VIII*, p. 332
23. *Ibid.*, p. 384
24. Wheeler-Bennett, p. 299
25. An American Resident, *The Twilight of the British Monarchy* (1937), pp. 13–14
26. *Ibid.*, pp. 30–1
27. *Ibid.*, pp. 40–43
28. Longford, pp. 60–1
29. Airlie, p. 203
30. *Ibid.*, p. 205

31. Baxter, p. 40
32. Wheeler-Bennett, p. 303
33. *Ibid.*, p. 305
34. *Ibid.*, pp. 312–13
35. *Time*, 22 March 1937
36. *Ibid.*
37. *The Listener*, 19 May 1937, p. 958
38. *Time*, 24 May 1937, p. 15
39. Wheeler-Bennett, p. 316
40. *Ibid.*
41. Keith Feiling, *The Life of Neville Chamberlain* (1946), p. 303
42. Wheeler-Bennett, p. 328
43. *Ibid.*, p. 349
44. *Ibid.*, p. 354
45. *Ibid.*, p. 356
46. *Time*, 15 July 1946
47. *Daily Mirror*, 15 April 1939
48. Eleanor Roosevelt, *This I remember* (1949), pp. 183–4
49. *Daily Telegraph*, 6 January 1970
50. Wheeler-Bennett, p. 380
51. *Time*, 29 May 1939
52. *Time*, 19 June 1939
53. *Ibid.*
54. *Ibid.*
55. Alaric Jacob, *Scenes from a Bourgeois Life* (1949), quoted in *News Review*, 13 October 1949
56. *Daily Mirror*, 23 June 1939
57. Wheeler-Bennett, pp. 392–3
58. *Ibid.*, p. 405
59. *Ibid.*, p. 407

Chapter 13
1. A. J. P. Taylor, 'The Improbable King', *Sunday Express*, 22 September 1957
2. *The Reign of King George VI, 1920 –25*, written in the year 1763, and republished in 1899, p. 14
3. *News Review*, 7 September 1939
4. Wheeler-Bennett, p. 420
5. *Ibid.*, p. 425
6. *Sunday Graphic*, 4 March 1951
7. *Daily Mirror*, article by 'Bernard Gray, *Mirror* correspondent with the B.E.F., 5 December 1939
8. *Daily Mirror*, 27 October 1939
9. *Daily Mirror*, 15 March 1940
10. Wheeler-Bennett, pp. 439–40

11. L. S. Amery, *My Political Life*, vol. 3 (1955), pp. 368–9
12. Wheeler-Bennett, pp. 443–4
13. *Ibid.*, p. 446
14. *Ibid.*, pp. 450–1
15. *Ibid.*, pp. 469–70
16. *Daily Mirror*, 10 September 1940
17. *Daily Mirror*, 24 April 1940
18. *Sunday Telegraph*, 18 March 1979
19. Longford, pp. 88–9
20. Wheeler-Bennett, p. 520
21. *Ibid.*, p. 531

Chapter 14
1. Wheeler-Bennett, p. 538
2. *Ibid.*, p. 550
3. *Ibid.*, p. 552
4. *Ibid.*, p. 553, quoted from the Logue papers
5. *Ibid.*, p. 558
6. Keith Middlemas, *The Life and Times of George VI* (1974), p. 143
7. *Picture Post*, 8 August 1942
8. Wheeler-Bennett, p. 566
9. *Daily Mirror*, 17 June 1943
10. Wheeler-Bennett, p. 578
11. *Ibid.*, p. 589
12. *Ibid.*, p. 594
13. *Ibid.*, p. 600
14. *Time*, 6 March 1944
15. Wheeler-Bennett, p. 602
16. *Daily Mail*, 29 March 1971
17. Wheeler-Bennett, pp. 619–20
18. *Ibid.*, p. 627
19. *Ibid.*, p. 633
20. *Ibid.*, p. 636

Chapter 15
1. Quoted in Middlemas, p. 158
2. C. R. Attlee, *As It Happened* (1956), pp. 242–245
3. *Ibid.*, p. 245
4. A. J. P. Taylor, 'The Improbable King', part 3, *Sunday Express*, 29 September 1957
5. Wheeler-Bennett, p. 651
6. C. R. Attlee, p. 171
7. Wheeler-Bennett, p. 638
8. A. J. P. Taylor, 'The Improbable King', part 3
9. Wheeler-Bennett, p. 645

10. *The Listener*, 23 August 1945, p. 205
11. Wheeler-Bennett, pp. 651–2
12. Bernard Donoughue & G. W. Jones, *Herbert Morrison; Portrait of a Politician* (1973), p. 557
13. Wheeler-Bennett, p. 703
14. *Ibid.*, p. 687
15. *Time*, 1 July 1946, p. 13
16. C. R. Attlee, p. 240

Chapter 16
1. Crawford, p. 59
2. Ex-Queen Alexandra of Yugoslavia, *Prince Philip: a Family Portrait* (1959), p. 65
3. Basil Boothroyd, *Philip: an Informal Biography* (1971), p. 12
4. Ex-Queen Alexandra, p. 72
5. Denis Judd, *Prince Philip; A Biography* (1980), p. 104
6. Wheeler-Bennett, p. 749
7. Longford, p. 102
8. Airlie, p. 225
9. Ex-Queen Alexandra, p. 84
10. Wheeler-Bennett, p. 755
11. *Ibid.*, pp. 754–5
12. Ex-Queen Alexandra, p. 102

13. Wheeler-Bennett, p. 755

Chapter 17
1. A. J. P. Taylor, 'George VI: the Improbable King', *Sunday Express*, 29 September 1957
2. Longford, p. 105
3. *Time*, 6 December 1948
4. *Time*, 21 July 1941
5. Dr Lennox Johnston, *The Disease of Tobacco Smoking and Its Cure* (1957), quoted in *Daily Herald*, 31 October 1957
6. *Daily Herald*, 31 October 1957
7. Wheeler-Bennett, pp. 786–7
8. *Sunday Pictorial*, 10 June 1951
9. *Ibid.*
10. *Sunday Pictorial*, 9 September 1951
11. *Daily Express*, 22 September 1951
12. *Picture Post*, 13 October 1951
13. Wheeler-Bennett, p. 790
14. *Sunday Express*, 6 February 1972
15. Quoted in the *People*, 18 June 1967, in a letter written by Sir Geoffrey Marshall
16. *Ibid.*
17. *The Times*, 12 April 1957
18. Airlie, p. 235

INDEX

ROYAL LINE FROM
QUEEN VICTORIA AND PRINCE ALBERT

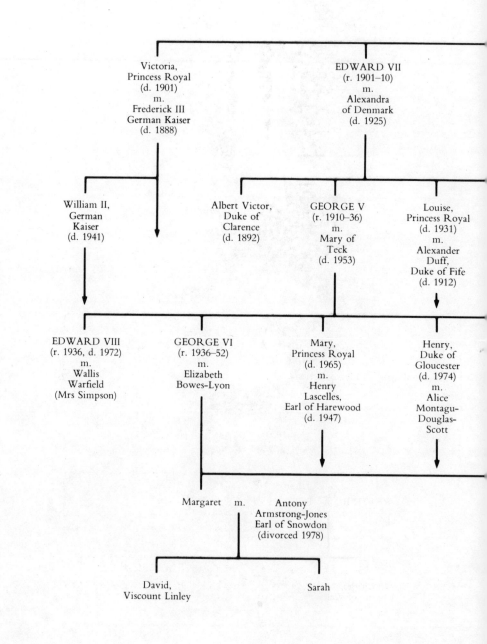